ROWING
FOR MY LIFE

ROWING
FOR MY LIFE

TWO OCEANS, TWO LIVES, ONE JOURNEY

KATHLEEN SAVILLE

Arcade Publishing • New York

First Edition

Arcade Publishing books may be purchased in bulk at special discounts for sales promotion, corporate gifts, fund-raising, or educational purposes. Special editions can also be created to specifications. For details, contact the Special Sales Department, Arcade Publishing, 307 West 36th Street, 11th Floor, New York, NY 10018 or arcade@skyhorsepublishing.com.

Arcade Publishing® is a registered trademark of Skyhorse Publishing, Inc.®, a Delaware corporation.

Visit our website at www.arcadepub.com.
Visit the author's site at https://kmsaville.wordpress.com and www.facebook.com/KathleenMSaville.

10 9 8 7 6 5 4 3 2 1

Library of Congress Cataloging-in-Publication Data is available on file.
Library of Congress Cataloging-in-Publication Control Number: 201604451

Cover design by Brian Peterson
Cover photo courtesy of Kathleen Saville

ISBN: 978-1-62872-688-6
Ebook ISBN: 978-1-62872-689-3

Printed in the United States of America

For Curt, my partner and best friend in the road not taken.

For our parents, Ida and Bartley McNally and Eugenia and Lloyd Saville. They always stood behind us, no matter where we wanted to go and how we wanted to get there.

For Christopher, whose gentle spirit welcomes me home every year. I love you.

"It is easier to sail many thousand miles through cold and storm and cannibals, in a government ship, with five hundred men and boys to assist one, than it is to explore the private sea, the Atlantic and Pacific Ocean of one's being alone."

Henry David Thoreau

Contents

PART III: SOUTH PACIFIC OCEAN

PART IV: NEW IDENTITIES AND NEW LIVES

Preface

IN 2006, I WENT TO Laos for an education conference and a week-long kayak trip to celebrate my fiftieth birthday. A chorus of cicadas filled the humid, musty air where I stayed in Vientiane before heading to a river in the southeast of the country. Geckos with transparent skin darted furtively along the walls and ceilings of my guesthouse. Banana, mango, and palm trees poked their branches under the eaves of the red tile roof. In the evening and early morning, the ethereal sounds of monks chanting at the local Buddhist wat drifted over the walls.

In the five years since my husband Curt's death in Egypt's desert, I had traveled at an almost frenetic pace to places like Laos (twice already), Hong Kong, Brunei, Singapore, and Malaysia, with regular trips back to the United States from my job in Cairo, Egypt. It was as though I was searching for something so elusive that I couldn't make myself stop long enough to find it. Now, though, I was going to go slow, by boat, with a young Lao guide by the name of Eing and take the necessary time. We would kayak the dam-controlled waters of the remote Hinbon River. I was hoping the experience would help me settle down so I could finally begin to write this book about the ocean-rowing trips that Curt and I had undertaken in the 1980s, a story I had tried to tell so many times in the past.

A week later, as the setting sun became a soft reddish smudge in the western sky, I was back in Vientiane sitting at my favorite outdoor food stand, having a Beer Lao by the Mekong River. I felt let down and missed the Hinbon River and kayaking with Eing; he had been a good travel companion. Idly, I watched a group of saffron-robed monks cross the large sand bar extending far from the river's bank, while a couple of fishermen in broad-brimmed straw hats walked slowly through the shallows, dipping their triangular nets in and out of the still water. Across the Mekong, on the Thai side, lights began to twinkle through the branches of the trees.

Here, at the end of my trip, I realized how much of a *memsahib* I had become over the years, focusing on my jobs and acquiring more material goods as my salary increased. Everything about me felt soft. I thought back to the year Curt and I rowed across the Atlantic, when I sat for hours on the port deck of *Excalibur*, our homemade rowboat, and wondered if I had the strength and courage to keep rowing day after day toward the western horizon and our intended landfall in the Caribbean. I also thought of our South Pacific rowing adventure, when the only instrument we had to navigate with, the sextant, was lost after Curt fell overboard. As we foolishly carried no spare, we were forced to navigate by the stars alone, using our hands to gauge their angle in the sky and a simple compass. I remembered pushing back on the paralyzing fear that every decision we made, based on where we thought we were, might be undermined by inaccurate sightings with the implication that we would never find land again or, ultimately, survive. I reflected on how my life had changed when our son was born and, through my own dogged efforts to adjust course, we traveled to South Asia and the Middle East as a family to live and work overseas.

Nothing within me had changed since those years of rowing the Atlantic and Pacific Oceans with Curt. I was pursuing the life I had chosen. I was still ready to get on a plane and go anywhere. And if I was to revisit those past journeys, it would be not so much to relive them as to seek a new understanding. Curt and I had taken on challenges that many thought impossible or at the very least fatal to our young marriage. We sought to face life alone in an ocean wilderness, exposed to natural forces we could barely conceive of, as well as unimaginable wonders. How had the experience shaped me? How had the rows shaped our marriage, and what had they meant in my life?

To prepare for the writing, I reread our unpublished manuscript about the Atlantic row and our self-published book on the Pacific row, as well as our diaries and personal logbooks from both expeditions and other shorter voyages we had taken. I also reread the words of our fellow New Englander and favorite transcendentalist, Henry David Thoreau, whose motivation for going to Walden Pond matched ours perfectly in undertaking our journeys: "I went to the woods because I wished to live deliberately, to front only the essential facts of life, and see if I could not learn what it had to teach, and not, when I came to die, discover that I had not lived."

Our ocean-rowing expeditions were small and personal, unlike those of our favorite old-time explorers, Ernest Shackleton and Robert Scott, whom we loved to read about. Except for one expedition for which Curt obtained partial support from National Geographic, our voyages were funded with relatively limited private sponsorship and our own earnings. We built our ocean-going rowboat *Excalibur* ourselves, with the help of friends, in order to undertake the Atlantic crossing, and later we refitted it for the Pacific row.

Rowing for My Life explores who Kathleen McNally and Curt Saville were, from when we first met in 1977 on the banks of the Connecticut River at a rowing race until the time in 2001 when Curt walked into the Egyptian desert to hike between the monasteries of St. Anthony and St. Paul and failed to return alive. What had driven us constantly to put ourselves in situations that required we depend on each other for our very survival? Did we bring something out in each other that impelled us to take such chances? Why was I eventually able to adapt that daring lifestyle into something as adventurous but less dangerous, while Curt remained unwilling to give up flirting with extreme risk? Did that say something about who I had become or who I already was?

While working on this book, I came across old correspondence from my mother dating from March 1981, the month we began the row across the Atlantic Ocean. She was struggling to let me go when she wrote, "Stay safe and happy—I do give you my respect for staying with your convictions. My feelings towards your venture are all necessarily predicated on the possibility of my not seeing you again or you being ill and so on. At least I am sure that you are in good health. That has served to calm some of my thoughts and should give you confidence as well."

I realized that the seeds of resiliency and the desire to be self-reliant had been sown in me long before I rowed an ocean. Perhaps they were in my genes. Mom confirmed as much when she wrote in another pre-rowing letter from 1981, "I see you as a positive young girl who [has] already separated herself from her family." At the time, I was hurt that she was suggesting our family was not as important to me as my rows with Curt. Now, I see that she was telling me, as Curt did years earlier, "When you go, don't forget to come back because we're waiting for you." It was a good lesson that I haven't forgotten.

In the end, writing *Rowing for My Life* has been part of the healing process over Curt's death, for it has helped me better appreciate the relationship that made us so successful as partners, how we evolved as individuals, and how those rows jump-started my life and contributed to making me the person I am today. As Mark Doty writes in *Heaven's Coast*, "What is healing, but a shift in perspective?"

Isle of Portland, England
Cairo, Egypt

Acknowledgments

THERE ARE MANY PEOPLE WITHOUT whose help this book would not have been completed. Curt's and my family have played a huge role, from the moral and financial support our parents gave us to the contributions of my sister-in-law, the photographer Lynn Saville, who was with us from the very beginning in 1980. Ed Montesi, who designed and helped us to build *Excalibur*, was with us one hundred percent of the way, as was Peter Wilhelm, who worked on the boat and provided brilliant ham radio communications, along with his father, Kurt Wilhelm. We might have been only two people on our rowboat on the oceans, but there were so many others on land that made it possible for us to be there. Companies gave us products in support of our expeditions, ham radio operators held regular radio schedules with us, yachties across the Atlantic and South Pacific Oceans shared their expertise and kept an eye out for us. Good people we encountered in Morocco, the Canary Islands, Antigua, various ports of call on the South American coast, the Galápagos, Marquesas, Society, American Samoa, and Vanuatu Islands, and Australia, helped us. Without their collective help and encouragement, we would never have been able to row all those miles from one side of the ocean to another.

Telling the story of these rowing adventures has been a long time coming, and I thank my mentors Cait Johnston, Barbara Hurd,

Debra Marquart, and Scott Wolven at the University of Southern Maine's Stonecoast MFA program for providing their invaluable feedback. Without the expert guidance of my editor, Cal Barksdale at Arcade Publishing, my stories might have been told lightly, without the reflections that he pushed me to. It would have been far easier to narrate only the events and not dig deeper into the reasons and motivations behind each journey.

Part I

Learning to Row

CHAPTER I

Joining the Team

Fall 1974

I WAS A FRESHMAN WITH TWO papers to write and a hundred pages of reading waiting for me in my dorm room. I ate my cafeteria dinner as slowly as I could, putting off the moment when I'd have to go back and start working. I wondered if my roommate, a senior with a full-time boyfriend, would be around this weekend.

I took one final bite of my Swedish meatballs, scooped up the rest of the rice, and drank the last drops of milk. I was restless. What I really wanted to do was catch a ride to Providence so I could spend the weekend at home. I was lonely for familiar faces and for my parents' company. Most of the students at the University of Rhode Island regularly returned home on the weekends, leaving the campus virtually deserted. The thought made me sad with homesickness.

I pushed open the exit door to the cafeteria and started down the stairs. That's when I saw the poster:

WANTED: ROWERS FOR THE WOMEN'S CREW TEAM
JOIN US TONIGHT AT 7 PM
STUDENT UNION

I didn't know anything about crew or what one did on a crew team, but the directness of the message grabbed my attention. I imagined it might include traveling by boat somewhere, maybe on the nearby Narragansett Bay. The idea of rowing sounded kind of sexy and a good way to meet guys. I looked at my watch: it was 6:30. I decided to check it out.

Three days later, I waited in my dorm room for Jess, a senior on the women's crew. I was wearing what I considered appropriate workout clothes for rowing: red hot pants, an orange-red stretchy knit top, a zip-up sweat jacket, and a pair of sandals. I stubbed out my cigarette when the knock came.

In the back of a truck owned by one of the experienced men's rowers were the other new recruits, including my friend Marion who was dressed in gray sweatpants, a blue pullover, and Adidas sneakers. Marion had been a field hockey player on her high school team in West Hartford, Connecticut. Maybe she knew something I didn't know about crew.

The wooden dock, attached to the banks of the Narrow River, rocked gently with the weight of new and returning crew members. I stood with Marion and the other women on the grassy riverbank and watched the men's crews carrying their rowing shells past us. I shoved my hands deep into the pockets of my sweat jacket. It was cold, and my legs were as red as the tip of my nose. Almost as red as my shorts.

Jon Beamer, the coach, stood at the far end of the dock, giving a pep talk to a group of new male recruits. He leaned toward them, eyes wide, voice loud. Each freshman stared back, intimidated. But he was connecting with them, and they were ready to do whatever he wanted so they could be part of his crew team. Jon, a recent graduate of an Ivy League university, had rowed lightweight for the varsity men's crew. His private university pedigree was an odd fit with our state school, and our University of Rhode Island crew did not have the history or the impressive funding of his former team. Every boat that the URI crew rowed and every piece of equipment it used was purchased only after arduous fund-raising by each dedicated crew member. Unlike the URI football team, which had a million-dollar budget, the crew subsisted on minor contributions from the athletic department.

I learned pretty quickly that day that whatever equipment the crew had was doled out according to gender. The men's crews rowed the lighter and newer boats. Their oars were also lighter and less beat-up than the women's. With a push on the boat and oars, Jon sent the new rowers and returning rowers off in the lightweight Schoen-broad. He turned back to glare at our little women's group, huddled between the riverbank and dock.

"Sue, send them up there to get the Pocock. Get the oars and shell down here."

Sue, the women's captain, and Jess, the senior, gathered all the new women and led us up the boathouse hill, its side gouged out with railroad ties for stairs. It took care not to trip on those steps. In the boathouse, Sue led us over to a huge, wooden eight-person row-ing boat. Its outriggers were chipped, blue-painted steel piping with bubbly welded joints, an indication that it had been repaired many times. The boat looked enormously heavy.

"The Pocock used to be the men's, but it's our boat now," Sue explained. "It's heavy, but it's one of the best. If you get used to rowing this boat, you'll be able to row anything." We all nodded, though we didn't have a clue what she was talking about. I don't think any of the new recruits had ever rowed before, never mind seen a barge like this Pocock. Images of Roman galley slaves came to mind, heaving at their oars while a brute of a slave driver flicked a whip about their shoulders.

"First, you need your oars." I tore my eyes from the boat. "Pick out an oar and bring it down to the dock and come back."

I chose the smoothest-looking sweep oar and tried to pull it out of the storage bay with one hand, but it was too heavy and its twelve-foot length made the balance extremely awkward. For the first and last time in my rowing career, I carried my eight-and-a-half-pound oar down to the water with two hands. Some of the men's crew who hadn't gone out with the first men's boat, egged on by Jon, thought it was hilarious to moo like cows as the women walked by with their oars. Eventually, like the experienced women rowers, I learned to carry my oars and our boats with no expression on my face. If any woman ever gave the slightest indication of how heavy the boat was, the men would be right on us, mooing and catcalling.

Back in the boathouse, ten of us lined up on one side of the Pocock and pulled it halfway out. At Sue's command, Marion and her group ducked under and stood up on the other side. Then, at the next command, we lifted the 61-foot, 285-pound boat to our shoulders. Again at Sue's command, we marched forward, some of the new people staggering under the weight of the boat, the gunwales digging into their shoulders. It was hard to believe that we weren't going to fall down the hill with the Pocock crushing us to the ground. As we began our descent, the experienced rowers gripped the gunwales harder while the new women cringed under the boat's weight. Just when the boat began to dip precariously toward the ground, a loud voice boomed out, "If you're going to fall down, make sure your body is *under* that boat. I say again, *make sure your body is under that boat!* That boat is worth more to me than you are."

That was Jon, of course, who was waiting for us at the bottom of the stairs. I straightened my legs and climbed downward, stepping carefully over the railroad ties. At the dock, Sue told us to push the boat up and over our heads while grabbing for the footrests in the center, all in one fluid motion. The boat plopped into the water, with the new people letting go at the last second when the boat's weight was the heaviest.

"Hold on to that boat and don't let it go!" Jon again. I didn't recall hearing him scream so much at the men.

Marion went out with the first group, coached by Sue, while I waited with the others. I stuck my hands in my sweat jacket and looked at Jon. He had a scowl on his face.

"Most of you *girls* are here for a scenic tour of the river." *The guys aren't too bad looking either.* "Most of you won't be here tomorrow because all you want is a pretty little trip down the river." He scowled some more and stepped away.

He was beginning to irritate me. This guy didn't know me at all, and he had just lumped me into a general category of useless people that he obviously wanted nothing to do with. Maybe his plan was to discourage the women rowers so he wouldn't have to coach us.

The next day, I exchanged my little red shorts for gray sweatpants and joined Sue and the other women for the next practice. After one afternoon's scenic row on the Narrow River, I was hooked. And Jon was just going to have to put up with it.

CHAPTER 2

The Night We Met

November 1977

I<small>T WAS DRIZZLING LIGHTLY AS</small> I walked along the soggy banks of the Connecticut River carrying a couple of oars. My crew team had just posted a solid third-place finish among ten women's fours at the Head of the Connecticut, a two-and-a-half-mile rowing race. Despite the cold rain, I was buoyed by the excitement of the race as I shoved the wooden sweep oars onto the boat trailer.

"Hey, Kathy!" When I looked over, I saw an old friend waving and drinking beer by a couple of single rowing shells in boat slings. Next to him was a man I didn't know. I strolled over, and Ron introduced me to Curt Saville, the newest member of the Narragansett Boat Club, a Providence, Rhode Island rowing club that I had been a member of since my sophomore year, in 1975. We shook hands and surreptitiously looked each other over as Ron chatted about the latest NBC gossip. Curt Saville, whom I later learned was ten years older than me and had come to Providence to teach at Brown University, was about my height with a stocky build. He must have been cold, because his blue eyes were startlingly bright in his pinched white face. The hood of his sweat jacket was tightly knotted under his chin, making him look older than his thirty-one years.

Amid all the bustle of competing rowing teams carrying long, sleek rowing shells to and from the river, I chatted with

Ron and Curt about rowing and the Narragansett Boat Club. When Maggie, our women's coxswain, strolled by to say it was time to pack up our boats and return to Rhode Island, I said a quick goodbye and left.

A week later, with nothing special to do, I caught a ride to Providence with a rowing buddy to go to the annual fall Narragansett Boat Club cocktail party, held at their boat club on the Seekonk River. There, amid the cases of tarnished silver trophies and old wooden oars fixed to the walls, was Curt Saville standing by the bar with a drink in hand. I threaded my way through the crowd to the bar and ordered a Coke. When I looked over at Curt, he smiled. I smiled back, and we began a conversation that went on throughout the cocktail party. We moved to the center of the room and continued talking, while friends occasionally came by to say hello. I learned that Curt had planned to go to a Peace Corps interview in Boston the evening of the cocktail party but the call confirming it hadn't come in time for him to catch the bus to Boston. When I asked him why the Peace Corps, he replied it would be his second stint if he got in; his first had been in 1968 to Bolivia and El Salvador.

"What did you do there?" I asked.

"I was first horn in the National Orchestra of Bolivia and trained local musicians. One of my students, in fact, came to the US through a fellowship I helped him get." He added, "I also did a lot of climbing in the Andes before the Peace Corps was kicked out, and I finished up in El Salvador."

I looked at him, my interest piqued. That was a lot of information. "That's really cool. How did you manage to climb and play in an orchestra at the same time? I mean, didn't you have to be in La Paz?"

He smiled and looked happy at the memory. "We did a lot of tours to villages outside of La Paz, in the Amazon basin and to remoter areas of the Andes. My Peace Corps friends and I played informal concerts and did some climbing."

He went on to tell me about climbing 21,122-foot Illimani and others in the Cordillera Blanca range, and the one that he was most proud of: 22,841-foot Aconcagua. He had done Aconcagua with his fellow Juilliard graduate and Peace Corps volunteer Richard

"Dobbs" Hartshorne, who was also on those local concert tours with his double bass.

I was impressed. My only travels outside the United States had been to Spain and Portugal as a teenager with my mother. When he told me his family had lived in Italy a couple of times during his parents' sabbatical years while on the faculty at Duke University, I was even more impressed. His years living overseas were so exotic to me and his attending schools like Juilliard and Yale for an MA in music so prestigious that I wanted to know more, as though by knowing how he did it, I might someday have such an adventurous life too.

After an hour of solid conversation, I was looking at him, his face framed by his lanky, straight blond hair and arms sketching out the shape of a mountain or length of a note he would play in a Mozart concerto, when I noticed he was outlined in a soft glow from the dim lighting. At that moment the entire room shifted and tilted. I blinked, and the room was upright again. There had been no physical earthquake, but a seismic shift in my being had left me breathless. I was falling for this man.

Peter Plimpton, a friend from my high school days at a Quaker girls' school that shared classes at the nearby boys' Quaker school and now a fellow member of the boat club, came up to us. Curt knew Peter slightly, so we three chatted together for a short while before Curt and I moved off to the deck of the boathouse to continue talking about his Peace Corps days and his climbing adventures on Baffin and Ellesmere Islands in the High Arctic. In the dim yellow light cast through small square panes of the French doors, he described his travels among the Quechua in Bolivia. He spoke so passionately about the muscular arms and strength of the Quechua women compared to American women's arms that I felt I had to defend myself. My arms were strong and muscular too, I said, pulling up my sweater sleeve. There had to be something I could best him at in his storytelling.

"I row crew, and I'm pretty strong. Here. Feel my muscles," I said, making a fist and flexing my forearm. He nodded and agreed that I was strong like those Quechua chicks. I smiled, and before I left to go home that night, I accepted his invitation to meet at the boathouse the next morning for a row on the Seekonk River.

The crisp fall air felt fresh and invigorating the next morning as I waited for Curt on a wooden bench on River Road, across from the NBC. I was reliving our meeting at last night's cocktail party and thinking about how much fun it was talk about adventurous travel, when I was startled out of my reverie by a guy dressed in white shorts and a blue sweat jacket who came running up to me. For a moment I didn't recognize Curt, and then I was so happy when I realized this smiling guy was here for me.

We crossed the road, undid the lock to the chain fence that secured the boathouse along the riverbank, and signed out a boat to row together. We took our oars down to the dock, then lifted the double rowing shell from its rack in the boathouse and carried it down to the water, where we set out to row our first miles together on the flat, calm waters of the Seekonk.

CHAPTER 3

Learning to Row Together

1978

B Y THE OFFICIAL START OF the rowing season in the spring of 1978, Curt and I had decided to train together for a race in the mixed (one woman/one man) double category. We had found that we could depend on each other to be at the boat club for practices. Though we liked rowing together, sometimes rowing the double with two oars apiece, it was a challenge to combine our styles and make the shell move smoothly through the water.

My three and a half years of rowing on a university crew team, along with summers spent rowing singles at the NBC, had endowed me with a certain amount of expertise over Curt's homegrown style of rowing. I had the benefit of almost daily coaching and the experience of numerous races competing against college and club teams in boats with four and eight rowers. After my freshman year and a summer of rowing and competing in singles at the NBC, I had decided that rowing stroke, the position nearest the stern end of the boat and the most competitive seat to win, was where I belonged. I rowed stroke for two and a half years until my plummeting GPA took precedence over my rowing career. In later years, I would facetiously tell people I had majored in rowing and minored in textiles and history, my real majors, at the university.

Curt had experience kayaking and rowing simple wooden row-boats, but his training at the Narragansett Boat Club was limited to a few coaching sessions in singles and doubles. After we had spent part of the fall of 1977 and early spring 1978 rowing together on the weekends, I felt we worked together well enough to compete as a mixed double in races in the New England area. Curt had no idea what he was getting into when we began racing together. It was at our first event that he learned how competitive I could be.

"Come on, sprint! Dig those oars in, put some power on!" I shouted from the stern rowing seat of our racing shell as we approached the finish line of our premier 1500-meter race.

"I'm rowing as hard as I can," Curt gasped. He thought we were doing well because out of a field of three boats, we were in second place and holding off the third-place team by several boat lengths. In the last 250 meters, I increased the rowing stroke, the number of times per minute the oars are pulled through the water, and we glided across the finish line to come in a close second. Curt dropped his oars and let them drag in the water. He leaned over the gunwales with a sick look on his face.

"Pick up your oars and keep going!" I yelled, turning back to glare at him.

"I thought the race was over!" he protested, but we rowed another ten strokes before I deemed it was OK to put the oars down. If I had tried to drop my oars right after reaching the finishing line in my college races, not only would the coxswain who steered the boat yell at me, but I might have gotten an oar jammed in my back from the rower behind me who had kept on rowing.

One afternoon, after work in his new job as a photographer with the city of Providence and before our daily rowing practice, Curt decided to stop for a beer with a mutual friend at the old Met Café in downtown Providence. Though he didn't tell me, I sensed something was wrong with the balance of the boat when we started our practice.

"Come on, you're throwing the balance off! Pull through evenly." There's nothing worse than an overly competitive college rower, which I was at the time.

"I *am* pulling through evenly! You're leaning to one side and tipping us over." And so it went, back and forth, until Curt got so angry and aggravated that he just wanted to jump overboard and leave me to get the boat back to the dock by myself. But since we were nearly at the NBC, he held his temper and said, "All right, let's just go in. This practice is not working out."

We put the boat and oars away in silence. But the next day at 5:00 p.m., we both showed up at the boathouse for practice. We knew we had made a commitment to train and enter other races together, and neither of us would let disagreements stand in our way.

A few nights later as the metal window fan pumped away in the small living room of Curt's second-story apartment in Providence, we had a long discussion that would begin to define what our relationship would come to embody.

"You know, rowing in a double can be frustrating," he began, while mixing up a couple of the Black Russians that had become our favorite summer evening drink.

"Yeah, I know," I interjected. "We're bound to have differences. I've been rowing and competing for over four years, you know." He nodded as much to himself as to me as I added, "And I think that I know the sport better than you."

"Yeah, but I've put in a lot of time on the water in the last year, so I think I know how to row."

"Right," I said, "just like if I started playing the French horn a year ago, I would know as much as you do?"

He laughed, and I had to admit to myself that it was a weak rebuttal, because four years of college rowing couldn't be compared to fifteen years or so of conservatory and graduate-school training in classical music.

"Okay, okay, we're bound to have different ideas on rowing styles like we do on life, right?" I countered. "So let's leave any differences at the boathouse and not carry them into our relationship." Neither of us liked to fight. We understood that about each other. Later on, when we were to spend long periods of solitary time in each other's company, this ability to resolve differences amicably helped us enormously. But early on in our relationship, I wondered if this almost compulsive distaste for fighting when one or both people lost control of their tempers, especially on my part, would result in issues that would never be worked out.

We toasted our new understanding with a click of Curt's yard sale glasses filled with Black Russians, and the issue was closed. For the next few rowing seasons, we continued competing as a mixed double, though we never won a race. Instead, it was becoming apparent to both of us that our forte was in our ability to row long distances, albeit at a slower but steady pace than our competitors, who would leave us in their wakes as they sprinted to the end. Knowing that we were on our way to developing a strong relationship where we could always depend on each other helped to push us over those finish lines.

CHAPTER 4

A Penobscot River Paddle

September 1979

I N EARLY SEPTEMBER WHEN THE autumn leaves were turning shades of deep gold and claret red, I grabbed my backpack and joined Curt Saville as he packed his old Pinto station wagon full of camping gear for a week-long canoe journey in northern Maine. When we arrived at the foot of Moosehead Lake, at the small town of Greenville, we drove over to Holt's Flying Service where we met John Holt and rented one of his sixteen-foot aluminum canoes. Curt arranged for us to be picked up by a floatplane ten days later at the foot of Chesuncook Lake. We pushed off from the dock, with the canoe outfitted with rowing seats that Curt had brought along from his family's summer camp and a boatload of carefully packed dry meals and camping equipment. Amid the festivities of the annual Greenville floatplane rally, we pulled at our oars, skirting the edges of the course where one noisy floatplane after another landed like an oversized loon, kicking up choppy waves and a cold spray.

Over ten days' time, in cool temperatures and occasional rainy days, we followed Henry David Thoreau's route memorialized in a trilogy of essays that make up his book *The Maine Woods*. It was the first time I had ever gone on a long-distance rowing trip and in such a remote area. Curt, who was an old hand at canoeing and camping, loved being out in the wilderness again. Every night, after the food and cook kit were packed up and hung in the trees away from the bears, we settled on our down sleeping bags while I read passages from *The Maine Woods*, comparing our experiences in 1979 with Thoreau's in 1853, nearly 130 years earlier. The banks of the present-day Penobscot River, I had noticed, were still cluttered with standing and fallen pine and spruce trees that sheltered the moose we would spot slipping into the river. All along the shorelines of Caucomgomoc Stream and the Lobster and Chesuncook Lakes were enormous piles of bleached gray driftwood left over from the days of heavy logging. Time in the Maine woods, it seemed to me, had stood still since Thoreau's journeys.

Every day we spent rowing and camping in the cool fall air of the North Country softened any uncertainties of the future of our relationship, though Curt was now considering a move to New York state for a new job. I had strong feelings about what teamwork consisted of that came from my years rowing in college. To me, it was about unwavering commitment and giving your all to the team, whether it consisted of two people or a shell of eight rowers. If we were going to continue this relationship, possibly long-distance, could I count on him to "stay with the team" and be a good partner? Did I even want a long-distance relationship? When Mr. Holt arrived ten days later, first circling overhead with the floatplane's two, large, boat-like feet protruding from the wing struts, I felt pangs of wistfulness and regret. I was sorry my days as a novice explorer of remote, uninhabited rivers and lakes of the Maine woods had come to an end. I looked at Curt and realized he felt the same. It was then that we became aware of how well we'd gotten along over the past week and how much we'd been able to count on each other during the times when the weather turned foul and the boating conditions rough. Working together had come naturally for both of us.

On Curt's last weekend in Rhode Island, he proposed that we should marry. Starting the following Monday, he was moving to New York state, where he would begin a job as a medical photographer. With the prospect that the nature of our relationship could change, I wasn't sure what would happen next.

In the tiny kitchen of his Providence apartment, amid the half-filled packing boxes, Curt sat with his back to the wall, his arms akimbo. Our normally easy conversation had died out, and I looked at him. He had something to say as I stood in front of the sink, my arms crossed too. We were at a crossroads, and what happened next was going to affect us for the rest of our lives.

"Will you marry me?" he said in his soft voice, and I smiled.

"Sure. I'd love to." And that was it. My life had been changed forever by that simple exchange.

CHAPTER 5

Building Our Boat

Rhode Island, 1980–1981

Mᴀ PARENTS WERE SURPRISED WHEN I returned to Rhode Island less than six months after marrying Curt. Though my father had predicted great success for my marriage, he hadn't thought we would quit our jobs in New York so soon and move into their house as unemployed full-time explorers.

For several months, as we settled into married life in Tompkins Cove, New York, Curt and I had talked about a summer rowing adventure in the Bay of Fundy or along the East Coast of the United States. None of the ideas inspired me, though, until one day I delved into the most creative side of my brain and said, "Why don't we build a boat and row it across an ocean? We could row across the Atlantic. That would be the ultimate sort of voyage in a rowboat." Curt looked at me like I was crazy, but I could see the idea was intriguing to him, the little wheels of adventure cranking slowly as he tried to imagine the two of us rowing a boat in big ocean waves. Could it be done?

It gave me a flutter in my stomach to think about rowing across an ocean. I had never rowed on the open ocean, though I had rowed and sailed on Narragansett Bay and gone out on fishing boat trips off the coast of North Carolina. Did that qualify me to make such an absurd proposal? I had rowed for three and a half years in college and more at the Narragansett Boat Club. Did that qualify me to row an ocean?

Over the last year since the rowing journey in the Maine North Woods, we had both read a great number of adventure books about climbing mountains, paddling canoes in wilderness areas, and traversing oceans in a rowboat. There were Harbo and Samuelson, who successfully rowed a simple dory across the Atlantic Ocean in the late 1800s for prize money, and the Brits who flew to America in the 1960s, bought a dory, and rowed out of Chatham on Cape Cod. More interesting to me, though, was the story of a British woman and two men who began their row in Gibraltar, only to end in Casablanca, where the woman parted company with the men, who continued the row to the Caribbean.

What I was proposing was to become the first woman to row across the Atlantic Ocean, and the two of us to be the first Americans to do so. The wheels of adventure started turning faster. There was a boat and sponsorship to be worked out. Rowing the Atlantic was going to be a problem-solving task of the first order. Each of us would need to learn new skills, such as ocean navigation and radio communication. We would have to do the hard work of finding sponsors for the boat and supplies to offset the costs of our endeavor.

The final decision to organize an expedition wasn't made easily. We would be giving up good jobs, a questionable move in the poor economy of the early 1980s, as well as an apartment in a community whose backyard was the 5,205-acre Bear Mountain–Harriman State Park, where we regularly ran the cross-country trails and on weekends camped out on the high ridges overlooking New York City. But, in the short time we had lived and worked in New York state, Curt's job at Helen Hayes Hospital was a constant concern. He liked the medical photography work and was good at it, but he and his colleague, another photographer who had been assigned to collaborate with him, didn't work well together.

One day, I pulled out the black pattern composition notebook that I had filled with menu plans and itinerary notes from our northern Maine row the year before and found a few blank pages. One of our favorite activities together was planning out camping trips in great detail as Curt had done in his Peace Corps days when he and his buddies climbed in the Andes. I took a ruler and divided the page into a Tompkins Cove column and a Project Row Across the Atlantic Ocean column. Over a period of several weeks, sometimes sitting by a fire at our favorite lean-to on the part of the Appalachian Trail that runs through Bear Mountain–Harriman State Park, we listed the pros and cons of staying in or leaving New York. Financial concerns went into both columns. My job at the local police station went in the Tompkins Cove column. Each time I thought about leaving my secretarial job, I felt guilty and unsure. My new friends there wouldn't think much of me for breaking my nine-month contract after only five months, and I liked working for my boss, Sergeant Jackson, who saw me, at twenty-four years of age, as capable of doing far more than clerical work. Though very junior, I had shown a keen interest in the aspects of criminal law that the police deal with in their everyday work, and he had suggested that, when my contract ended, I should seriously consider applying to law school.

In the Project Row Across the Atlantic Ocean column, Curt felt time was of the essence. At our low rate of income, we could look forward only to a better used car and a new home mortgaged to the hilt in the next ten years. We should strike while the iron is hot and do the Atlantic row while we were young, in good shape, and capable of planning a successful expedition. His arguments and the fact that his job situation wasn't getting any better swayed me more and more. Though my ocean-rowing suggestion had been made, in part, in response to Curt's restlessness, I was optimistic that our marriage would survive the uncertainties ahead.

Finally, in May 1980, I closed the door to the apartment in Tompkins Cove for good while Curt waited in the packed Pinto wagon. In the end, my new self-image as modern-day explorer won out, inspired by the words of our favorite Transcendentalist, who had accompanied us on our northern Maine row through his writings. Thoreau wrote, "It is easier to sail many thousand miles through cold and storm and cannibals, in a government ship, with five hundred men and boys to assist one, than it is to explore the private sea, the Atlantic and Pacific Ocean of one's being alone."

Nonetheless, our decision made little sense to our families and our friends at the Narragansett Boat Club. My parents' idea of their daughter's happy marriage to a Yale-educated man was faltering while Curt and I spent days trying to determine the parameters for the design of an ocean-going rowboat. Worse, I asked them if we could build it in their garage in the backyard of their home on the exclusive East Side of Providence. My parents agreed while looking nervously out their back window into the open doors of the garage, where wood and other boat supplies were steadily accumulating. Stacked on the left side was a stash of oak and mahogany planks purchased from a marine store in southern Connecticut with our job savings, while boxes of tools from Curt's father's workshop in their Vermont summer home lay on the right. The boat, I pointed out to Mom and Dad, would be built in the middle. They nodded uncertainly.

Peter Wilhelm, a good friend from the boat club, was enlisted to work with us to build the double-ended Swampscott dory design we had decided on. The Swampscott dory was not only aesthetically beautiful, with its gently rounded lap strake sides, but it was known for its extreme seaworthiness. It had been originally designed in mid-nineteenth-century New England as a lifesaving boat, and many life boat stations along the New England coast still used them.

For days the band saw screamed away in the garage, until one day it came to a screeching halt. Late that afternoon, while going over the calculations for the boat ribs, we found that the measurements for the boat were off by a full third. The boat frames, costing a few hundred hard-earned dollars, had been cut for a vessel that was approximately one-third smaller. Instead of for a twenty-two-foot boat, they had been cut for an eighteen-footer. We were all upset, and for a brief time we parted ways with our friend to rethink the boat-building project.

There were so many things to do to prepare for such a voyage that the whole idea seemed vaguely improbable to some people. At a rowing regatta one weekend, we approached a well-known rowing coach and asked him about the kinds of rowing equipment that might stand up to a long transatlantic row. He thought for a long moment, and then surprised me by saying, "That sounds like a good way to break up a marriage."

"Oh, I don't think so," I responded. "We get along pretty well."

"I'm sure you do. But it can be tough out there. I was in the Pacific during the war. We went for days without being able to take a fresh-water shower. . . . We were covered in salt, . . . Even the big ships move around a lot in the waves.

"I've been around boats all my life," he continued, building to an obvious lesson, "and I get seasick. And you want to be out there in a small boat for months? You won't be out there for long and you'll be wet and tired. I can see it: 'It's your turn to do the dishes!' 'No, it's yours!'"

I could see he was really getting worked up over the idea of a married couple aboard a small boat for days on end. His parting shot was, "You'll regret that you ever thought of the idea!"

The reaction from Ed Montesi, another boat club member, was different. Ed said, "If I were going out there, I would only do it with the best or close to the best equipment and technology available." He was a proponent of building with fiberglass, wood, and a synthetic material called Airex foam core. He offered to design an ocean-rowing boat that would be twenty-five feet and five inches long with a five-foot–three-inch beam. Two enclosed cabins, fore and aft, would provide shelter and storage respectively. In the center of the open deck, the two rowing stations would be set up. Watertight storage compartments below deck would be used to keep fresh water, food, and gear, such as a medical kit, cooking kits, clothing, fishing gear, and navigation equipment.

The best part of Ed's plan was that the boat would take only six to nine months to build if we worked full-time. He gave us the name of a boat builder who he said might work with us in the initial stages. A week later, we tracked down Rob O'Rourke, a middle-aged Irish American in an old cow barn owned by a retired Portuguese farmer in Touisset, Rhode Island. Rob was lovingly sanding his J/24, a popular recreational fin keel sailboat, for the upcoming racing season on Narragansett Bay when we met him. His son from an estranged marriage was coming to stay for the summer, and Rob was working hard to get the boat ready for the June opening of the summer sailing season. Rob also needed money. He needed it so much that the little we offered him to work with us on the boat hull was accepted without argument.

Within the week, we had struck a deal with Tony, the Portuguese farmer, and moved into another part of the barn, which was terribly dilapidated from years of disuse and lack of upkeep. The ceiling of the long, one-story, cedar-shingled structure was covered with moldy sheetrock loosely nailed to the cobwebbed ceiling joists. Frayed wires poked through holes in the sheetrock, with low-wattage, excrement-covered light bulbs dangling off the ends. We replaced the ones hanging directly over the boat-building area with clean, one-hundred-watt bulbs and suddenly the barn looked worse. On either side of our boat-building platform were the poop-covered remnants of wooden cow stalls. Tony still kept hay at the far end next to the bunny hutch, where Lucy, a sweet-tempered beagle mix, had her unending litters of puppies. Tony's boat-building space cost $100 a month, a sum we could barely put together after daily expenditures on fiberglass, marine plywood for the deck and hatches, stainless steel bolts and nuts, and various other marine items. To build a boat and meet minimal living expenses, we needed to live frugally and eventually find sponsors.

Beginning in June 1980, we worked for more than seven months building the boat. One hot morning in early July, Ed, Peter Wilhelm—who was a fellow member of the NBC and collaborated with us the whole time—Curt, and I met at Tony's barn to fiberglass the outside of the hull. We unrolled long pieces of fiberglass cloth and mat so Curt and Peter could cut the fiberglass to the shape of the boat. Ed and I mixed buckets of resin and everyone then furiously spread the pink-tinted resin over the hull with paint rollers before it hardened.

Another weekend we divided efforts, and I took the train to New York City to buy charts and arrange transportation for the boat and ourselves aboard a Yugoslavian freighter to Casablanca, Morocco where we had decided to begin the row across the Atlantic. When I returned, Curt and Peter proudly showed me the major changes that had taken place while I was gone: the hull had been released from its frame, turned over, and put into a receiving cradle. It was beginning to look like a real boat!

By the end of July, it was time to put the bare hull on the water to see how well she rowed. Early one warm, muggy morning, Peter Wilhelm showed up with a borrowed trailer. Ed, Curt's sister Lynn from New York City, and Saville family friend Peter Thomas came down to help us with the launching of the boat. It was turning into a brilliant summer day as we drove the big pink hull the short distance down the road to the town's landing on Rhode Island's Mount Hope Bay. Since we wanted to know how the boat would row when fully laden, everyone pitched in to load bay water in the hundred empty gallon milk jugs that Peter Wilhelm had brought with him in his VW van. Each gallon weighed slightly over eight pounds, and, combined with all of our weights, the simulated weight was nearly 1,400 pounds, which Ed and Curt thought was close to what the completed boat with all the supplies and us in it would total. Everyone took a turn rowing on the makeshift rowing platform, including Tony, the farmer, who had the most fun of everyone. The day was a great success: the first major test of the boat design and its construction had been met.

Money, however, was now a problem. There was a boat hull but little savings left to fund further building. All of our time and resources were going toward the project. For the rest of the summer and into the fall of 1980, I spent my days divided between writing sponsorship letters and working on the boat. Some days, when it got too cold to sit in the car and type on my old college portable Smith Corona, I would drive over to my Portuguese grandmother's house in nearby Somerset, Massachusetts. Grandma never asked me why I wanted to row across an ocean. Or why my clothes were smelly, since I lived with my husband in the barn on a half-completed boat or camped in the car in the cornfields behind the barn. I would come into her kitchen, which was fragrant with the smells of *calde* and *linguiça* sandwiches in fresh Portuguese bread, and soak up the warmth and comfort she gave me so I could go back out to the boat again. She always gave me a soup container or two of *calde verde* for Curt.

Tony Rodriguez, our barn landlord, never ceased to find humor in the situation. He thought it was the funniest thing to see me typing away in the front seat of the Pinto station wagon. But he was impressed when the results of all that work started rolling in, in the form of boat equipment from sponsors like Frank Beckerer, president of Beckson Marine, who came to see us in October 1980. To prepare, we gathered Curt's color slides from a long distance row in the unfinished boat we had taken on Narragansett Bay in September and set up a projector and a screen presentation in the barn. As soon as Mr. Beckerer arrived, Tony went out to greet him. The two had a lot in common, since they had both grown up on farms.

When Mr. Beckerer had seen our slides and examined the boat hull, he declared, "I have to tell you, you have a good boat here. But you have a lot of work to do to finish it."

Curt explained we were working on the bulkheads and expected to put the cabin structures in next. Mr. Beckerer seemed satisfied. He took out a catalog that profiled their plastic deck and cabin hatches and said, "Beckson will be happy to supply you with anything you need in exchange for mentioning us on any sponsorship publicity you do." When Mr. Beckerer had come and gone, we were buoyed in spirit for days afterward, and that night we celebrated at the Old Venice Restaurant in Warren, Rhode Island, with the cheapest and most affordable pasta dish on the menu: a heaping plate of $1.99 spaghetti dressed in oil and sautéed garlic. To fill our stomachs with more carbs, we shared a can of Budweiser beer.

For the fall, to break the tedium of working in the barn day after day, I had offered to fill in temporarily as a coach for the women's crew at my alma mater, the University of Rhode Island. Curt and I had rowed all our belongings in the incomplete boat hull south through Narragansett Bay to the wooded shoreline of the Narrow River in southern Rhode Island, where we camped out in a tent. By chance, Peter Wilhelm, our boat-building friend, was coaching the men's heavy weight crew, so the three of us lived together like hobos, camping, coaching, and boat-building on a shoestring budget, since our coaching positions paid nothing.

The lack of pay for coaching the women's crew was all the more irritating when some of the women complained about my coaching skills to the team's university advisor. When summoned to his office, I explained to Dr. Mottinger, my old crew team advisor, that I set our crew practices for 6 a.m. because during the day my husband and I were building our ocean rowboat to cross the Atlantic next year. While I agreed that they might have trouble hearing me call instructions from the launch I used, with Curt at the engine, to travel beside the women's eight and four, I pointed out that I had no megaphone because the men's lightweight coach would take it for his team. I was mortified when he told me I was fired. On my last day with the URI women's crew, most of the girls were shocked to learn that I was building an ocean-rowing boat with my husband, the launch driver, and living in a tent beside the boathouse because we couldn't afford to live elsewhere. Some even came down to see the boat after our last practice.

Setting off early the next Saturday morning so we could catch the tide going out at the mouth of the Narrow River, Curt and I rowed the thirty-five miles along the southern Rhode Island coastline back north to Mount Hope Bay and Tony's barn. For a brief time, we spent our nights either in the 1978 brown Pinto wagon that we would park on the abandoned cornfield behind the barn or in a tent. When snow began to fall, we moved from our car/tent home into Tony's barn. Tony and Edith, his wife, never questioned our living in their barn in the partially completed boat cabin. They offered cheerful encouragement when our spirits were low. Edith's home cooking often warmed our frozen insides when we came into their cozy kitchen for a break.

There were lots of ups and downs during this period. A former president of a rowing organization heard about our project and declared, "Row across the Atlantic? It can't be done. It simply can't be done." He didn't want to hear anything more about it. Curt filled out an application to the Explorers Club in New York City for a travel grant. Surrounded by stuffed animal heads, paintings of famous male explorers, and exotic memorabilia from past expeditions, we made a personal plea for why we should be funded to row across the Atlantic. One man responded that I didn't look strong enough to row any boat, never mind an ocean-rowing boat. I fixed him with my best steely look and said that I had been rowing since 1974 and I knew what I was doing. Curt outlined the plans for the expedition and impressed his former Arctic-climbing buddies. A few weeks later, a note on the famous red-and-blue letterhead of the Explorers Club informed us that they had decided to give us a travel grant.

To round out the sponsorship we had received for boat products and now an Explorer Club travel grant, we wrote to the oceanography school at the University of Rhode Island to ask if there was any sort of ocean water sampling we could do while at sea. Curt's parents, professors at Duke University, had convinced us that conducting oceanographic research on board our unique platform would be a good project to break up the monotony of rowing. We succeeded in contacting an oceanographer, who asked us to collect periodic water samples in small bottles partially filled with formalin.

When the weather became colder, Curt wore his favorite old orange down vest from his climbing days over the same blue hoodie every day, all day long. He worked with the single-minded dedication of someone driven to succeed at all costs. I wore layers of T-shirts, turtlenecks with sweatshirts, and corduroy pants to protect my skin from the fiberglass while continuing to alternate between boat-building and typing letters to potential sponsors from the front seat of the Pinto. In the evenings we would walk out of the barn to crystal-clear skies with the constellation of Orion, the hunter from Greek mythology, transiting above us. Later on, Saiph or kappa Orionis in the cluster that forms the shape of Orion would become crucially important to our survival at sea.

By late January, the boat was finished and sitting pretty in her shipping cradle, ready to be taken down to the port of Baltimore. One evening before climbing into the forward cabin for bed, I leaned against the gunwales in the silence of the empty barn and looked over what we had built in the past year. The twenty-five-foot-five-inch boat, which we had painted a bright red with a blue undercoat, was long and sleek, with gently rounded curves that mimicked the graceful lines of an expanded racing shell. The boat's lightweight, uncluttered fiberglass sandwich construction, with a half-inch Airex foam core between two stiff layers of fiberglass cloth, meant there was more storage space above and below deck in so compact a vessel. I remembered the hours we'd spent fitting the bulkheads that covered the front of each cabin, fore and aft, and the ones that divided the space below the nine-foot open deck where we rowed. All the bulkheads were heavily fiberglassed into place. The deck area where we rowed was fitted with two sets of rowing tracks, one after the other like a racing shell, and the oar locks were screwed into metal plates that were bolted into four square openings in the gunwales of the boat. When I worked with Curt to bolt one-inch-thick mahogany planks to the deck side of the starboard and port gunwales to give them extra strength and a place to put loops for tying down equipment, I was glad that Ed's design called for a series of five-inch scuppers, or square flaps, to drain the deck from breaking waves. The boat would sit so close to the sea that the three-foot height of the gunwales might be scooping water all the time.

Ed's extensive knowledge of rowing and boat design helped us outfit the boat in important ways that would make the voyage safer. For example, he designed the outside of the bow cabin to have a small overhang that protected the marine electrical plugs for the solar panels and give us a place to shelter when we needed to be on deck during a storm. On the sides of the overhang, we drilled holes and strung two-inch-thick polyester rope between the bow and stern cabins as safety lines. To charge a battery for lights in both cabins and power the radio and a small bilge pump, we attached eight solar panels donated by PD Labs, a California company, to the roof of the bow cabin.

As I stood there thinking of what it would be like to actually live on our boat at sea instead of in the relative security of a musty old barn, I felt the first pangs of excitement coupled with a tinge of anxiety. I could see Curt through the small rectangular port windows of the bow cabin in the glow of yellow candlelight, because we had yet to purchase a marine battery for electrical lights. The boat, I thought, looked very smart with its Beckson ports and hatches. Bolted and siliconed on deck were six eight-inch round hatches with metal safety tabs that Ed had made to prevent our below-deck fresh water supply, which would be housed in individual plastic five-gallon water bottles, and a small number of can goods from bursting out in the event of a rollover. In the bow cabin there were four port windows, two air vents located in the roof and in the bulkhead on the starboard side, and a large, white side opening hatch that functioned as the front door of the bow. The aft cabin had half the number of ports and vents because its space was limited by the rudder trunk that housed our extremely heavy one-piece, nearly five-foot-long rudder that ran through the roof of the cabin. Ed had pushed for such a heavy rudder, reasoning that its weight would give us more stability in stormy seas. Two dagger boards that ran through bow and aft fiberglass slots in the deck added to the boat's stability as well.

We had been lucky with the sponsorship of oars on the boat. Concept 2, a Vermont company run by Dick and Peter Dreissigacker, two brothers who had rowed competitively, donated two sets of their extremely durable carbon fiber singles oars and one sweep oar. The Martin Marine Company (now known as Alden Rowing), located in Maine, donated two sets of their foam-filled wooden oars that we used as backups. All the oars were stored on deck in a clever arrangement that Ed had designed so the oar handles fit into small round openings on either side of the aft cabin bulkhead.

At the beginning of February, word came from Jugolinia Shipping Lines that *Zvir* was ready to depart Baltimore, Maryland, in approximately mid-March 1981 or even earlier, in late February. Wanting plenty of time to drive to Baltimore with the old Pinto wagon and stop along the way to camp out and row the boat on Chesapeake Bay, we prepared to leave Rhode Island and Tony's barn well ahead of that date. At 11:30 p.m., February 3, 1981, the eve of our departure from Rhode Island, Ed Montesi came down to the boat to say goodbye. It was an emotional moment, because the three of us had been through so much over the year. Ed had stuck with us throughout the times when there seemed to be more naysayers than those who believed we could be successful. Now he wished us luck and gave us a knife, which he had designed specially for use at sea. He had made it with high-quality, rust-proof stainless steel with a special sheath. Handing it to us, Ed inadvertently gave us the perfect name for our boat when he said, "I present you with *Excalibur*." As in the legend of King Arthur miraculously extracting his sword from the stone, we felt that only we could pull off a successful row of the Atlantic Ocean.

The day we left, Tony, Edith, and their son came out into the snow-filled yard to wish us well and say goodbye. Tony told us he had seen us when we were building the boat and he wanted to see us when we got back. He had repeated this wish several times over the previous year, and now it felt like a good-luck mantra. The boat was ready to be loaded onto the passenger freighter and sent off to Casablanca, Morocco, the starting point for the Atlantic row.

PART II

NORTH ATLANTIC OCEAN

CHAPTER 6

The Expedition Begins:
Casablanca

March 1981

Z*VIR* MOTORED SLOWLY DOWN CHESAPEAKE Bay and into the stormy waters of Cape Hatteras, toward the ports of Charleston and Savannah where she would load additional cargo before heading across the Atlantic on what was to be her last voyage as a freighter. She would soon be sold to an Egyptian company, her name would be changed, and she would be relegated to taking tourists back and forth from Alexandria to New York.

During the week that *Zvir* stopped in several East Coast ports to take on cargo before motoring across the Atlantic, we went ashore to purchase last-minute supplies like more stainless-steel bolts and screws and dried food items too heavy to tow on the drive to Baltimore. In the evenings, we sat at our table in the small dining room for passengers, sipping our after-dinner coffees. One evening a ship's officer came over to our table and informed us that the first mate and captain requested our presence on the bridge. We were escorted into the darkness of the bridge—all the lights were turned off except for the glow of navigation instruments. The captain and first mate stood by the bow windows looking into the night.

"So I hear you are going to row across the Atlantic," the first mate began. "How long do you think it will take?"

"About three months." Our eyes were becoming accustomed to the dimness. I could make out the dark shape of the third mate at the wheel and half-full cups of coffee on the counters. An air of extreme seriousness and competency reigned over the bridge. Curt later told me he felt intimidated by these men of the sea.

The first mate spoke again. "I hope she is under control, because this voyage could take more than nine months." He laughed at his crude joke, though I didn't find anything funny about it.

Before either of us could reply, the captain interjected, "What course will you take?"

"We plan to go from Casablanca to the West Indies or Florida," Curt replied.

"Do you know what it's like out there? Have you ever been to sea?" the first mate asked.

Curt had an answer ready. "Yes, I've crossed the Atlantic six times by boat. We feel we've made all the necessary preparations." He didn't mention the six crossings were on passenger ships. For my part, I had only flown across the Atlantic.

We stood in silence. As the first mate, Lukin Zoran, carefully lit his pipe, I could see his rough features reflected in the nearby window. There was a frown on his face as he blew out the match.

"I've been at sea for nine years. I've looked at your boat, and it seems very well thought out. I think it will come through. But I want to give you some advice. It is you that must survive. You might want to be done with the voyage and jump overboard."

I didn't think this would be the case, but his next comment brought home the deadly seriousness of what we were proposing to do.

"They found *Puffin* with nobody on board. Maybe they were washed overboard, maybe they jumped off. . . . You *have* to think of the psychology of survival."

He knew something about ocean rowing, I thought. He knew about *Puffin*, whose crew had been lost in a 1966 attempt to row across the Atlantic. He went on to cite another ocean rowboat that had recently been found empty, floating upside down. Its rower vanished on his second attempt to cross the Atlantic.

As the *Zvir* traversed the Atlantic, a low-pressure system developed and we were soon in the middle of a full gale. Towering waves crashed over the bow, and the surrounding seas were blown white with foam. The scene in the dining room of passengers tipping over in their chairs and waiters walking Charlie Chaplin style as they balanced plates of food might have been amusing if it hadn't been for the fact that Curt and I could someday soon be rowing in such conditions.

Four days later we were in Casablanca. The decks of *Zvir* swarmed with Moroccan stevedores. We had taken the precaution of securing all our gear—such as the Autohelm, a self-steering device, sextant, charts and navigation books, TR-7 ham radio, life jackets and foul weather gear, cooking stove, the Norton medical kit given to us by Ed, marine battery, bilge pump, and other essentials—in *Excalibur's* cabins before *Zvir* docked first in the Arab port of Tangier and then Casablanca. Early on the first morning there, Curt went off to find port immigration officials who could stamp *Excalibur's* boat papers. Stevedores dressed in ragged, dirty *galibayah*s roamed the passageways of the boat, looking for loose items of interest and a bit of *baksheesh*. As it was, we were going to have to pay the Moroccans extra harbor fees for off-loading *Excalibur* into the harbor waters instead of to the dock.

When Curt returned with our stamped papers, I was giving the bottom of *Excalibur* one last coat of anti-fouling paint. We were standing together surveying my handiwork when Lukin Zoran came up and announced our "welcoming committee" was here. We turned to Charles Sten, the US consul, Jean-François Polizzi, president of the local rowing club, and Patrick Everarts de Velp, an oarsman and diplomat from the Belgian embassy. With joy and undisguised relief, we shook their hands and invited them to look at our boat.

With that, we were invited to moor *Excalibur* at the Casablanca Yacht Club for the week we expected to be in port before departure.

A few hours before the boat was to be off-loaded, Lukin Zoran invited Curt to his cabin. Handing him a glass of Yugoslavian wine, he said, "Now, you must be careful of compass deviation. How will you set your compass to stay on course when you are out to sea?"

Curt replied that he planned to consult the lines of magnetic deviation on the charts and apply them to our course.

"But you have solar panels, wires, and electricity," Lukin Zoran said patiently. "These can disrupt the magnetic field and cause additional compass error. Now you will copy these tables." He handed Curt a Yugoslavian volume on navigation and indicated the pages we would need. He translated the instructions for Curt so he could check the boat's compass using the bearings of the sunset and sunrise. "We cannot have you zigzagging your way across the Atlantic." He laughed as he pulled out a set of vector drawings that he had made for Curt to use in plotting direction and speed on the chart of the Atlantic we would be using.

When the permit arrived, *Excalibur* was lowered into the dirty harbor waters by boat crane, and a rope ladder was unfurled. Lukin Zoran went down first and stood on the gunwales, bouncing up and down. The boat was so heavily laden and well balanced that it barely tipped either way with his weight. Curt and I followed, legs shaking slightly from the new experience of climbing down a rope ladder into *Excalibur* with all eyes watching.

A week later, amid departure festivities, we stepped onto *Excalibur's* nine-foot-long deck. I sat in the bow rowing station and Curt went to the stern deck and leaned against the cabin. As I began backing the boat away from the docks of the Casablanca Yacht Club, Curt suddenly put up his hands as if he wanted to say something. In the rowing station, I sat facing backward, toward the stern, and watched Curt; I rested the oars. A feeling had come over him that he had to say something significant to the people assembled to bid us a bon voyage. Jean-François, Patrick, their families, Norberto, a Moroccan ham radio operator that the US consul had arranged for us to be in touch with throughout the row, and many others who had so generously hosted us during our week in Casablanca, and well-wishers who had come for our departure looked at him expectantly. He looked nervous, I thought. Holding on to the cabin edge, he began, "Why . . . ?" People on the dock became silent and looked at him. "Because through exploration, people and nations can learn to live and work together in peace," he said. The crowd broke into applause, and he waved his hand and added in French, "*Merci beaucoup*. Thank you for your help. We love Morocco!"

Curt took his seat in the stern rowing station, and together we continued backing the rowboat away from the dock of the Casablanca Yacht Club. Maneuvering *Excalibur* forward, we began the long row toward the harbor entrance, past the phosphate plants spewing white clouds of dust as it was loaded onto ships, and past the anchored, decrepit wooden fishing trawlers. A number of small motorboats, sailboats, and competitive rowing boats escorted us. A large French cruise ship steamed by, her deck crowded with passengers clicking away with their cameras and waving madly. Horns sounded all around. We passed a French aircraft carrier with the crew standing at attention in their bright white, pristine uniforms. A few minutes later, an old Russian trawler came into port and cut very close to us, sending a wake that tossed *Excalibur* back and forth. Russian seamen looking down from the deck saw our American flag mounted on the cabin top and laughed. Curt shouted, "It looks like you need a paint job!!" The rowers in our entourage added their comments in the form of obscenities.

I remembered something I had forgotten. Paula, the teenage daughter of Jean-François, had asked me for the words to the Beatles' song "Yellow Submarine." I had written them out but neglected to give them to her, so when we came to the end of the sea wall, I beckoned to Jean-François to draw closer in his single rowing shell. Carefully putting the notepaper with the words to the song on the tip of my oar blade, I passed it over to Jean-François, who grabbed it quickly and pushed off. Once again alongside us together with his son and Patrick, all three singles matched *Excalibur* stroke for stroke.

We rowed on and came to the end of the breakwater. The ocean waves were choppy, and conditions became difficult for the smaller boats. Bailing frantically, they turned back, one by one. We waved a last farewell, and in a short time we were alone at the beginning of our voyage. The date was March 18, 1981.

CHAPTER 7

Lights under the Water

March 18, 1981

I SAT HUNCHED ON THE ROWING seat, pressing my lips tightly together to keep from vomiting all over the deck. The minute we left the calm of Casablanca harbor heading into the heavy swells of coastal Morocco, *Excalibur* had started a horrible seesaw motion, throwing my body back and forth like a limp rag doll. My stomach heaved, and I could barely keep my eyes open. "This is nothing like Narragansett Bay!" I gasped, leaping for the gunwales. The worst sea conditions I had experienced on the rowboat were on the relatively shallow waters of Rhode Island's Narragansett Bay. To move anywhere on the boat, I had to hold tightly to the safety lines strung between the fore and aft cabins. Now I leaned over the side of the boat, hanging on to a safety line for dear life, offering my breakfast to the waves.

Later, although the lights along the Moroccan coastline twinkled dimly through the ocean haze, the weather deteriorated. The change began deceptively, with a light breeze out of the southeast, but within an hour, conditions were so bad that we could barely wrench our oars in and out of the building waves.

Crack! There was a terrifying noise above my head, and, as I twisted around to look up, the overburdened oar-shaft mast supporting the radio antenna, flags, radar reflector, and navigation lights tilted perilously in my direction.

"Look out!" Curt screamed, and I threw out my hand as the mast came down, barely missing both our heads as it crashed onto the starboard gunwale, nearly splitting in half, and then dropped into the sea. For a few nightmare moments, the green and red lights blinked eerily below the ocean's surface. I scrambled to my knees to grab the wires and mast before the waves pulled them away from the boat, then carefully got onto the cabin top, fighting to keep the mast upright again while Curt retied it using ropes in place of the broken wire cables.

Huge storm waves built all night, their white crests breaking thunderously in foaming masses that rushed toward the boat. I had never felt so vulnerable in my life.

By the second day, the mast had landed twice more on deck, each time barely missing whoever was rowing. Each time it came down, the wires for the radio antenna were torn apart and we had to retwist the wires and wrap them again with electrical tape. Our three-times-a-day schedule with Norbeto, the Moroccan ham radio operator arranged by the US consul's office, was not off to a good start either, because we were so busy just trying to survive our first few days at sea that we were late for some call-ins. When Curt calculated our position in relation to Casablanca harbor with his new plastic Davis sextant, he found that the boat had been blown back over most of the distance we had rowed that first day. Worse yet, *Excalibur* was less than five miles from the pounding surf of the shoreline that was just over the eastern horizon.

Stomach clenched with fear, I turned to him and said, "My God, we're going to end up crash landing on the coastline! We're going to be rolled over and dumped on the shore!"

In a barely controlled state of panic, I crawled back into the cabin and dug through my clothes bag, to find heavy cotton long underwear and a sweat suit to protect my body from being raked over the rocky beach that guarded the Moroccan coast.

"Do you want your sweats? It's safer with them on!" I yelled out the bow hatch door. Curt's mouth moved, but all I could hear was the wind.

"Here! Put them on!" I handed out his sweats while he grabbed our life jackets from the stern cabin. If the boat tipped over, we didn't want to be caught locked in the cabin, so we huddled together on deck with our backs to the cabin hatch door. For hours, we watched the seas slam hard against the boat—until I remembered something.

"What about the sea anchors?" I said, wiping the spray from my glasses.

We carried at least three of the pointed, parachute-like devices with holes at the end. Each curling wave pushed us along with what felt like the energy of a freight train, but by using a sea anchor to control the boat's speed, there was a chance the drift could be slowed.

"I don't know. I've never used them before . . . but I'll try it. Anything is better than this out-of-control ride." Curt got up carefully, grabbing the safety lines, and, walking like an old man, his shoulders hunched high, went to the aft cabin where the sea anchors were stored. Within minutes of him setting a brand-new sea anchor off the stern, *Excalibur* began drifting northward rather than toward the shore. The Autohelm, the electronic self-steering device that was attached to the tiller of the rudder and ran off batteries powered by the solar panels on top of the bow cabin, was adjusted so that our course was even more northward along the coast rather than toward the northeast, where the wind was pushing us.

During lulls in the wind, Curt took in the sea anchor, and we rowed to gain distance from the shore. But the boat was still in danger. Louder than the wind was the steady beat of a ship's engine from the constant stream of maritime traffic that plied the Moroccan coast. From time to time one of us would sound the Freon foghorn to signal our presence, and we left the navigation lights on all night.

CHAPTER 8

Birthday on the Barbary Coast

March 22, 1981

I SAT IN THE BOW CABIN alone, fingering the delicately wrought gold pendant in the shape of the hand of Fatima, wife of Muhammad, that Curt had just given me for my birthday. Thank you, I'd said, and leaned over to give him a kiss. He smiled and reached below deck on his side to pull out the SLR camera for a couple of photos. Twenty-five years old and at sea, rowing across the Atlantic Ocean. I slipped it on the braided gold chain with the St. Christopher's medal that Curt's sister Lynn had given me before we left the United States. With Fatima and Christopher together, I hoped we'd be lucky.

Each morning, after putting away the one sleeping bag we used since the cabin was so small, and firing up the Optimus stove for coffee and bowls of instant oatmeal, I would take a marker, lean over to Curt's side of the cabin, and write the month and day under year 1981: 3/18, 3/19, 3/20, 3/21, and 3/22, my birthday. The space was so small in the cabin that I could reach over and write on the wall with my left hand while holding on to the handle of the pot with the other. For a few minutes it seemed to me, the day held still as I printed the numbers.

I thought about this new life to be marked by the most alone time with another person I had ever experienced. Apart from the limited daily contact we had had with Norberto and the ceaseless rocking movement of the rowboat, the most significant aspect of the trip so far was the solitude of our community of two. For the past two and a half years, we had shared a common fascination with Thoreau's writings on nature and the solitary life. I had read *Walden, On Walking,* and *A Week on the Concord and the Merrimack Rivers* out loud as we rowed, hiked, and lived together. Thoreau's transcendental flirtations intrigued me, and I felt that his words spoke to me. It was how I wanted to live my life: through the challenge of being self-sufficient in nature.

By the day of my birthday, with the foul weather finally moderating five days after leaving Casablanca, I had lost my seasickness and had gotten my sea legs well enough to sit on deck again and appreciate the ocean environment. Curt, it had seemed to me, was not as bothered by seasickness as I was, though I imagined how hard it must have been for him, even somewhat nauseous, to keep up with the navigation and read the tiny print of the Nautical Almanac he used in his calculations.

Later, when I rowed, I saw long-tailed black cormorants swooping low around the boat, diving for the small fish hiding in the shade cast by the boat's bottom. These cormorants, *Phalacrocorax africanus*, I read in the *Pilot Guide to the Atlantic Ocean*, were seabirds found along the African coast, especially south of the Sahara. I rowed for a while and then pulled in my oars to watch glistening black-and-white short-beaked Atlantic dolphins jumping in front of the boat, flinging white necklaces of water droplets into the air. Sighting these graceful creatures was like a birthday gift.

A few days later, Curt wrote in his logbook:

March 25 We have to be extremely careful of Cape Beduza, a large rocky promontory of land that extends out into the sea between Casablanca and the Canary Islands. We've been putting in long hours at the oars. When I crawl back into the cabin afterward, I have only to close my eyes when vivid, dream-like scenes flash before me. I'm not quite asleep but I've seen scenes from my childhood, though I haven't really been thinking about them.

On March 27, the dawn began with a soft rose tint in the eastern skies and barely a breeze in the air. The sea was calm and silent. We took advantage of the conditions to swim and wash clothes. But by afternoon, the wind had found its strength again and was soon pushing three-to-five-foot breaking waves hard against the boat. It became too choppy to row and the boat's yawing motion was so rough that Curt put out a sea anchor again. It was too scary to go on deck, and we spent the next couple of days in the bow cabin reading to each other, writing up terse entries in our journals, and looking nervously out of the hatch while the weather worsened.

One morning when I went out to pee, the waves looked more threatening than ever. All around me as I perched on the edge of the port gunwale, bottom extended and my back pushed against the safety line, were heavy, lime-green waves that roared by the boat and broke with a nasty hissing sound. I finished and hastily stuffed the zip lock bag with toilet paper behind the tied down oars and scuttled back into cabin where Curt waited with a dry towel. Starting the first night, we'd gotten into the habit of drying each other off when we came into the cabin when conditions were stormy.

When the wind veered to the northwest on the 29th, the troughs between waves started looking like mountain valleys. The sea anchor off the stern was causing too much resistance against the prodigious force of the waves. With each wave, the boat would go forward only to be quickly jerked backward by the anchor's pull. It would struggle to the top, then be yanked back and forced into an almost sideways motion.

Finally, Curt said, "I'm going out. I've got to do something," and began to fasten on his safety harness.

I sat up, exhausted from the lethargy of days of rotten weather with no rowing, and said, "Wait! Why do you have to do that? It's crazy out there. Just let the boat drift."

"I can't just sit here and let the boat be jerked around. Besides, I'm sick of being in this cabin."

I understood his deadly boredom with the enforced inactivity. The sea anchor had to be taken in. I flopped back on my pillow after he went out and tried to imagine myself out on deck trying to set the sea anchor myself, but it scared me too much. So I waited and watched out the cabin door.

In the pitch dark of night, with his safety harness tied around his waist, Curt went to the stern deck where the sea anchor was tied off. Bracing his feet on the aft deck, he pulled laboriously, hand over hand. The wind was blowing hard, and ten-foot waves towered above the boat. When they broke some distance away, the boat rode easily, but when they broke right beside us, it created a foaming surge. I could see Curt cringing as gallons of cold seawater broke over him.

The storm went on for four more miserable days before Curt could go on the stern deck to take sights of a few stars that poked out from the clouds with the Davis sextant. As he caught each star in the mirror of the sextant's viewfinder, he called out "Mark" and I recorded the time from my wind-up Oyster watch that had been donated by Rolex, one of our sponsors from a contact at the Explorers Club. Later, in the cramped bow cabin, he worked out his calculations while I rowed: *Excalibur* had drifted two hundred miles off course. The boat was now south of Sidi Ifni and only a few miles off the African coast and Cape Juby. The American consulate in Casablanca had explicitly warned us to stay clear of the area south of Sidi Ifni because of the ongoing war between Morocco and Mauritania that extended into this region of the coast. The storm had blown us into a war zone.

Huddled together in the bow cabin, we looked at the vector drawings that Lukin Zoran, the first mate on *Zvir*, had made. With these, Curt could calculate the direction and length of time we would have to row in order to counteract the wind and current and make it safely out of this war zone. If we continued to drift in the southerly direction we were going, we would crash-land on the African coast north of Cape Juby in about thirty-six hours.

Curt looked up from his calculations and said, "We have to row northwest for about twelve hours if we are going to get out of here." I nodded unhappily, and we stowed the chart and went out on deck to row.

The new danger of the war zone after two serious storms put us on edge. Thoreau, our prophet for the wilderness, had not given us advice for dealing with fear and physical discomfort in such trying circumstances. In the nearly two weeks that we had been at sea, we'd been able to set up a fairly regular schedule of rowing both alone and together about eight to ten hours daily to keep the boat going in the right direction. But with the potential for problems in this remote area of the Moroccan coast, we were going to have to put in more hours at the oars. Curt began to complain of salt sores on his bottom from sitting on his wet rowing seat for so long, and my leg and arm muscles were achy all the time. Both of us had blisters from the first days at sea, but now we were developing new ones that stung badly in the salty living conditions. As much as I loved the beautiful lines of *Excalibur* that made her so easy to row, it seemed her extreme tenderness in the waves at sea was causing us to develop muscles in places we didn't know we had. In time, I would develop a dull pain in my hips from rocking back and forth in the bow cabin at night that only went away when we got off the boat.

One night in the dampness of the tiny forward cabin after a tedious day of rowing, we sat, feeling cramped and barely able to sit up straight with the low ceiling, eating another boring meal of macaroni and cheese; both of us were lost in our own thoughts. I scraped the last of the orange cheese sauce from my bowl, asked, "You finished?" and reached for his bowl.

"No, give me a few more minutes."

"Well, you can wash your own bowl," I snapped and opened the cabin hatch. Behind me, I could hear him muttering, "What's the difference? You never wash the dishes after dinner anyhow."

"Oh, shut up," I said, and slammed the hatch behind me. He was right: I never washed the pot or dishes after dinner, but then, he wasn't the one sticking his hands into a black sea in the dark. How did I know what was down there, as food bits drifted into the water at night? I had visions of fierce sharks leaping out of the dark to bite off my hands.

As evening descended, there was a violent splashing near the boat. I looked around and saw a large school of yellow fin tuna breaking the surface of the sea in the moonlight. It was a fantastic display, enormous tuna jumping completely clear of the water.

The wind died down and the seas subsided. Being blown onto the shores of Cape Juby was no longer an immediate threat because of the long hours and days we had spent rowing, but getting clear of the war zone and Moroccan coast was still important.

CHAPTER 9

Approaching the Canary Islands

Late March 1981

Fueteventura, the easternmost island of the Canary Islands, slowly came into view under clear skies dotted with fair weather cumulus clouds. We had read in the *Planning Guide for the North Atlantic* that the terrain of this island was similar to the Sahara Desert, which was only sixty miles away on the West African coast. After three weeks at sea, the sight of land mesmerized us. As we rowed closer, the dry barren hills and a group of fishing villages came into sight.

"Let's get something to eat," I said, putting down my oars.

Both of us were feeling tired and out of sorts as we put away the oars. I opened one of the round Beckson deck hatches to look for a can of Underwood luncheon meat, and when I put my hand down below, I touched liquid. There was a significant amount of water in the hatch with the food stores, sloshing back and forth. I pulled up a plastic bag with cans that I had protected with marine varnish while *Excalibur* sat on deck of *Zvir* on the Atlantic crossing, and saw they were rusty and the bag filled with saltwater. I looked over to Curt and at that same moment it occurred to both of us that the other hatches could be waterlogged as well. We began opening all the deck hatches, and indeed they all had at least three to four inches of saltwater sloshing around. We took turns pumping out the six deck hatches and leaving them open to dry in the afternoon sun.

Soon it was time for our regular radio contact with Casablanca. The battery, below deck in the stern cabin and wired to the solar panels on the bow cabin, had run down and never recharged more than halfway because of our initial, three-time-a-day schedule with Norberto, so we had reduced communications with him to once a day. We also wanted to maintain a schedule with a newly found ham radio maritime net out of the UK.

"CN8AP, CN8AP Casablanca, this is *Excalibur* KA1GIN, over." While we were building our boat, I had earned a Novice amateur radio license that allowed me to transmit in Morse code and receive in code and voice. I wasn't very good at it, though, as I translated each message into code and then slowly tapped it onto the 1960s-era Morse code key that our friend Peter Wilhelm's father had given to us.

"KA1GIN, hello *Excalibur*! Your signal is very faint. What's the problem?" Norberto, CN8AP, responded in voice.

I leaned out the cabin hatch to call to Curt and gestured impatiently back at the TR-7 radio transmitter wrapped in white padding and tied to the cabin ceiling. It had been making scratchy sounds for a few days, and now green lights were flittering unevenly across its front panel as I tried to answer Norberto.

When he couldn't hear my response, he guessed the saltwater might have eroded the wires of our electrical system because we were so near the water. He made a suggestion in Spanish that was to become one of our favorite mantras: *Pone en el sol!* Put it in the sun!

It was a memorable suggestion that we would repeat when our clothes and sleeping bag grew damp and wouldn't dry in the cabin. Sometimes we were laughing our heads off from the more inventive things to "pone en el sol," like a bowl of moldy oatmeal or the old threadbare towels scavenged from Curt's family's summer camp and especially chosen for their light weight.

Meanwhile, Norberto was still trying to reach us and repeating his "Pone en el sol!" suggestion when the green lights of the radio flickered once, twice, and then disappeared for good.

"Hold on," Curt said from the door of the cabin. "I'll go check the batteries."

He turned and went to the aft cabin to find the batteries were nearly dead and not charging. He came back to where I sat, and traced the problem to the wires leading from the solar panels mounted on the roof above. It must have been the pounding of the waves from the storms combined with the salt in the water that had corroded the wires. There was nothing to do but try to repair the connection.

I turned off the radio and reached behind it to unscrew the coaxial wire. I crawled out of the bow cabin, and together we began taking apart the wiring of the solar panels above our living quarters. After all of the eight panels had been unscrewed from their mounts, dried in the sun like strips of meat jerky, the wires replaced, and the panels remounted, I pulled out my trusty Morse code key and contacted Norberto once again. He was obviously so pleased that his suggestion had worked well that we couldn't help but smile at the excitement in his voice.

The wind and waves had been in our favor during the emergency maintenance session, for the deck had remained dry. That day, though, I was reminded how fragile our lives were at sea, and how tenuous our connections to the outer world.

CHAPTER 10

Near Miss

Early April 1981

[Letter to Kathleen's parents and siblings that was never mailed.]

Dear Family,

Looks like I might get this letter mailed on Fueteventura, Canaries. I'm actually 19 miles south of Fueteventura but we are hoping to go ashore tonight or tomorrow. We're finding out through our radio ham contacts what towns we are looking at and also we're trying to clear our way through customs on the islands before we get there. Our luck in Casablanca was tremendous, we made very good friends who bought food for us, drove us around to do our chores and fed us for a week straight.

When we arrived in Casablanca, we were met by the American consul, Charles Sten, and two members of the Casablanca Rowing Club. Each of the two rowers, about 40–50 years old, took turns having us for dinner. There was so much they wanted to do with us that sometimes we had to plead tiredness. The American consulate was very helpful: through them we met a ham radio operator who wanted to be our contact. We said OK but we didn't have the voice [capacity] so Norberto, CN8AP came down to the boat and set up a dipole antenna and fixed up a microphone! We have been on schedule with him every day at 11:30 am GMT.

During the first few days we were in touch three times a day! That cost us a lot in power so we cut it to once a day at 14,250 MHz at 1130 GMT, I believe 0530 GMT for you. Of course, once we discovered voice, we had to talk to someone else, since Norberto speaks no English; contacts [with him] are made by Curt in Spanish. We quickly found out one day during a three-day storm when all you can do is stay inside the cabin and rest (??) about the British Maritime Net at 0800 and 1800 GMT and at 14, 303 KC on the dial. It was a lot of fun checking in with them.

They all have English accents and are so polite. I tell you it's addictive this radio. QSOing. I enjoy it a lot but the dumb thing is I haven't said a word to Norberto or the UK net yet! Curt does the talking, I send the code. But I'm getting my courage up because this morning when Ernie, British net head, called us, I responded in code. So with all these hams listening to the Kat and Curt story, we can't be off the air too many days without people getting worried. Every day we give our position to the British net.

Well, anyways back to business at hand. We are doing fine. I've found my sea legs more or less. I did get seasick within two hours of leaving Casablanca and had problems for a few days afterwards. I thought I had strengthened my stomach after going thru the gale on the *Zvir* but that was not the case. I'm much better now; in fact, these last two days have been so calm I've felt a bit of motion dizziness being so still!

I have finally come to accept my cooking job as 1st cook (chef) with a reasonable amount of responsibility. Even though my menus are best suited for one without teeth, lots of potato flakes, soups, meat spreads, the crew of the *Excalibur* is not in danger of scurvy or starvation. In fact, I made a very good French onion soup seven days ago: Spanish onions fried in Moroccan olive oil, two cups of beef bouillon topped with slices of Edam cheese. My fish chowder made with canned sardines was an excellent fare of those who trod the decks of *Excalibur*.

My only reservation about cooking I have is the washing of the dishes at night. We see lots and lots of pinpoints of bioluminescence in the water at night. I suppose the same creatures are around during the day but I don't know what's out there besides that at night!

The fishing detail has not been so successful yet. Almost every day we cast lines. On Monday, we spotted a solitary fish swimming under the boat as I washed the breakfast dishes. I got so excited. I named him Harold and we set about trying to catch him. The bait was a can of Underwood liverwurst spread. He came so close we decided to try to get him with the dip net.

The routine was: I would drop liverwurst in the H2O and as the wind carried it away, Curt placed the dip net in its path. The fish was supposed to go for it, which he did but later figured it was better to wait for the morsel to float past the range of the net and go for it then. Curt said, "He's eating it, he's eating it all." And I laughed so hard.

We stopped the handouts and tried to catch him 'legitimately' as Curt put it. Two lines and five hours later, Harold was still swimming beneath our hull and nibbling at the hook ever so delicately. Before I gave up, I tried smearing liverwurst on the side of the boat right at the water level. I almost got him but . . .

The next day all stops were pulled out as Curt fashioned a spear from the boat hook. I even got out his wet suit so he might go below to confront the bugger himself. Unfortunately, Harold did not show up; perhaps he thought better of it.

This morning, however, Harold is back, but we are preoccupied with getting to the Canaries so we are giving him a break.

I'll keep in touch via Wilhelm or telex from Casablanca [through Norberto]. I started to say the American consulate is very helpful, they will send telegrams for us anytime. They have notified many people along the way of our row. Mr. Charles Sten is Consul in Casablanca but it is his assistant, Mr. Hadi who is helping us quite a bit. Mr. Hadi is a Moroccan and he is very good friends with Norberto. This Norberto was the radio contact for the Ra Expedition with Thor Heyerdahl.

Got to go now. It's raining!

Love, Kathleen XXOO

Our latest navigational challenge was to pass between the African coast and Fueteventura south of the Canaries and straight into the Atlantic Ocean, but one night a German ham radio operator, Fritz, whom we had met on the air through the British Maritime Net, told us that a low-pressure system was building over the entire Canaries archipelago. I looked at Curt in dread as Fritz described the predicted large seas and high winds.

"What about the hatches below deck?" I asked Curt, remembering the mold and seawater I had found earlier. "I think we might have a problem in another storm." Fritz, hearing my question, responded with an offer to help re-outfit the boat but at his home base in Tenerife, where he lived on a yacht with his girlfriend. When I hesitated, he said they would sail out to meet us in two days, after the storm, and tow *Excalibur* to his port. We agreed, but it meant that we had to maintain our position for a couple of days offshore from Fueteventura, not going any further south where the worst of the storm was predicted to hit.

Late into the night, we rowed out away from Fueteventura and into the wind. A line of bobbing lights appeared in the distance, growing brighter and brighter until a single spotlight seemed to be bearing straight down on us.

"Hey, they're going to run us down!" I dropped my oars and grabbed the foghorn attached to the wall above my bunk. Curt threw open the bow cabin door and plugged in the spotlight. He waved the light up and down and sideways—anything to get the attention of the ferry.

"Watch out! We're here!" I knew they couldn't hear us, but it was impossible not to scream. At the last minute, the ferry's lights veered away to port. We narrowly escaped being run over. In the surreal blue-white lights of the ferry, we could see human figures and rows of trucks lining the decks.

The next day, Fritz reported that conditions in Tenerife were still too stormy. "It's just too rough for us to leave port and cross over to Fueteventura. You have to hold on another night."

I turned to Curt, who was listening intently. "I hope we don't run into a ferry again." But in the evening, it seemed that the very same ferry was threatening to run us down once more.

When it was time to change rowers and I replaced Curt in the middle of the night, I asked him, "Do you know where we are?

How long do we have to keep rowing to be safe?" He pointed to a single solitary light that was Punta Lantilla on the southeast shore of Fueteventura.

"We have to keep rowing to clear that point because if we stop, we'll end up on shore with this south wind. You don't want to crash on the rocks, do you?" He spoke with what sounded like condescension, and when I gave him a dirty look, he muttered, "Sorry," and slunk into the bow cabin.

A cold rain carrying sand particles from the Sahara began to fall, and I pulled the hood of my rain gear tightly over my head. Out of the corner of my eye, I saw to the port side a long trail of greenish bioluminescence moving back and forth beneath the boat. This wasn't any small school of fish causing the glow; it looked like a very large fish—maybe a shark—longer than *Excalibur*'s twenty-five feet, swimming directly below us. I tightened my grip on the oar handles and looked straight ahead into the darkness.

Curt's log: April 7, 1981

Kathleen crawled into the cabin to sleep after her two-hour stint at the oars. She passed out a bottle of brandy, which I sipped to keep warm. As I rowed, a mass of green bioluminescence appeared beneath the boat. We were vulnerable, so close to the sea. I had the impression there was a very large fish, larger than *Excalibur*, swimming directly below the two dagger boards of the boat.

When I woke Kathleen to take over again, I did not want to alarm her, so I said, "You might see a big school of little fish exciting the bioluminescence beneath the boat. If you see them, wake me up, okay?" But she said that she had seen them too.

On April 8, Fritz on *Jangada* radioed that they were finally on their way, and on the 9th we rendezvoused by waving and flashing a mirror. At the last minute, with *Jangada* still way off in the distance, I decided to wash my hair. After three weeks at sea with only one person to see me, I was afraid of how wild I might look. I whipped off my T-shirt and lathered up my salt-stiffened hair with a sweet-smelling bar of saltwater soap. Though it was guaranteed to work like soap in fresh water, our clothes and bodies never quite felt as clean or soft as the advertisement predicted. Later, when I looked at Fritz's photographs of our first meeting, I wasn't surprised to see that both of us had hair that stood up stiffly around our tanned faces.

Jangada sailed smoothly up to us and put down rubber bumpers so *Excalibur*'s red hull wouldn't mar the sky-blue gel coat of their boat. When we climbed aboard, both of us could hardly stand up straight after so long on rocking-and-rolling *Excalibur*. Fritz and Kerrie, who was from New Zealand, presented me with a large bouquet of orange birds of paradise that I relished for its ambrosial scents of land.

For an hour, the four of us sat in the cockpit and talked—or rather, Curt and I talked, because we found there was so much to say to new people after twenty-one days at sea. Fritz and Kerrie listened in polite silence, smiling pleasantly, and then Kerrie invited me to go below deck to chat with her while she made a delicious lunch of rosemary spiced potatoes and fried minute steaks. Fritz went on board *Excalibur* with Curt to check the electrical wiring, where they found the damage was extensive. Fritz once again invited us to come back to Tenerife to make repairs and replenish the damaged food supply. We agreed, and after lunch and a quick swim we began the bumpy overnight tow to Puerto de Santa Cruz de Tenerife.

CHAPTER 11

Tenerife and Hierro

April 1981

O UR WEEK-LONG SOJOURN SPENT BUYING supplies and exploring Tenerife ended all too soon. One day Curt and I had taken a break from working on the boat to hike in the forests surrounding Pico del Tiede, a 3,718-meter volcano in the interior of the island. The trail wove its way through a cedar-scented forest that reminded us of the woods around Curt's parents' summer house in northern Vermont. For a short time, we were tempted to extend our visit, but the hurricane season was approaching and we had to be on our way.

We left Tenerife for Hierro Island in mid-April, with *Jangada* towing us once again. Between Fritz and *Jangada's* owner, who was visiting from Brazil, and ourselves, we had come to the conclusion that Hierro, the smallest of the Canary Islands and in the most southwestern quadrant of the archipelago, would be the best jumping-off point to resume the row across the Atlantic Ocean.

A few hours later, after anchoring in Puerto de la Estaca, with the bright sun wafting streams of hot air over us, Kerrie and I walked along the dirt road that led from the port to Val Verde, Hierro's capital city high above the ocean. Though we chatted about mundane things as we carried our empty string shopping bags, I couldn't help but think how something as normal as walking and chatting with a friend was an activity that I was going to have to treasure for those times at sea when the confined life on *Excalibur's* nine-foot-long deck became too limiting. Higher and higher we climbed as Puerto de la Estaca steadily diminished in size, until it was only a small bite out of land where *Excalibur* and *Jangada* were anchored.

"Hey, that's your rowboat, isn't it?" Kerrie said, pointing to a red dot in the blue water.

"Yeah, I think so," I said, and thought how nice it was to be on this dirt path in the hot sunshine with the astringent scent of acacia bushes in the air. Just before we reached Val Verde, small cement houses appeared, and young men working the rugged hillside gardens looked up at us and hooted as we passed. We were both wearing T-shirts without bras and short shorts, but there wasn't anything to hoot about, we thought. Kerrie looked at me and shrugged, and I shook my head as if to say, "Guys—what can you expect?"

In Val Verde, I pulled out my scribbled list of last-minute food items for the ocean row while Kerrie took out her list for the return sail to Tenerife. We stopped at all the open-air market stalls and filled our string bags with vegetables, fruit, and the special red wine that Hierro Island was known for throughout the Canaries. Before siesta hour when all the businesses shut down until 4:00 p.m., I bought one last ball of the local white cheese, and we began the winding downhill walk to the port and our boats.

Before starting the crossing on the morning of April 21, we needed to wedge pieces of rubber tubing between the extremely heavy rudder and its fiberglass housing that ran from the top of the aft cabin to the bottom of the boat. From the beginning when we left Casablanca, the rudder had banged back and forth in most conditions at sea. It was a problem we worried about, because the weight of the rudder might crack its half-inch fiberglass housing and cause a leak in the aft cabin. I remembered how much work the rudder and its housing had been to make in the barn in Touisset. When we had finished the repairs, we were better prepared than we had been in Casablanca.

I looked up as we completed our work and saw a French couple, François and Corinne, motoring in our direction in their inflatable dinghy. "I've brought something for you!" François called out, and he handed Curt a spear. "I think this will be interesting for you because when you see a fish, you can kill him and eat him. Sharks are good to eat, too, and their teeth are valuable."

There was a loud whistle from the quay above, and the harbor-master waved cheerfully as he held out a huge bouquet of orange bird of paradise flowers for me along with our stamped departure papers. I looked at him and the flowers, a happy smile plastered on my face, though I hesitated to reach out and take them. Accepting the flowers meant the beginning of the row was coming closer and our time on land was ending. It had been exhausting rowing down the Moroccan coast because of the adverse weather and the constant threat of being run down by the relentless stream of shipping traffic. Sometimes the ceaseless motion of the boat threatened to toss us off the deck or drive us crazy with its lack of stillness. Now, almost a month after leaving Casablanca, on this warm, serene, and sunny April morning, I was in our homemade rowboat at the edge the open Atlantic, ready to row out into the unknown again. This must be what exploration and adventure are all about, I thought.

I looked over at the harbormaster.

"*Muchas gracias, señor,*" I said, and took his bouquet.

Presently, Fritz came over and gestured to the ocean beyond the breakwater. It was time to get moving. We waved goodbye to people on the quay as François and Corinne cast off *Jangada*. Fritz started the engines while Kerrie, Curt, and I hauled in the two anchors. We were underway! *Jangada* would tow us to a safe point south of, but within the longitude of, Hierro, where the row would recommence.

Excalibur was still tied alongside *Jangada*, the two hulls protected by rubber bumpers. Curt and I kept looking over the gunwales of *Jangada* to make sure *Excalibur* was riding well. As we motored out of the fishing village at Puerto de la Estaca, François and Corinne ran along the breakwater, keeping pace as long as they could. "*Bonne chance! Bon voyage!*" they shouted. The harbormaster stood nearby waving farewell.

Once safely clear of the port, we climbed down to *Excalibur* while Fritz prepared a long towing rope. With it securely tied to

Jangada's stern and *Excalibur's* bow, we untied the lines that held us to the port side of their boat. The rowboat gave a sudden jerk when the slack on the towrope was taken up by the forward motion of the sailboat.

Finally, after watching the island recede for a short while, Curt turned toward *Jangada*, waved his arms, and shouted to Fritz to stop and let us off. Fritz once again cut the engines and pulled us in with the tow rope. We reached up to shake hands and thank him and Kerrie for all the help they had given us in the islands.

"Good luck, man," Fritz said, clapping Curt hard on the shoulder, "and remember to check your batteries once a day and watch your power consumption."

Kerrie ducked below deck and came back with an envelope containing a transparent white shell she had found on a beach back home in New Zealand for me. "Here's something for you; I hope it brings you good luck." I thanked her, and we hugged and kissed goodbye. We had become good friends in a short time.

Curt cast off the tow rope, and I sat down to row. It was 1600 GMT, April 21, 1981. The open Atlantic portion of the row had begun.

CHAPTER 12

With the Atlantic in Front of Us

April 21, 1981

W E ROWED ON THROUGH CHOPPY seas away from Hierro. Soon, the local south wind effect caused by the island gave way to the persistent northeast wind of the stationary North Atlantic high. We rowed smoothly together in spite of the three-foot waves and occasional breaking wave crests. As our sliding seats that faced aft like a regular racing boat moved up and down the tracks, the pressure on the oar blades strong, we felt happy to be on the move again. The rowing stations were actually the most comfortable places in the boat. Here, we could watch the waves and compensate for their motion by leaning to one side or the other to slip the oars in and out of the water. And here, in our rowing seats, sometimes on top of the specially made foam pads an acquaintance had created for us based on the contours of our bums, we could best control the motion of the boat as we pulled steadily toward our goal.

As we watched the green-gray mass of Hierro recede in the distance, Curt said, "Last land for a long, long time." I said nothing in response but continued to row, setting the pace from the stern. But occasionally both of us would look toward the distant hillsides.

No turning back

Curt's log: April 21

I knew there was no turning back. The persistent trade winds and waves were too strong to row back against. Hopefully we would follow them far out into the Atlantic and across to the other side. I wondered about voyagers long ago. How many had seen that last island recede in the distance and wondered what lay ahead for them? Columbus certainly. But Columbus was unique. He came back. Some of his men thought they might sail off the edge of the earth, though they believed that chance preferable to life in prison. [Many sailors of that time were convicts offered a way out of prison by crewing on the government-funded ships of exploration.]

We rowed on for two hours until we were safely clear of the island. Then we stopped, took in the oars, and tied them to the edge of the deck. "I'm hungry," I said, and Curt agreed he was as well. I went forward to the bow cabin to get out the stove, and Curt went back to the aft cabin to get fresh food supplies. He later told me, as he leaned into the cabin, bracing himself against the motion and looking for potatoes and carrots, a wave of fear passed through him as he thought of the distance of this undertaking. Even if we steered a reasonably straight course, more than three thousand miles lay between us and the nearest islands in the West Indies. It was a very weird sensation. He said he felt as though he had been here on the open sea before and died many times.

Enough of such thoughts! It was a time to celebrate. We were at sea again in *Excalibur*! Taking the fresh food, he closed the hatch and moved toward the forward cabin holding on to the safety lines. I leaned out of the forward hatch, and Curt passed the food in to me.

"Are you coming in?" I asked.

"No, I think I'll stay out on deck for a few minutes," he answered. The sky was beginning to grow dark, and he wanted to sit on deck and think.

Kathleen's log: April 21

I was glad to have a few minutes alone, even in the cramped little cabin. A lot had happened this day, and there was much to think about as I organized the kitchen equipment below deck. We had finally started out across the Atlantic. I felt a little scared about what could happen out there. Did we really know what we had gotten ourselves into? I thought of my family and wondered what they were doing now. Even though it was getting dark now, it was still light at home, in Rhode Island. I felt so far away.

The space in the forward cabin where we spent part of our days out of the sun, did the navigation and radio communication, slept, and ate was tight. The interior was about six feet in length, with four under-deck compartments for stowing clothes, navigation equipment, and immediate food stores. It was approximately three feet wide at the widest point and six inches across at the very bow, where it was so narrow that when we rolled out the sleeping pads and pulled the sleeping bag over us at night, we had to stack our feet on top of each other's. Along the sides it felt like a pup tent, but it had a rounded ceiling that allowed us to sit up completely only down the middle. The bulkhead or front of the forward cabin was canted slightly toward the bow so the bow rower would have room to lean back at the end of a stroke. The cant of the wall was so slight, though, that it didn't really diminish the space inside.

As we sat in the cabin after dinner, Curt remembered it was time for the UK net. We had agreed to meet Fritz on this DX maritime ham radio network operating out of the United Kingdom in the evenings. Curt reached up and switched on the radio, tuning it to the right frequency. The round of amateur ham operators checking in had already begun. Soon we heard Fritz.

The net control who was leading the evening's meet said, "Jolly good, perhaps Fritz can tell us more. What news do you have of the rowers? Over to you."

"Well, yes, we've done our best to kick them across the Atlantic. I wonder if *Excalibur* is copying us?"

"Roger, roger, this is *Excalibur*. We copy you loud and clear, we're doing fine on our first night out on the Atlantic." We looked at each other, smiling. We could just imagine Fritz and Kerrie sitting in *Jangada*'s salon below deck.

The next voice we heard was familiar to us. John Wilhelm, our friend Peter's brother from Rhode Island, checked in. The reception was remarkably clear considering the great distance and the boat's closeness to the water. John had talked to Curt's father in North Carolina, who said all was well at home but expressed some concern about the state of our solar panels. Apparently, details in the press had been sketchy about *Excalibur*'s problems with the wiring. The Rhode Island papers had been following us through the Wilhelms' ham radio contacts with us and sometimes through my parents, though the primary source of information about us came from the Wilhelms. The Explorers Club had initially put out press releases about our row, and some of their press contacts regularly contacted our parents and the Wilhelms. Stories in the Vermont papers as well as the Rhode Island and North Carolina papers were picked up by the wire services. I was beginning to suspect that the hams we spoke to and the many who just listened in were probably sharing what they heard with their newspapers as well. I was glad when Fritz explained the work he had done to correct the corrosion issue. John responded by promising to call our families. I could tell Curt was happy to hear that, because he didn't want our families to worry too much.

When the net schedule was over, we switched off the radio to save power and sat back, basking in the glow of good news, and smiled at each other. It meant a lot to receive these good wishes and the news from home. We were on the Atlantic, and all was well.

CHAPTER 13

Night Stories

April 1981

CURT AND I STOWED THE kitchen equipment below deck in the center hatch. While he rolled out the sleeping pads that took up all of the cabin floor space, I went on deck to stick the dirty dishes in a cloth bag with the intention of washing them later. The odds were probably very small that a shark would come up and grab me and those dishes when I stuck them in the water, but I was never sure. The same went for calls of nature. Curt was lucky he could stand on deck, holding on to a safety line to pee. I had to take my chances by sitting carefully on the gunwales, bottom extended just far enough.

I opened the cabin door and crawled in. Curt was stretched out, writing in his log. When I finished filling in mine, we turned off the light and pulled the lightweight sleeping bag over us. In companionable silence, we listened to the wind and waves slapping against the hull. The conditions were choppy, because the islands nearby disrupted the regularity of the waves.

We kept waking up during the night due to the incessant rocking of the boat back and forth. Each time one of us woke up, we would open the hatch and scan the horizon for ships. *Excalibur* was still close enough to land that the danger of being run over by a freighter was real. Once, in the middle of the night, Curt went out on deck to check the Autohelm autopilot and compass. He clipped his safety harness to the lines suspended between the cabins and worked his way back to the aft cabin. I switched on the anchor light that Fritz and Curt had fixed with a brighter bulb. The added brightness would enable us to check on things on deck at night without carrying a flashlight.

Curt made a small adjustment with the autopilot's compass setting to improve our course. Even though we did not drift with any speed when we weren't rowing, the Autohelm, attached to the tiller of the rudder, helped us to drift in the right direction and probably gave us better time, which meant increased safety. In the past, seafarers would tie off the rudder to approximate the direction they wanted to go in and hope for the best.

Curt's log: April 22, 1981 0630

This morning when I woke up I expected both of us to row but Kathleen said she wasn't feeling well; seasickness was bothering her again. I went on deck and untied the oars and fitted them into the oarlocks, and looked around at the choppy waves pushed by a steady breeze. I began rowing and enjoying the warmth of the sun filling the air. There were a few clouds on the horizon to the east. They looked as though they were hovering over land since there was a dense quality about them. I looked closer and could just make out the distinct profile of Hierro Island. Gradually the sun climbed higher in the sky and the cloud formations above land grew thicker until I couldn't make out the shape of the island from the thickening clouds. I thought how this last sight of land made me feel sad.

After about three hours, I took a break to see how Kathleen was doing. I left the oars tied crosswise on deck so they would be ready to go again. In the cabin, I saw that she was already up and making breakfast.

It was later in the day when I saw the faint purple smudge on the eastern horizon that was to be the last sight of land for two months. I sat on deck, the ocean waves jostling the rowboat from side to side, watching with apprehension as we drifted steadily in a westward direction, away from land. Though I had the advantage of a few hundred years of history behind me, I was sure that my feelings were the same as other mariners when they left the Canary Islands with the ocean in front of them as an immense mystery. Would we survive our row in twenty-five-foot *Excalibur* from Hierro Island, the smallest and most western island in the Canary archipelago, to the Caribbean?

Later, after we left the boat to drift in a westerly direction, I followed Curt into the bow cabin, ducking under the orange bird of paradise flowers tied to the ceiling that the Hierro harbormaster had given me. I would study them every night above my head and think of land. In the morning, in a passion play of my own making, I would take a flower, drop it overboard, and watch as it slowly drifted off. The informal ceremony helped me to readjust to life at sea again while saying goodbye to land. In the end, the tiny bugs that lived in the flowers quickened the rest of the bouquet's departure from the cabin. The cellophane covering that mimicked the sound of raindrops was stuffed in the back cabin for possible reuse.

For a half hour, we wrote in our logbooks until I turned off the overhead light and pulled the sleeping bag over us.

The next morning, I still couldn't row because of my seasickness and I called out to Curt, "My stomach doesn't feel so good. I don't know if it's from the boat's motion or a bug I picked up in the islands." I was sitting up cross-legged in the cabin, opening the deck hatches below where we slept to take out the stove to make breakfast in the cabin.

"Sorry to hear that." He called back. "Are you going to have some breakfast?"

"Maybe something light. Want some hot chocolate and bread? We should keep eating the bread before it goes bad."

"Sounds good to me. Let me know where I can come in."

When the flame was blue and steady, I put the cook pot on to boil.

"Is it ready? Can I come in?"

I held up a finger. "In a minute . . . Okay, be careful, I'm holding the hot chocolate." I turned the stove off and put it below deck.

"God, my legs are killing me. They're cramping."

"Stretch them out. I'll hold your cup until you're settled. Phew! That's awful," I told him. His feet smelled terrible. "Can't you move your smelly sneakers out of here? I feel awful and your stinky socks in my face aren't helping either."

He responded defensively. "I'll try to put them out of the way. But they need to hang up to dry properly." He had taken off his damp socks and hung them in the yellow hand straps attached to the ceiling.

"Right, but they're not doing me any good! You know," I decided to goad him, "you don't really need shoes. You should go barefoot. It's healthier."

"No, it's not! We're going to be here for a long time, and we have to be careful of salt sores."

I could tell I wasn't going to win this one. Someday he would realize I was right. For now, all I could do was look out the port window and watch the waves go by.

In the late morning I rowed, stretching out my leg muscles by pushing back hard against the weight of the waves, and soon my stomach began feeling better. I loved the craziness of rowing through rough, tumbling waves in the emptiness of the ocean landscape. With each stroke, though, the wind increased and the waves crested white while the sky took on a gray blanket of thick overcast.

When I crawled into the bow cabin, I saw that Curt had already turned on the radio for Norberto time and was tuning to the right frequency. There was a lot of static today, but there was no problem finding our friend. We were delighted to hear Fritz was also on the frequency. He explained to Norberto the new radio schedule that we devised while in the Canaries.

"I have told these Americans that they use too much power without any thought as to where it is coming from. They have to be very careful of their power consumption." We were interested in Norberto's response, since a good part of our "too much" power consumption had been due to our initial, heavy, three-times-a-day schedule with him until we had reduced it to once a day.

"They will be making contact with you on Mondays and Thursdays at 1130 hours GMT (Greenwich Mean Time), over."

"*Si, si, muy bien.* I will be on the air with them on those days. I will tell Mr. Hadi at the American consulate. They always look for information on the rowers. They have put up a map of their course." Norberto's English was improving.

Curt couldn't stay silent any longer and got out the microphone. He sent 73s—or "greetings," in ham radio parlance—to Norberto and the others in Casablanca.

After a light lunch of liverwurst, two overly ripe tomatoes, and some stale cookies bought from a Val Verde bakery, we went out on deck to row.

"Curt, do you think the wind has picked up any?" I asked.

He thought about this for a few moments, turning his face to both sides to feel the wind, as we pulled the oars through the water, and then said, "Yeah, it has." After a few minutes he added, "The clouds don't look too good either. I wonder if the bad weather in the Canaries will catch up with us."

A small twinge of anxiety touched my stomach. Curt was anxious about the weather too. We rowed on for most of the afternoon, pausing to have a snack of figs and prunes from the food stores we had bought in Casablanca and cups of sweet instant lemonade from the Gilster-Mary Lee food company, one of our sponsors. By the early evening, the sky was almost all overcast. The increasing winds pushed the waves to six to seven feet high.

"We better make sure to tie down these oars good."

I took the rowing seats, put them in the stern cabin, and grabbed a packet of noodles and cheese for dinner. Before leaving the Canaries, we had taken the new precaution of putting perishable foods in the back cabin or on top of the water containers below deck so that any water that leaked in could be pumped out before rising high enough to damage the food. I worked my way across the deck to the forward cabin, holding on to the safety lines. As I ducked under Curt's arm where he was holding on to one of the safety lines, I saw the worried look on his face. He was looking out across the sea. When I was back in the cabin, I called out, "Do you think you'll get any sights tonight?"

"I've seen Jupiter through breaks in the sky. Pass me the sextant, and I'll give it a try."

After dinner, Curt worked out his sights of Jupiter and Capella using the HO 249 Sight Reduction tables. Though the HO 249 tables come in three volumes and were originally designed for air navigation, volume one is used by marine navigators as well. Because volume one contains the altitude and true azimuth values of seven selected stars that are considered first-magnitude stars whose brightness is sufficient for navigation, HO 249 has always been considered an easy and fast way for sailors, or ocean rowers in this case, to calculate their positions. Satellite navigation was in its infancy in 1981, and we didn't have the money for such a system. Our navigational tools consisted of a sextant, a compass, the *Nautical Almanac*, and the HO 249 tables.

"If the sights are right, we are at 26 degrees 54 minutes north, 18 degrees 40 minutes west. I think we're rowing at about three knots or a little over three miles per hour."

It was another uncomfortable night amid the increasingly building seas.

On April 24, Curt got up at 0700 to start rowing. He remarked on how sick he felt and that his stomach hurt. He thought the fresh air would do him some good because he probably had the same bug I had had. I was feeling fine now that my stomachache and seasickness was gone.

After breakfast, I told Curt that he should rest and I would go out to row. It wasn't really too hard to adjust to life back out at sea. Though the waves had gotten bigger, I felt challenged by them as I worked at adapting my style to the rolling waves.

With the skies overcast, the wind had shifted to the northeast. A black-and-white petrel flew by in the near distance, and I called to Curt to come and see it, but when he emerged from the cabin, I saw that he was drawn and tired-looking. As long as he was up, he said, he would try shooting the sun through the clouds to get an estimated position (EP) from a line of position (LOP). By combining the observed angle of the sun that he got using the sextant with the exact time of day, he could produce an LOP that told us we were somewhere along that line. In a few more hours with the sun's angle changed, he could do another one to get a "running fix." The most accurate way to determine our position, however, was with the stars and planets to obtain more than one LOP that would accurately fix our position where the lines crossed. Navigation like this was complicated, and Curt was getting better at it all the time.

Later in the afternoon, we rowed together for a couple of hours. Sometimes we had to pause in the rowing strokes to let a large roller go by. The shifting wind was making the waves more confused and blowing cold spray that drenched both of us. By early evening, the sky was gray and dismal.

Curt's log: April 25.
I awoke at first light and saw that Kathleen was still sleeping. She had rowed more than I had the day before and needed the rest. I dressed quietly and crawled past her onto the deck. I clipped my harness onto the safety line since conditions were far too rough to risk going without it. Right away I could see why we were rolling so much. Most of the waves were at least ten feet high. Even as I stood bracing myself against the forward cabin structure, the top of a wave broke over the side of the boat and partially filled the open deck area. I watched as the water drained out through the square scupper openings at the edges of the deck and through the drainpipes in the foot wells at the center of the rowing stations. Cold seawater sloshed back and forth on deck.

I was concerned about the autopilot because it was mounted above the aft cabin structure and exposed to all the elements. Attached to the tiller, it had been running continuously since we had left Hierro. As we rolled around in the waves, I could hear its little electric motor inside the housing, whirring first one way, then the other, as it tried to compensate for the motion. I did not want the motor to overheat and burn out because of heavy use this early in the voyage. Perhaps it needed to take a rest and cool off.

I unlashed a pair of oars at the stern rowing station and switched off the autopilot and tied off the tiller. Then I quickly sat down and began rowing. I would try to keep us on course by rowing and watching the compass. The waves were much larger than anything I had ever rowed in before. Another breaking wave came along, rolled over the gunwale, and landed in my lap. I had to stop rowing for a moment because the water felt so cold that I was shivering. I started rowing again but the boat had drifted off course. I pulled harder on the starboard oar to get us back on course again, but the wind and waves had caught the side of the boat and we continued to drift broadside to the waves. I pulled hard on the starboard oar but I could not point the bow downwind.

Then I saw the wave coming but could not do anything about it. We were broadside to the waves now, as a greenish wave built beside me, arching upward and splashing over my head, filling the deck area with foaming turbulent water. It tasted very salty.

I heard a scream from the cabin.

"I'm trying to row without the autopilot," Curt shouted toward the bow cabin where I was sleeping. "It's not working too well." An understatement, I thought. Though the boat had remained relatively stable and the deck area drained well, it was better to put the autopilot back on. Within a few minutes, with the autopilot reattached to the tiller, the boat was back on course. Curt continued rowing on the more optimal downwind course.

After lunch, I came out and joined him. We seemed to be making good time rowing in the waves. Off in the distance, Curt spied a large fishing boat that appeared to have a crane on deck. We stopped rowing and stood up to get a better look.

"I bet they're going to the Endeavor Bank," Curt said.

This was a good sign, because he had calculated our position to be a mere few miles from the great mountain peaks on the ocean floor that made for excellent fishing. Though the water was probably about twelve thousand feet deep where we were floating, the Endeavor, Echo, and Papp Seamounts rose thousands of feet from the ocean floor. At the Endeavor Bank, the depth is less than six hundred feet.

By late afternoon, we were feeling so tired from rowing in the rough conditions that we took in the oars and went into the shelter of the forward cabin. Soaking wet and yet exhilarated from the row, we dried each other off with the threadbare "*Pone en el sol!*" towel and put on dry clothes. We crammed our wet clothes through the hand straps on the ceiling and hoped they would dry.

After dinner, Curt turned on the radio so we could listen to the weather report. Colin of the UK Net came on with the forecast that he had just picked up from the BBC weather service. We listened closely for the various regions, beginning in England and working down the European coast to Africa. Then it came to our part of the world.

"Force 4 to 5, increasing to 6 to 7, winds veering to the northwest, choppy seas, increasing to very heavy seas, repeat: very heavy seas . . ." He continued to give weather for other regions.

I switched off the radio, and we sat staring at each other for a long moment. The famous Beaufort wind force scale that the BBC used to announce the weather went from the calm of a Force 1 all the way up to the hurricane-force wind of Force 12. According to Colin's weather forecast, in our region of the Atlantic Ocean this coming week, we could experience a moderate breeze of Force 4 or as much as a moderate gale of Force 7. Either way, *Excalibur* and her crew were about to be tested again.

CHAPTER 14

Adjusting to Life at Sea

Curt's log: April 26

I THOUGHT AGAIN OF THE FIRST mate of *Zvir*. When conditions grew bad, it helped to think of him.

It was dark out there and I did not want to go on deck. I was tired and it was comfortable inside the cabin. Besides, the wind outside was steadily increasing in force; I could tell by the sound it made in the guy lines surrounding the oar shaft mast. What had been a low moaning sound was now a high pitched whistling.

I told Kathleen I was going on deck. I asked her to turn on the deck light when I crawled out, blowing spray greeting me as I emerged.

At the back cabin, I checked the compass and autopilot settings. Then I checked the lashings that secured the autopilot to its mounting, and the tiller in case it had become loose. The oars were the next order of business. I was thinking that it was a good thing I was checking these things because we didn't tie all of these ropes when we finished rowing. I was concentrating so hard on the knot I was tying when . . . *bam* . . . a wave crashed against the boat, throwing me off balance. I fell on the deck and the cold water rushed over me. Shit!!!

I wiped the saltwater from my eyes and tried to get up while grabbing hold of the safety lines. I went back to the oars and finished tying them in. Through the cabin hatch window at the opposite end of the deck, I could see Kathleen sitting in the corner holding on to the straps on the ceiling. When I came in, she quickly reached over and closed the door behind me. I took the towel she handed me and dried off. "You poor boy, let's get you dried," she said.

Curt began peeling off his wet clothes. Though we were approaching the Tropic of Cancer, it didn't take much to get cold on a stormy night like this. We decided to call it quits for the night and get under the sleeping bag. I reached up and turned off the cabin light.

"What's it like out there?" I wanted to know. The waves sounded ominous.

"It's pretty dark, and you can't see much except for a white blur from the waves that are breaking near the boat. There're streaks of bioluminescence in the waves. I think they're pyrosoma."

"Really? The same ones we've been seeing since Casablanca?"

Boom!!! Another wave broke against the boat. Instantly, Curt was thrown to the opposite side of the cabin against me as *Excalibur* heeled to a precarious angle. Whoosh!!! The foam of the breaking wave gushed around the boat, creating a cacophony of water bubbles popping against the hull.

"Aaghh!" I screamed. "Get off my arm!" He had landed with his elbow digging into my forearm. The sleeping pads, sleeping bag, and everything else in the cabin seemed to be in a jumble. I reached up and flicked on the cabin light. In the violent lurching of the storm, we did our best to straighten things up, wishing for the umpteenth time that we had some sort of seatbelt to strap ourselves down in bad weather.

"Do you think everything is all right out there?" I asked and switched on the anchor light. I pushed aside the rose-colored canvas curtains that Kerrie had made for our bow hatch to cut down on glare from the sun and we peered through the Plexiglas hatch window into the darkness, not wanting to open it for fear of flooding the cabin. Through the maelstrom outside the hatch, we could see the autopilot dripping wet but still moving the tiller back and forth as it steered through the waves. Once again we switched off the lights and braced ourselves.

Then in the distance we heard a sound of a freight train above the roar of other waves. It grew louder and came closer, crashing over the top of the boat with a harsh *kussssh* sound. We were both thrown across the cabin, and water streamed in the ceiling ventilator above our heads. Curt reached up and shut the vent with a quick twisting motion. Water was now sloshing around inside the cabin. Water was also coming in the hatch cover through a slot by my head where the radio antenna went out.

"Quick! Stuff something in the slot!" Curt fumbled for the light switch, and I grabbed the towel and rammed it in the slot. We surveyed the shambles in the cabin. Everything was soaking wet, ourselves included.

"That must have been a rogue wave." Curt looked at me. He was exhausted. I'm sure there were dark circles of fatigue under my eyes as well.

Once again we switched off the cabin light and held each other under the sleeping bag, our feet piled on each other at the narrow tip of the cabin. It was a terrible night.

I was sound asleep when Curt crawled out on deck, clipping the safety harness. It was starting to get light. The seas were still very choppy, but the fury of the storm was gone. He leaned against the forward cabin and looked toward the gray skies and gray-white seas. A flapping sound above drew his attention to the American flag at the top of the mast. Though now a little tattered, she looked majestic.

Feeling a little groggy and dazed from the night's activities, Curt had thought rowing might clear his head. He put out a pair of oars, retrieved a rowing seat from the aft cabin, and started rowing. He wasn't really thinking as he rowed; minutes seemed like hours. How long he was out there, he later told me, he did not know. He felt like a zombie, mindlessly pulling the oars through the water.

Anatomy of a Rowing Stroke

Kathleen's log: April 26.

I awoke to see Curt coming back in the cabin. I didn't even know he was gone. When I asked him how he felt, he said that I shouldn't ask and he needed to get some rest.

I put the sleeping bag over him and went out on deck, where there were high clouds moving out of the northwest. Lower cumulus clouds were coming out of the east-northeast with the surface winds and most of the waves.

I rowed for two hours. It was easier to row for a longer period of time when I didn't wear my watch and keep looking at it. I started talking to myself as I rowed. I imagined the tiller of the rudder on the aft cabin in front of me as a microphone. I wanted to explain what it was like to row out here. "We usually scan the horizon, perhaps from the habit of looking for ships on the Moroccan coast. We know there aren't any shipping lanes here but we keep looking. Maybe we'll see a sailboat.

"The rowing style is not the best but you have to do what you can do given the conditions. The waves are not regular—you have to watch them, they come in threes. You see one sometimes that catches your eye and it goes up and up. You wonder if it will go over the boat. You're lucky when it doesn't break where you are. When you're lucky, the stern will rise and the whole boat will glide over the wave. Then the second wave is sharper, most encompassing. It is usually the one that will manage to get you wet. It has more force packed behind it. The third wave is a shadow of the first two, a follow-up that spits.

"The waves also come in different directions. Mostly they come from the direction of the wind, but some come from other directions. You watch them, feel them and the motion of the boat. You can't pull through evenly. One oar has to come through before the other. I've learned not to put out my thumbs on the ends of the oar handles, having been bumped a few times in the waves. It's important to follow through at the end of the stroke too. Even if the oar blades don't come out of the water at the same time, they will move back toward the catch together."

Here I concluded my analysis of the rowing stroke used in ocean rowing.

Curt's log: April 26.
Kathleen finished her stint at the oars and came to the door of the cabin. I was awake now and feeling better than when she left me a

few hours before. "How about some breakfast?" I asked her, pushing the sleeping pads aside so I could get to the food hatch below. I fished out the granola and got some Moroccan nuts to sprinkle on top. While water was heating on the stove for hot chocolate, I worked on my logbook that I had hardly written in since leaving the Canaries.

After breakfast, I announced I was going to "hygienize" myself. This was my code word for washing up. We had agreed early in the expedition that we would keep ourselves as clean and tidy as possible. Not only would this make us healthier, but also it would probably improve our mental outlook. I took a bar of pumice soap and a tube of Suave shampoo and went out on deck.

Early in the afternoon we rowed together for a few hours. It was about 72 degrees F but it felt cooler with the north wind. We wore sweatpants rolled up to the knees and long cotton shirts. I still wore my socks and sneakers on deck despite their being soaking wet from last night's weather. I knew Kathleen thought I was crazy to be wearing them out here because she often commented on how uncomfortable they must be, since most of our clothing items were in a constant state of dampness.

Before going into the cabin after our row, I needed to check on the fifteen-meter whip antenna for the ham radio because Kathleen had been unable to make contact with the Wilhelms in Rhode Island at the scheduled time. Maybe there was another problem with the antenna. I unscrewed it from the round aluminum base and examined the threads, and to my dismay I saw that many of them were eaten away from the corrosion of the saltwater. I cleaned off the white powder with sandpaper and applied Vaseline to the remaining threads, hoping for the best. With an old crampon strap left over from my climbing days, I secured the antenna further with a few climbing knots.

Just as I put the tools back in the aft cabin, Kathleen asked what I wanted to drink and I told her that some Johnny Walker with spring water would be good though she didn't plan to have any with her stomach occasionally sensitive from the boat's motion.

After dinner, Kathleen switched on the radio and tuned in to the fifteen-meter band. She sent out a series of CQs [Morse code for

"Calling any station"] for anyone to respond, for a few minutes but no one responded. We were about to turn off the radio and settle in for a quiet night when we heard, "KA1GIN MM, this is G4AYO in England."

Kathleen transmitted back and forth with Mike, a ham radio operator she had met while we were rowing on the Moroccan coast, for a few minutes, ascertaining that our signal was good. When she told him we were in a boat rowing across the Atlantic, he seemed to have his doubts as to whom he was really responding to. We later found out he went to the trouble to look up Kathleen's call sign and correspond with her mother, who confirmed we were, indeed, crossing the Atlantic in a rowboat.

CHAPTER 15

Red Sails in the Morning

Late April

I AWOKE FEELING STIFF AND CRAMPED. "I feel like I've been run over by a truck!" I said, turning over.

"What's the problem?" Curt mumbled, half asleep.

"I have bruises on my shins from the oar handles bouncing off them, and my knuckles have scratches from my nails from when I pull through at the end of the stroke." Curt stuck his hands out from the sleeping bag in response. They looked the same as mine.

This morning it was too hard to go out and row right away, so I decided we would have a leisurely breakfast. I opened the cabin hatch and reached for the hand pump that was attached to the front of the cabin by the door. Every morning one of us would pump a couple of gallons of fresh water into the flexible Nalgene plastic container by the hatch door. The cooking water was from the supply we picked up in the Canaries and could only be used for cooking because, without boiling it, we would have stomach problems. Our bottled drinking water supply was in liter bottles.

While I cooked up a pot of mushroom soup with pork and beans, Curt worked out the star and planet sights he had taken the evening before. They were tedious to work out, but we needed to know our position before the noon sun sights. So far, it looked as though we had logged sixty miles from the previous day.

After breakfast, inspired by the impressive mileage, Curt put away his navigation materials and went out to row. According to a small handheld anemometer given to us by Davis Instruments, which had also supplied the sextant, the wind out of the northeast was blowing a brisk Force 4 knots, giving us choppy seas. The sky was clear, and the sun reflected brightly off the breaking whitecaps. The deep red of the boat cabin tops glistened from the blowing spray.

The next set of strokes were hard ones. Curt was into doing the power pyramids we used to do when we trained for races on the Seekonk River: ten, twenty, thirty hard strokes and an equal number of easy strokes in between. He tried to get me to do them when I went to join him later in the morning, but I wasn't in the mood. Our rowing session culminated in our oars clashing and becoming entangled, so I gave up, tied my oars across the deck, and went back into the cabin.

At lunch, Curt commented on the granola with raisins we were having: sort of a reversal of breakfast and lunch meals. I knew he was trying to be funny, but there wasn't anything amusing about our meals, I thought.

"Well, when we get up in the morning, sometimes it's cool and I want something warm to eat, but in the middle of day, it's hot and a cold lunch tastes good, don't you agree?" Curt only shook his head. Maybe he thought I was still mad at him for banging into my oars when we rowed together earlier.

The seas continued to calm down, and it was a good time to give the autopilot a rest. Switching it off and tying off the tiller, Curt started to row by pulling hard on one side and then on the other. This worked fine for fifteen minutes until a big wave slid under *Excalibur* and the boat was pushed off course. He tried to compensate by rowing harder on port but we kept going farther off course. He felt himself get angry at the sea that was pushing us broadside to the waves. Taking the port oar in both hands like a sweep rower, and letting the starboard oar trail in the water, he put in several hard strokes. Still it didn't do any good. Then he saw a fin slicing smoothly through the water. It was a fifteen-foot shark only a few feet away, with another shark appearing behind him. They started circling the boat; maybe they had come to see what all the splashing was about.

I was reading *My Ántonia* by Willa Cather in the cabin, enjoying having all the space to myself, when I heard, "Hey, Kathleen! We have visitors!"

I put the book aside and stuck my head out of the cabin, expecting to see a ship.

"There're sharks out here! Should I throw something to them to eat and see if they come closer?"

I looked at him as if he were crazy. "No! Are you kidding? We'll never get rid of them if we do that!" In fact, two years later on our Pacific Row, we did have problems with sharks along the Peruvian/ Ecuadoran coast. Apparently, every potato peel and onion skin we threw out was eaten by either the sharks or other fish and earned us a steady following as we rowed north to the Galápagos Islands.

By early evening, it was blowing Force 2, with gusts of five knots. It was turning out to be a beautiful, calm night of floating gently along in the seas. But later on, the wind came up again, and the boat resumed its incessant rocking, back-and-forth motion, making it hard to sleep. A big wave breaking into the deck area forced cold water into the opening for the antenna by my side, waking me up abruptly as the water poured in over my head. I crammed the last dry towel in the open slot. With our fresh air supply cut off, the cabin was stifling.

In the early morning, I wondered if we would ever catch up on our rest. "Actually, I think we've adjusted to the conditions very well," Curt said. "The cabin isn't any bigger, but there seems to be more room than when we were in Casablanca."

Sometimes Curt irritated me with his brand of "Isn't this fun, this tough-ass expedition stuff we're doing?" Rubbish. I responded with what I imagined was a definitive putdown: "No, it isn't! The cabin is as cramped as ever. We still have to pile our feet on top of each other when we sleep, *and* it's impossible to find a comfortable position because we're bouncing and rolling around so much, *all—the—time*!"

Curt didn't really have an answer to that, but he knew when to lay low.

We took a break from rowing for the noon sighting. I went into the forward cabin and handed out the Davis sextant. One after another, I recorded the measurements as Curt called them out. We tuned in for the Rhode Island radio schedule and spoke with Peter Wilhelm's father Kurt in Rhode Island and sent him our noon position: 24 degrees 16 minutes north and 22 degrees 54 minutes west.

With the waves rolling out of the northeast, we found the afternoon's rowing more pleasurable. The waves were regular and helped the boat build speed that let us glide on the backside of the breaking waves. The equal distance between each wave meant we could easily time our power pyramids to peak at the top of the waves and then enjoy sliding down them as they pushed us along. Curt said he thought the boat was actually reaching seven knots during the surges. It was an exhilarating feeling.

As we tied the oars for the evening, we stopped to watch the sun dip below the horizon. Deep reds and pinks bathed the cumulus clouds, and colors of the sky reflected on the surface of the sea.

The next day's navigation fixes showed *Excalibur* to be only forty-four miles farther along our course. The course change that Curt had made seemed hardly to make a difference. He was afraid we were headed too far south and a storm could blow us south to the Cape Verde islands.

"Could we be farther south already than your navigation shows us?"

"I hope not."

"Could those white birds we're seeing have come from the Cape Verdes?" I thought they might be jaegers.

"I don't think so. I doubt we're so far south."

"But we see them every day. They must come from somewhere."

"How do I know where they come from?" With that he dumped the navigation books into the hatch and went out on deck to row. He was concerned about his navigation but unwilling to bring it out in the open. How dependable was any sight with a sextant taken from a rowboat at sea? We'd counted on contacting ships with the handheld

VHF that *Jangada*'s owner had given us to verify our positions, but we hadn't seen any ships. And now these damn birds.

It was obvious we would have to row harder and longer to make better mileage. The longer it took us to get across, the greater the chance of being hit by a hurricane before we made landfall. Fritz on *Jangada* had said that the boat looked very strong, but he doubted the crew of *Excalibur* would survive a hurricane.

I came out to row, and together we put in two hours at the oars. I kept trying to think of other places and people to take my mind off what we were doing. Then, out of the corner of his eye, Curt saw a reddish purple thing that looked like a plastic container. He had seen one earlier, but this one was much closer than the other had been. It was about six inches long and was actually tacking back and forth like a sailboat in the wind. It was some kind of sea creature, and Curt wanted to catch it.

The thing was astern of us now. With the autopilot detached, we backed the oars as hard as possible to gain on it. I reached over and grabbed the dip net at the edge of the deck, but the creature tacked to the south. Then Curt jumped up and shouted at me to row while he reached out to net it. I rowed as hard as I could, but it was getting away from us.

Finally, I said, "Curt, you'll never catch it!" That did it. He was already in a testy mood from the afternoon's navigation session.

"What do you mean, I can't catch it?" he yelled. I screamed back and stomped off as best I could on the cramped deck, heading to the forward cabin and slamming the hatch after myself. He tried to open the door, but I'd locked it. We were starting to drift broadside to the waves, but Curt was mad. He reached down to the edge of the hatch and ripped it open, not caring if he tore it off the hinges or not.

"Don't ever tell me I can't do something when I'm trying to do it," he yelled in the door.

At that moment, I felt such disgust because he had lost control of himself, something I had been brought up never to do. All I could say was, "You broke it, damn you!" and slammed the door shut again.

CHAPTER 16

A Gift from the Sea

Curt's log: April 29

The wet deck slipped from under my feet and I went down, landing hard on the rowing tracks. I winced from pain and rolled over to stare up at the sky. "Damn it," I thought. I was mad at Kathleen, mad at the boat, and mad at the sea. Pulling myself up by the safety line, I stood at the edge of the deck and thought I would just jump overboard. The dark blue waves were rolling the boat around aimlessly. Then it occurred to me that if I jumped, most likely I wouldn't be able to get back to the boat. The waves were moving too quickly. I rubbed my hand over my face and tried to get hold of myself.

With the autopilot reattached, I sat down and started rowing. The familiar, repetitive motions calmed me down. I thought of the rowing coach at the Narragansett Boat Club and our conversations on the banks on the Seekonk. He was right. In a small, confining boat, far out to sea, two people could be at each other's throats. Depending on how we handled the situation, we could be a danger to each other.

That evening we didn't have much to say. We ate our ham and potato flakes in silence and went to bed early.

There was an east wind blowing the next morning with rain showers. Curt had gone out early to row and left me to stretch out alone in the cabin. I thought about the fight we'd had the day before. Though I was not about to blame myself, I could understand Curt's frustrations. It *was* difficult navigating on *Excalibur*. Sitting hunched over in the small forward cabin of a rolling rowboat, reading small lines of numbers, and plotting them on a folded-up chart was definitely not easy. Our positions had to be approximations, given the height of the rowboat above the sea. The baseline calculations from the navigation tables started at about sixteen feet above sea level and had to be adjusted for dip error that was caused by the height of the eye relative to the horizontal plane, which made the observed angle between the horizon and the star or planet too large. We were less than sixteen feet, no matter where we stood on the deck. With the sextant in hand, Curt had to "grab" those sights, as he called out the instant he put the sun, planets, or stars on the horizon with the sextant. If he was off, the calculations were off. To compensate, he would take several sights of the same object and plot them on the chart.

It was obvious that the success of the voyage would rely on the navigation and our ability to get along and work together.

By the time it was breakfast, the rain clouds had moved off to the west. The sun was shining, and my mood lifted. It was amazing how the weather and seascapes affected us. When Curt came in for breakfast, the air between us had cleared measurably, but as usual we didn't talk about our disagreement once we spent some time apart cooling down. I still thought he had been an idiot for losing his temper over actions that were beyond our control. And I never understood where his anger from being told not to do something came from. Since we got along well most of the time, it seemed moments of disagreement like this one wouldn't impact the safety of our lives or the success of the row.

"I think we must have crossed the Tropic of Cancer last night," Curt remarked, sipping his coffee.

I looked out the port window. "I hope we see more marine life out here."

"Did I tell you I saw a flying fish this morning?" Sure enough, as he was rowing, off the port stern cabin a streak of silver flashed by in the far distance. It looked like a silver arrow flying through the air.

I reminded Curt of the fishermen on Hierro Island who had told us that where there were flying fish, there would be bigger fish following in pursuit.

I resolved to catch a fish today after my morning row. The day had turned out beautiful—the wind was down to Force 3, and the waves were only a few feet high. As I pulled at the oars, the seas were long and following.

The sun climbed higher in the morning sky; its warmth felt good on my shoulders as I rowed wearing a loose T-shirt and bikini bottoms. I was getting a good tan. I was lucky that way, because Curt tended to burn in the sun, but he was adapting well to the exposure.

The time had come for a little fishing. I had found that I liked sitting on the starboard side of the deck, facing aft, where the water-proof bag containing the spare butane gas canisters for the backup stove made a rather comfortable seat. With a flasher attached to the hand line and the other end tied to a thick piece of oak, I let the line out about forty feet. It trailed slowly behind as the boat inched along in the waves.

I didn't catch any fish, but it didn't matter. The afternoon on the deck, in the sunshine of a perfect day, gave me time to think and look out at the sea. I always lost myself in these extended sessions of reflection. Maybe I was meditating; the waves were certainly mesmerizing enough.

Later in the afternoon, Curt came out to row with me. I rowed in the stern, facing the aft cabin, and he was in the bow. I was always curious to know how far we'd come, so I asked him about the noon sights.

Without missing a stroke, he told me we were most likely *not* below the Tropic of Cancer yet. We seemed to be making more progress west, because the boat was responding well to the westerly course that he had put us on since yesterday.

I glanced at my watch and saw that it was almost 1800 hours GMT. It was time for the maritime net in the United Kingdom. Though we weren't planning to check in, we could at least listen.

As I tuned into the frequency, John, a ham radio operator in the United States, was calling to Net Control in the United Kingdom. "Have you heard anything today from the rowers?"

Net Control responded with a "Negative, John, we haven't heard a thing lately. Just a minute, and I'll put it up and see if anyone has heard from them."

"Splendid, Fritz is on frequency. Go ahead, Fritz," Net Control continued.

"I heard from them today, and they say they're doing fine. The weather must be cloudy, because they gave yesterday's position again. I estimate they are now at 24 degrees north and 23 degrees 35 minutes west. You copy?"

John wanted to know how many hours we were rowing a day.

"Five hours together," Fritz said.

"About five hours, I think." Steve at Net Control relayed the information to John. However, in the transmitting, the info was jumbled, and John asked again, "Does that mean they are each rowing five hours or five hours together?"

Fritz was clearly losing patience with the exchange. "Curt is rowing five hours and Kathleen is rowing eight hours!"

That time the message got through and there was silence on all ends. Then Steve said, "I guess that's women's liberation."

John's only comment was, "No, I don't think that's women's liberation at all."

I was still asleep when Curt got up the next morning. But as he started moving around, pulling on his shorts, I woke up. "Are you going out to row? How did you sleep last night?"

"Much better. I think I'm adapting to the motion of the boat." I had to agree. Once you found a comfortable position to sleep in, the boat's rocking wasn't too bad. I usually slept on my right side with one leg drawn almost completely up to my chest. My other position was wedged against the side of the boat, the little angle between deck and wall holding me in place. My stuff-sack pillow rested on top of the emergency bilge pump. Curt didn't have a water pump to put his stuff sack on, but six inches above his head, on the port side, was the electricity box where the wires from the solar panels on the cabin roof connected. More than once I had tangled my hair in the protruding wires when we moved around the cabin. I much preferred my bilge pump to his wires.

Curt opened the hatch door and started out. "Hey, Kathleen! Look! Guess what we have on board!" He went out, and I followed. There in the bow foot well was a flying fish. How exciting! I reached for the frying pan in the cooking bag we always left secured to the deck.

It was a lovely silver-blue fish worth documenting on film as well. I handed out the camera and light meter that Curt requested and posed with the fish, spreading out its wings above the sea and then above the frying pan.

Curt's log: May 1

It was May 1st and we agreed to have a special May Day breakfast with the fish, potatoes, and coffee. Kathleen sent me to the back cabin to get onions and potatoes. Oh boy, I said to myself, as I opened the hatch and reached in to get them where they hung suspended from the ceiling. This would be the first fish dinner at sea since leaving Casablanca 45 days ago.

It was a memorable feast. Kathleen fried up the fish in Moroccan olive oil with thinly sliced onions. This was followed by potatoes and onions fried with rosemary, salt, and pepper. To drink, we had hot chocolate, coffee, and fresh lemonade.

Later, as we sat at our rowing stations, renewed and refreshed, Kathleen remarked on how something different could happen out here to change our perception of the sea. It was like arriving in a new place, a tropical sea, where the landscape was completely different. Then, as if the environment around us agreed, a fish jumped 50 feet astern of the boat. We watched the fishing line that was trolling behind the boat, but the fish didn't grab a hold of it.

We rowed a little longer when Kathleen remembered the little purple and silver fish she had seen while washing the dishes after breakfast. It had come up and grabbed a food morsel that was drifting away. He was only four inches long. And then there was another one up by the bow and he was bigger, about six inches. "Have you seen them before?" She asked me.

I hadn't but I knew they were pilot fish from my readings of marine life at sea. It seems boats and large sea creatures acquire whole colonies of these fish that eat barnacles or any refuse generated by their hosts. It was nice to think we had our own school of pilot fish accompanying us as we traveled. It was good not to be so alone out here.

Later in the day, I saw one of the reddish-purple creatures sail by. My first thought was, "Forget it, we can't get it." But Curt and I were rowing, and the conditions had calmed down considerably.

We backed oars hard on the starboard, and after a couple of minutes of intense rowing, we managed to get upwind of it. Curt stopped rowing and went to the tiller to grab the dip net. As I pulled hard on starboard, he pushed the tiller over and we closed in on the creature. I stopped rowing as Curt reached over and scooped it up.

We had finally gotten one. I took the net from Curt while he reattached the autopilot to put us back on course. I carefully lowered the net into the bucket that Curt had filled halfway with saltwater. Looking closely at it, we realized that it was a Portuguese man o' war jellyfish whose long purple tentacles were highly poisonous. It was fascinating to watch as it tried to get out of the bucket by twisting itself over the rim.

"I knew it had the ability to sail, but I didn't know it could climb," Curt remarked. The sail was actually the fin part of its jellylike mass. It was an amazing creature to examine close up; it was so well adapted to life in the trade wind belt of the Atlantic Ocean. By twisting its sail-fin, it could move from place to place, taking advantage of the ever-present wind.

Gingerly, Curt put it into one of the sample bottles with formalin to take back to the University of Rhode Island oceanography program. The bright sail slowly turned a darker purple, like the deepening colors of the evening sky. I recorded the date and location for our records.

Curt's log: May 3
Tired from the motion of the boat of the night before, I did not feel like going out to row when I woke up at 0800 GMT. I lay there under the sleeping bag for another hour, dozing. Images of my childhood flitted through my half-asleep mind. The smell of breakfast cooking in the kitchen. The sound of dishes and silverware clattering. The muted voices as the family began to stir. Hurrying to the bathroom for a quick shower before breakfast. That feeling of fresh water splashing over my body. Now, that was a nice memory. That would sure feel good now.

Kathleen was still asleep when I went out to row. The sky was clear and the wind was coming out of the east-northeast at Force 3. The temperature was a pleasant 27 degrees centigrade. But I felt tired. The pain in my back from the other day when I fell on deck was still nagging me. There was also the pain that ran from the left shoulder up the left side of my neck. That one had started on the Moroccan coast. There was something wrong in my right elbow. It hurt when I bent my arms too soon at the end of a stroke. As I rowed, I watched the clouds come in from the east. They were not heavy clouds but high clouds that blanketed the sky and covered the sun, turning the water from a warm blue into a steel gray.

There was not a single person, not another boat, just the ocean, the rolling waves, and an occasional peek at the horizon from the top of a wave. The sky met the sea in a flat circle that formed a ring around our boat. Beyond that, we couldn't see anything. It felt as though we just rowed in place, the center of a circle.

I heard a sound, like the voice of another person. I stopped rowing and scanned the horizon, the circle that was our world. But there was no one, not a ship, not another person. Then I heard the sound again. I turned. The sound was Kathleen.

Later, as we rowed together, I said, "Why don't you go in and have some lunch? I'll row for a while." Curt was tired today, and without protest, he stood up and moved past me to change places.

Where are the flying fish? I wondered as I pulled at the oars. Curt had seen them as they flew through the air, dodging in and out of the waves. The only one I had seen was the eight-incher that we ate on May 1. I wished another one would land on board or that I could catch one from the hand line I left out every day now. Normally, on land, I could take or leave fish, but out here I had developed a taste for them. Our fresh food supply was getting low, and fish was becoming something I increasingly craved, maybe because of a vitamin deficiency.

The day was perfect for a bath. For both of us. I stopped rowing, tied the oars across the deck, and stripped down. I filled the bucket with the cool seawater and got out the saltwater soap.

As I leaned back to splash more water on my body, I could see Curt watching. I gestured for him to come out: I needed him to pour water down my back and maybe his. As we splashed double handfuls of seawater over our bodies, the water on deck ran in little eddies, back and forth in the gentle rolling of the boat, seeking the scuppers and drains where it flowed back into the sea.

We stood on deck, holding on to the safety lines, letting the wind dry the seawater from our naked bodies. It was a perfect moment with the lightest of touches from the warm ocean air.

By early afternoon, the wind had lessened to Force 2 from the east. Only slow-rolling, three-foot waves passed under *Excalibur*. We had just finished a lunch of potato flakes mixed with beef bouillon and freeze-dried peas and carrots in the cabin when I turned to him and said, "You know, it's time to change your hair style."

He frowned. "What's wrong with my hair?"

"Well," I told him, "it's gotten entirely too long for life at sea. I'm going to give you a haircut. It'll be fun, you'll like it!"

Curt didn't look convinced.

"No, really, don't worry. I won't cut it too short. It'll be out of your eyes."

The scissors I found in the compartment below my pillow were covered with grease and dried fruit that had fallen out of an old plastic bag. I cleaned them off with toilet paper dampened with rubbing alcohol. When I started to comb his hair in preparation for his haircut, he said I would get hair all over the cabin and led the way onto the deck.

"Hey, I have my doubts about how even the lines will be," I told him on deck. "I don't guarantee anything with your straight hair and the wind blowing." He rolled his eyes. Even in the calming seas, there was still considerable motion on the boat.

From the back cabin, he retrieved one of the inner tubes we brought to use as flotation in case of damage to the boat. He blew it up and settled himself on it as I braced my feet on the deck and stood over him with the scissors. Soon, snippets of his blond hair were blowing away in the wind. "Be careful of the points." he kept saying, worried that the boat might make a sudden motion. I was finding the experience increasingly funny, though I tried hard to not laugh out loud. He was being such a good sport, and my spirits were lifting by the minute.

As I was cutting, a green ball floated by some forty feet off the port side. Curt watched it for a second and then decided he wanted it. "Look, there's a ball, I want it!"

We watched the ball drifting away. I wondered what it was and where it had come from.

"Look, it has things growing on it," he said, pointing. I stopped snipping and focused on the little green object now amidships. He was right; there was a little world floating by our boat and we had to go after it. I went for the tiller. He untied the oars and began rowing. I kept an eye on the ball, telling him which side to row harder on. There it was, on the port side.

He let go of the oars and grabbed the dip net to scoop the ball up. A school of purple black-striped pilot fish following it looked momentarily disoriented when the ball rose high into the sky, disappearing from their sight. Curt later claimed that he saw the pilot fish from our boat swim out to the new pilot fish and guide them back under *Excalibur*. It did seem as though our contingent of pilot fish beneath the boat was growing larger.

Our attention now turned to the green ball that was swinging in the air in the dip net. I filled the bucket for the second time that day and put the ball, with its tiny crab, sea urchins, barnacles, and a slimy fungus-like growth, into it. While Curt photographed the ball from all angles, I tapped it lightly and found it was hollow. Crustaceans had formed wiggly lines all over the surface, and the barnacles had formed conical houses. The green ball looked just like the little planet in Antoine de Saint-Exupéry's *The Little Prince*.

I peered hard at the raised printing on both sides: PLASTICOS 800 ML MORELL. Not much to go on, but it might have come from a fishing net and was originally made in Spain. I decided to keep the green ball, and watch its creatures as pets.

My attention turned back to the haircut; it was only half done, though from Curt's point of view we were finished. When it was over, I gave him the two-inch-by-two-inch mirror on the sighting compass: he had to admit it looked different. It was shorter and definitely was not in his eyes anymore.

Curt's log: May 3
With the conditions improving, I wanted to look at the bottom of the boat for barnacles. In tropical seas, barnacles have a remarkable ability to grow in short time spans. I also wanted to see how the rubber pieces we had jammed in the rudder trunk back in Puerto de la Estaca were faring. Were they still there? I asked Kathleen if she wanted to go for a swim.

She wasn't interested and I didn't blame her because she had quite a scare off Fueteventura when she and Kerrie had gone for a swim from *Jangada*. They were a short distance from the boat when two brown sharks appeared. Fritz and I yelled to them to come in quickly, but they had been oblivious to the proximity of the sharks. With only two of us on the boat now, it was a good idea for one of us to remain on board and keep a lookout.

I took my sleeveless wet suit out of the back cabin and got suited up. In the hatch below the bow rowing station, I found my mask, snorkel, and fins. Kathleen had tied a rope to the inner tube I had used while she was cutting my hair. I was to grab it if she needed to pull me in quickly.

With the mask on, I dipped my head in the water from the deck to check for sharks. There weren't any, so I slipped into the sea beside the boat.

The water was alive with all kinds of sea creatures. Small jelly masses floated by, held in suspension by the blue ocean water. On closer inspection, they looked like colonies of many one-cell organisms, some of them the size of a dime, others no larger than the end of a pencil eraser.

I did a surface dive and swam deep beneath the boat. As I turned to look up, I was startled for a moment when I saw the shape of the sea anchor out of the corner of my eye, trailing behind *Excalibur*. We had put it out to further slow the boat down while I was in the water. It was shaped like a conical coffee filter with a hole in the end.

Under the boat, the school of pilot fish came right up to my diving mask and looked me curiously in the eyes. The oxygen in my lungs was running out so I shot up to the surface to get another breath. The pilot fish, startled by the sudden movement, scurried away to hide behind one of the dagger boards.

On the surface, I told Kathleen what I had seen. She was curious to know if it were possible to catch one of the pilot fish for dinner. Sure, I'd give it a try. François in the Canaries had said they were good eating. On my second dive down, I grabbed for the biggest one. He must have been able to read my mind because he darted away as my hand came toward him. He stopped about six feet away and looked back at me. Was that a reproachful look I detected?

I swam over and examined the hull of the boat. It was clean except for a few tiny barnacles. I tried to pull them off but they were stuck fast. I could have scraped them off with the knife but I was afraid the anti-fouling paint would come off with it. Then we would have more barnacles, most likely bigger ones.

I swam over to the stern of the boat and looked at the rudder. I could see one of the rubber inner tubes partially hanging below the rudder slot by the string Kathleen and I had tied it to. I cut the string with my knife because I didn't want any drag.

The next morning the seas continued to calm down. With the cabin hatch open and the cool morning air drifting over us in gentle wisps, we languished in bed, reluctant to get up. The sun was rising, and there is something truly inspiring about a sunrise—or sunset—at sea. I got up and went on deck with Curt close behind. We settled ourselves against the bow cabin wall, and watched the sun, holding the promise of bright heat that would spread quickly, rise above the tropical sea. The reflection of the rising sun slowly turned the surface of the water from a diffused soft pink to silver white.

CHAPTER 17

A Calming Sea

May 5, 1981

Aᴄᴛᴇʀ ʙʀᴇᴀᴋꜰᴀꜱᴛ ᴀ ᴄᴏᴜᴘʟᴇ ᴏꜰ days later, I washed the dishes off the side of the deck and then sat down to row. Curt stayed in the cabin, enjoying his chance to stretch out and rest after his stint at the oars. I heard the stove start up and knew he was making a cup of coffee to go along with his navigation work.

I thought of how rowing day after day could be a very tiring business. The weight of the boat and its supplies required a pulling action by both the arms and back compared to a racing shell where the legs drove the boat. Long hours were required to make any sort of distance. The increasing heat of the day as we moved farther south in the tropics was having an effect on us as well. Blisters suffered early in the voyage had now healed, and we had tough calluses on our hands. But I wondered if the strengthening process of our muscles would reach a point where our bodies could build no further and then weariness would take over. It would become a battle to keep the boat going day in and out.

Late in the morning, Curt came out on deck. "I want to get some shots of us rowing while the conditions are calming down." He showed me a contraption he had designed for taking remote photographs while we rowed.

He had taken one of the rectangular plastic containers we had brought along to store odds and ends and cut a hole in the bottom for the camera lens, shutter release, and a nylon cord. I was skeptical about its working.

"I'm going to pull it to the top of the mast where the flag and radio wires are. As we row, I'll pull on this string, the clothespin will come out, and the elastic will pull on this lever and depress the shutter release." I stopped rowing so Curt could rig his pulley system.

After a couple of minutes, he sat down and we began rowing. On the second stroke, he pulled the string to take the picture. When he brought the camera down to advance the film, he said, looking happy, "It works!" I had to hand it to him: it was an ingenious technique for taking self-portraits. After a few shots, we went in the cabin to get out of the sun. The wind had died down to almost calm, making the air hotter than ever.

The noonday sights showed us to be at 22 degrees 32 minutes north and 28 degrees 38 minutes west. We were getting close to the Norfolk (Virginia) to Dakar (Senegal) shipping lane; it was only about seventy miles away on the calming seas.

Rowing in the late afternoon seas was pleasurable. With the sun at a lower angle in the sky and the barest whisper of a breeze, the boat glided smoothly along. From the corner of my eye, I caught a glimpse of silver in the water. We stopped rowing and leaned over the side. Down deep, under the boat's bottom, was a school of pompano dolphin fish. One of them would make a fine addition to the evening's meal.

Curt went to the aft cabin and got out his wet suit while I pulled the oars in and lashed them crosswise over the deck. As Curt leaned against the aft cabin while putting on his wet suit, I considered going in the water too—I was so hungry for fresh fish. But when I looked down into the sea, its blue depth limitless and so clear, I reconsidered. Though we were in a calm, I didn't like the idea of both of us swimming in the water at the same time. What if one of us suddenly needed help? When I caught sight of the school again, they appeared very small; they were at least thirty feet below the boat now.

Curt climbed overboard while I dropped the sea anchor off the stern to keep the boat stationary, though it seemed unnecessary because the sea was now completely calm and the boat barely moving.

Curt's log: May 5

While Kathleen spotted for sharks from above, I dropped over the side into the beautiful other dimension that surrounded *Excalibur*. It seemed to stretch indefinitely below. For years before the voyage, I had wondered what it would be like to swim far out at sea. I dove down as far as I could until my eardrums could take no more pressure. I stared into the deep blue depths of the sea. Somewhere far below was the ocean floor, locked in perpetual night. The water was more than eighteen thousand feet deep. I tried to imagine the Great Abyssal Plain stretching for hundreds of miles like a great desert under the prodigious pressure of the ocean.

I turned and glided toward the surface. *Excalibur* looked small; the hull was like a racing shell as it floated silhouetted against the sky. There was no sign of the silver fish. I must have scared them away. I decided to take pictures instead with the Nikonos.

With the camera that Kathleen had given me from the bow cabin, I swam away from the boat to get an overall view of Kathleen and *Excalibur*. Under the water, I saw the pilot fish that were again following me. When I stopped swimming about forty feet from the boat to take photographs, the pilot fish stopped too. They seemed disappointed that I wasn't going any farther—they must have thought I was leading them on a great expedition. After taking several photos, I decided to play a game with the fish. Turning abruptly, I swam quickly away from them. Looking back, I saw they had followed faithfully. It was impossible to get away from them! Even when I swam after them, they would dart away and hide behind the rudder. If I looked quickly around the rudder, they would swim off to hide behind the dagger board. But if I floated motionlessly in the water, they peeked out from their hiding place and then swam cautiously up and peered at me through my diving mask.

It was great fun playing with the pilot fish but presently my attention was diverted to the pompano dolphin fish that had returned.

Ten of them were circling the boat. Some of them were a foot or more and a couple were nearly sixteen inches long. Slowly I swam over to the boat and asked Kathleen for François's spear.

"Go get 'em, buster," she said, and I saluted as I returned to the sea on my mission. I adjusted the piece of nylon cord that attached the spear to my wrist and tested the rubber strip that would propel the spear into the dolphin. Now I was ready.

The pompano dolphins were coming closer. I floated motionlessly on the surface, breathing through the snorkel. As the school passed about ten feet below me, I dove down and released the spear in the direction of one of the larger ones. But I had fired too soon. Startled and scared, the whole school swam away.

I would have to be more careful. The inner tube rubber had not given enough velocity; next time I would try jabbing with the spear as I held it in my hand. I could see the school coming back; I swam toward them. The pilot fish were close on my heels. I singled out the leader of the dolphins, waited until the latest possible instant, and then thrust the spear hard into its back. It gouged a hole in its back but failed to penetrate far enough to fix him to the spear. I followed him deeper but I couldn't get closer for another try.

I hated to injure the dolphin and not finish the job. The school swam away, with its leader spewing white clouds of excrement into the water.

By now, the sun was going down and I was starting to get chilly. I headed back to the boat where Kathleen asked how the spearing had gone. She looked disappointed, but said nothing. I took off my wet suit and dried myself off with the towel Kathleen handed me.

We leaned against each other by the deck cabin, watching the sun meet the ocean on the western horizon. The seas rolled gently around us and were smooth and shiny as glass. The surface showed not the slightest indication of air movement. The sky and water were blue, and then the sky turned yellow and both melted into soft pinks, blues, and grays. As the seas flattened out, the colors spread from the sky to the water and finally over to us until we felt as though we were part of the sunset. The feeling was so peaceful and the sight so idyllic, I felt we could stay there forever.

I saw that the pompano dolphins had come back. It was getting dark, but they were just below the surface of the water, their blue-silver bodies glinting in the last light of the evening sky. Curt leaned over the gunwale, spear in hand, waiting for them to come closer.

I went into the cabin to get the fishing book so we could identify exactly what kind of creature we were trying to catch and maybe glean a hint or two on the best technique for spearing them. The book indicated they might be yellow jack instead of dolphin and light tackle could be used.

Curt took the fishing pole, which we had attached to the bow cabin roof to troll, and put a flasher on the end of the line. He cast it out and started reeling it in. *Bam!* He had one on the very first cast, twisting and fighting. In a moment, he had it on board, covered with the dip net. It wasn't the same kind of fish as the one he had injured earlier. We compared it to the pictures in the book. "It must be a pompano dolphin."

I lost no time getting the stove out and heating olive oil and rosemary in the frying pan. Curt handed in the cleaned fillets to cook. This time we saved the guts for bait for the next day.

In the yellow glow of candlelight, we ate our fillets of pompano and sipped at the Spanish sherry given to us by the port director in Radazul, Hierro. It was by far the best meal we had had yet.

The next morning, I woke up at 0730, feeling relaxed. It was perfectly calm, and the boat wasn't moving at all. I rolled over and looked at Curt. When he opened his eyes, I asked him how he had slept.

"Very well, thank you." I smiled back and pointed out the port window on his side. The sea was like glass. We decided to take a holiday—each of us doing what we wanted. Curt wanted to develop film, while I planned to fish and sketch in my logbook.

Leaving Curt to catch up on his sleep, I went out on deck. It was lovely to be alone on a calm sea. I was determined to catch more fish, so I assembled my fishing equipment and settled down on the starboard side. I baited my hand line and tossed it overboard. At first, the only fish I saw were pilot fish. They swam up and looked closely at the baited hook. They weren't interested, though. Their mouths looked too small for the hook anyway. I was just as glad because, according to an old fishermen's superstition, it was bad luck to catch the pilot fish—however tasty they might be!

As I sat on my favorite seat, I felt overwhelmed by the beauty of the sea that day. There wasn't a wave, not even a ripple. And the silence was the most complete I had ever experienced. When I sat perfectly still and held my breath, there wasn't a single sound.

I sat on deck until about 0930, enjoying the morning, trying to catch a fish. The silver fish returned, but not even they seemed interested in the baited hook I dangled in front of them. Eventually, I heard a stirring in the forward cabin. Curt leaned out of the hatch and asked if I wanted pancakes for breakfast.

"Sure, that sounds great." I sat fishing for a few more minutes and then put my line away when Curt handed out perfectly cooked pancakes with Vermont maple syrup. Pancake breakfasts were a Saville family Sunday tradition, and he was very good at making them.

After we had eaten our fill of pancakes, Curt called out from the interior of the cabin, where he had remained. Did I want to work with him to develop a roll of black-and-white film?

No, no, I didn't. I just wanted to change places with him and go in the cabin. I wanted my time alone there. Curt could work on his own developing the rolls of black-and-white film we had been taking photos with all along. We switched places, and I handed out the bag of photo developer chemicals from the forward hatch.

I settled myself down in the cabin, stretching out with the luxury of two pillows. I told Curt he should pretend he was doing a photography program on television and describe his actions as he went along. He agreed, and I "watched" the show audibly from my vantage point, propped up on the two pillows and folded-up sleeping bag.

In all, the operation took an hour, using three quarts of fresh water. The Perma-Wash film rinse was a great help because it reduced the amount of water needed after the film was fixed. He was pleased, and I was impressed when the film turned out so well.

As Curt was putting away the last of the chemicals, later in the morning, we heard a noise near the boat: *swoosh!* In the silence that surrounded *Excalibur*, the sound was startling.

"Whales! There's a pod of them off the bow!"

I dove out of my nest with the camera in hand. Off the port bow were two huge whales, the sunlight glinting off their black skins, expelling air from their blowholes.

The whales, probably the baleen North Atlantic right, took a few more breaths and left us, diving deep beneath the surface. We never saw them again, but later in the day I heard them. By then, a very light breeze had come out of the west, just enough to put little ripples on the glass-like surface of the sea.

We were curious to see if our position had changed in the last twenty-four hours in the calm conditions. We had rowed for a little while the previous afternoon, and the light breeze out of the west was probably pushing us back some. But the two forces had practically evened each other out. We were still in just about the same place, as was shown by the noon sight: 22 degrees 20 minutes north and 28 degrees 42 minutes west.

By the time night had descended over the sea, the wind was coming out of the northwest at about Force 1. We wondered if we were in for a weather change. But there was nothing we could do about it, so we didn't worry.

As usual when the dinner was done and the dishes stored in the red nylon bag on deck, we were both tired. I read aloud from a Travis McGee thriller, *The Empty Copper Sea*, which seemed appropriate, until we couldn't keep our eyes open any longer.

At about 0230, I woke up. The antenna wire was moving back and forth in the air vent by my head. I was afraid the abrasion might damage it, so I stuffed a towel in the slot to stop it from moving. This cut off the air by my head, so I went out on deck to breathe some fresh air and see why the antenna was moving around.

Out on deck, leaning against the bow cabin, I could feel a light breeze on my left cheek, coming out of the north-northeast. I looked around at the incredibly clear night. The Milky Way was spread across the sky in a great encompassing arc.

CHAPTER 18

Seed of a Hurricane

May

W E FELT REFRESHED AFTER OUR holiday in the calm. We'd needed it, for we'd worked steadily, without a break, for the two weeks since leaving Hierro. But we could congratulate ourselves on having covered nearly seven hundred miles of the row across the Atlantic during that period.

Curt's log: May 7

The oars seemed to be less heavy as I rowed alone in the early morning seas. I thought of the rowing schedule we had settled into: it was really working out well. I would row alone for about two hours in the morning, finding it a pleasant way to wake up. After breakfast, Kathleen would row alone for another two hours. In the afternoon, she would row another hour or so. The sun would still be high in the sky, but she wasn't as bothered by its heat as I was. Later in the day, I would get in a couple of hours and then, before shooting the stars in the twilight, we would row together. This way, the boat was moving under oar power up to eight hours a day. And we had plenty of time to be alone in the cabin and on deck.

The waves had not yet built up after the calm. The wind was blowing out of the east at Force 2, taking the edge off the morning heat as the sun climbed higher in the cloudless sky. We had originally planned to do much of the rowing at night to avoid the tropical heat. But this had not yet been necessary. In our preparation, we had overlooked the wind chill effect. How ironic that we had forgotten about that! All winter long, in Tony's old barn in Touisset, the freezing temperatures of the wind had plagued us as we worked on the boat. It never occurred to us that the wind chill effect could be a benefit in the tropics.

I saw something off the starboard that at first looked like a bird. On closer inspection, I saw it was a silver-blue flying fish in the low morning sun. It flew at least fifty feet through the air before plunging back into the water. A moment later, another one took flight.

The wings of the flying fish drew my attention. They seemed to be moving in a blur, like hummingbird wings. Were they actually moving very fast or did it look that way because of the way the sunlight was hitting them? I could not tell, but I had always thought that flying fish shot out of the water and glided with their fins extended.

The sun was climbing higher in the sky every day as we rowed south and the month passed by. As I recorded the noonday figures that Curt read from the sextant on the deck, I noticed the sun's altitude was 84 degree 30 minutes above the horizon. When he finished, he came back in the cabin to work the sights out.

By June 21, the sun would be at 90 degrees, or directly above the Tropic of Cancer. But as we traveled south, the sun would appear to be more than 90 degrees, taken from the south horizon. It was necessary for us to get an accurate sighting of the sun from the north and south horizon around that time, something Curt was still working out in his mind. He seemed exasperated by my questions about it, so I dropped the subject. I picked up my logbook and wrote in it for a few minutes.

"We're at 22 degrees 9 minutes north and 29 degrees 6 minutes west. We're getting even closer to the Norfolk-to-Dakar shipping lane. The middle of it's about fifty miles away. I don't know how close the ships stay to the lane—we might see a ship any time in the next couple of days."

That was an exciting prospect. According to John Fairfax, who had rowed across the Atlantic in the mid-1960s, he had met quite a few ships and been given all sorts of goodies. I got out the VHF radio to give a call, on the off chance that a ship was in the vicinity. Curt followed me out on deck.

We scanned the horizon but didn't see anything. I wasn't discouraged, though, because the handheld radio had a range of about forty miles. This meant we could talk to a ship even though we couldn't see it. Holding the radio up to my mouth, I pushed the talk button. "CQ, CQ, this is *Excalibur*, the transatlantic rowboat, seventeen days out from Hierro. Do you copy me? Over."

Silence.

I tried again. "Calling any ship in the Norfolk-to-Dakar shipping lane. Please come in. Do you copy, over?"

Silence.

"Let me try," Curt said, taking the unit. "*Esta es el barco de ramo Excalibur de los Estados Unidos llamando barcos en esta region. A ver si nos copia. Cambio.*"

Silence.

There weren't even any Spanish-speaking boats out there. We looked at each other in disappointment. I took the radio, crawled into the cabin, and put it away. Curt sat on the rope bag on deck and looked out at the sea. He felt as unhappy as I did.

The unsuccessful attempt to talk to a ship, filled with other people, left me feeling lonely. I reached over and switched on the ham radio. I wanted, needed, to hear other people. Tuning the 15-meter band, I could hear two hams conversing in Morse code. As I listened, I could tell that one ham was in Palm Bay, Florida, and the other in Alaska. I was impressed that the Drake TR-7 could pick up signals that far away. I thought of contacting them, but we needed to conserve electric power, so I listened a while and then turned it off.

Curt's log: May 7
I thought about the course. The autopilot was still set at 255 degrees true. Nevertheless, we were getting farther south than I wanted.

Should I change the course to compensate? No, I thought it was better to leave it alone for a few days. I noticed the little Xs on the chart showing our position for the past two weeks formed a slightly zigzag line. Maybe that was because I realized that altering the course too frequently had been a flaw in my racing strategy at regattas. It was better to make a decision on a course and follow through with it. The straighter the course, the more efficient.

But what if we went too far south? What would that do for us later in the voyage? Would the more southeasterly winds on the western side of the Atlantic compensate for this and push us back north in the later part of the voyage?

I went out of the cabin and we began the afternoon's rowing session. Both of us kept looking over our shoulders at the sun until the last point of light disappeared below the horizon. Then we watched for Jupiter, which was the first object to appear in the night sky except for the moon that hung where the sun had been. When Jupiter appeared, it was time for the evening sights. Curt wanted to doublecheck his navigation with additional stars and planets that evening, so when Jupiter became visible, we quickly took in the oars and tied them down for the night. We had grown so accustomed to this task that we could practically tie the oars with one hand and steady ourselves with the other.

That evening Curt was able to shoot Jupiter, Sirius, Capella, Arcturus, and Polaris. Polaris, the North Star, was particularly useful because it could give us a double-check of our latitude position. Since it is only a third-magnitude star, it was sometimes hard to focus in the telescope of the sextant. Polaris was now getting so close to the horizon, due to our southerly travel, that the earth's atmosphere was making it more difficult to see clearly. Its altitude for this position from where we were was 21 degrees 40 minutes. After Curt had applied corrections to the sights he had taken and plotted them on the North Atlantic chart, we found that we were 22 degrees 3 minutes north and 29 degrees 31 minutes west. From the pre-marked lines on the chart that showed the boundaries of the shipping lanes, we were indeed getting closer to the Norfolk-to-Dakar lane.

During the night, we took turns getting up every half hour to look out for ship lights. But each time the sky was dark and the sea empty.

One morning when I was taking my stint at the oars after Curt had already put in his two hours, I saw a pilot fish following my oars as I rowed along, playing around the tips of the blades as I pulled them out of the water at the end of the stroke. I was delighted that the pilot fish had stayed with us after the calm.

One of the purple-and-striped fish stood out from all the rest. It was about four inches long and seemed to have a sleeker body than the others. Or was it my imagination? I thought he was more playful than the rest, staying closer to my oar blades than his buddies. When I would take the blade out of the water, he would swim quickly forward to see what had happened to it. When the blade went back in the water at the bow end of the boat, he swam back to look. I decided to give him a name. Alpha: the first name that came to mind.

Alpha reminded me of *Excalibur*'s sleek hull. Ed Montesi had done a great job creating lines that made her such an easy boat to row. Even in the light winds blowing out of the northeast, the boat was smoothly cutting through the water.

We had told Ed that we preferred a low profile for the ocean-rowing boat. This, we felt, would give us greater maneuverability in windy conditions at sea. Ironically, we paid for this choice in the lower headroom and more cramped conditions in the forward cabin that were our tiny living quarters. Moreover, higher cabin structures could have probably enabled us to drift farther in strong following winds. But it had been a trade-off against the need for more control over the boat.

Throughout the day, the conditions remained stable. The wind was light and blowing from an advantageous direction. We finished the day feeling good about the progress the boat had made. After a dinner of curried rice and soy protein, I suggested we turn on the radio to see if there was any interesting news on the UK maritime net.

An amateur radio ham in the Caribbean came on and told everyone on the net that the first hurricane of the season had just formed near the West Indies. We looked at each other in shock. It was only early May. Normally, the hurricane season didn't start until June or July. "HI, HI, and the baby is born!" "HI, HI" was ham jargon for laughter. They were referring to Hurricane Arlene. We didn't think it was funny at all.

Curt reached up and turned off the radio. For several moments, we sat looking at each other in silence. We were stunned. Everything was going so well. The weather report, however, brought home the reality of our situation.

"This makes you think of where we are and what exactly we're trying to do," Curt commented, adding, "and how many miles we have yet to cover." He opened the navigation hatch and pulled out the chart, dividers, and a pencil. He began taking measurements and writing figures in the margins.

I asked him what he was doing, and he replied, "Trying to figure out how long it will take to reach the nearest island in the West Indies. I think it's Antigua."

"How far is that?" I wanted to know.

"More than seventeen hundred miles. It could take us into July to get there. And that's not allowing for adverse winds or a storm that could blow us off course."

I leaned over his shoulder and looked at the course he was pointing to. It was obvious we now had to think of the Atlantic row as a race—a race against an early hurricane season.

We talked again of rowing across the Atlantic as quickly, carefully, and efficiently as possible. We seriously discussed the ways to complete the voyage faster than anyone had ever before rowed across an ocean. It was a tall order. In 1869, Samuelson and Harbo had rowed *Richard K. Fox* from New York to France in fifty-five days. The closest anyone had come to that record in modern times was the crossing by the Allum cousins from the Canary Islands to St. Lucia in sixty-four days.

"If we can make it to 40 degrees west by next Sunday, May 17, then we will have been at sea for twenty-five days since leaving Hierro. I regard 40 degrees west as being approximately halfway across the Atlantic to the West Indies. We might then have a fighting chance to make Antigua or Barbuda in another twenty-five days," Curt said, still looking at the chart.

We agreed the new rowing regime was going to be a stepped-up version of what we were doing now. Instead of only seven hours combined rowing, we would each row six hours apiece and a few other hours together. With the good weather from the stationary high west of the Azores, it was possible that we could be halfway across by the following Sunday.

I reached up and turned off the light as Curt put the hatch cover over the navigation hatch. He pulled up the sleeping bag, and settled in for an uneventful sleep. Tomorrow would start early.

CHAPTER 19

The Big Push

Curt's log: May 8

I T'S 0545. TIME TO RISE and shine." Kathleen's voice jarred me awake. It was still dark as I rolled over and looked for my watch. It was 0545 but that was in GMT. It was 0345 local time.

Kathleen was already dressed. She opened the hatch and a cool breeze filled the cabin. I could see by the dim glow of the mast light that she had put on a red sweater and green pants rolled up to the knees. She was barefooted.

I reached in the stuff sack under my head and pulled out a pair of shorts, a T-shirt, and a sweatshirt. I grabbed my white cotton hat as I crawled out after Kathleen.

"It's pretty chilly at this time of morning," Kathleen said as she untied her oars with one hand, steadying herself with the other. I couldn't really manage a reply at this hour.

Settled at the oars, I reached in the cabin and switched off the anchor light before we started rowing. I could see Kathleen's back in front of me in the stern. She looked over her shoulder and said, "Ready all?"

"Ready."

Our seats slid forward in unison as the oar handles started forward. The Big Push had begun.

I kept my eyes on the stern cabin door in front of me as we rowed, watching my reflection rolling back and forth, partially mesmerized as I was still half asleep. The hardest part was out of the way: getting out of bed and starting to row. Within a few minutes, the action of rowing and a damp chill had awakened all my senses. The wind was blowing out of the northeast at Force 5, accompanied by rolling, six-foot waves. As the gray dawn spread slowly over the sea, I could see occasional higher-breaking waves, nearly nine feet high.

"These waves are good for rowing. They pick us up and push *Excalibur* along," I commented over my left shoulder as the stroke came to an end.

Curt didn't say anything right away. He seemed to be watching the waves and concentrating on his rowing. A few more minutes passed before he said, "It seems to be the waves more than the wind that helps boost us along."

Dark clouds raced overhead as rain came down lightly. "I don't think it's going to rain much because the clouds are moving quickly. There's a lot of blue sky." With that, we both fell silent, drawn into our own private worlds of contemplation.

The cumulus clouds on the rim of the eastern sky began to turn orange. Their colors spread and intensified. The waves rolling toward us from the direction of the rising sun reflected the colors of the sky and took on a three-dimensional quality. The vivid sunrise was over very quickly because in the tropical zones, the sun rises and sets almost perpendicular to the horizon instead of at an angle as it does in the temperate zones.

In a few minutes, the full disc of the sun shone brightly on our faces. Having rowed for an hour now, we took a five-minute break to shed our outer clothing and put on sunglasses and sunscreen. We shared an orange.

After the second hour of rowing, we had a breakfast of cold rice and soy protein pellets that were no longer crunchy, as they had been the night before. Now they were spongy and tasteless. Curt drank hot chocolate while I had pea soup; it was the taste of salt that I craved out here. On land I rarely had instant soup mixes, but at sea, they filled the need for salt and added bulk. Curt craved the hot chocolate out at sea, something he could take or leave on land. It was strange the way our food tastes had changed.

Another hour of rowing brought us up to three hours. A school of flying fish shot out of the water like a fusillade of arrows. More flying fish indicated we were getting farther down into the tropics.

By the time the third hour at the oars was over, it was burning hot in the sun. My lips were bothering me. They were sunburned, chapped, and hot to the touch. I crawled into the bow cabin and found the jar of white moisturizing cream. Sunburn on the lips had been an increasing problem. I had tried ChapStick, but it wasn't enough. If we were going to spend more time in the sun rowing, we would have to take better care of our lips and skin.

At noon, it was time for a radio contact with the Wilhelms in Rhode Island. We had traveled far enough west that the time of the noon sight in GMT was about 1400 hours, the same time as the radio schedule. We had to do the noon sight and the radio call at the same time. To accomplish this, I stationed myself at the radio with my Morse code key. Between sending and receiving messages, I had to jot down the measurements for the sun sights as Curt called them out from the deck. Since it took time to work out our positions, I could only send an estimate, but I wasn't sure they had received it because the radio propagation deteriorated and we lost contact as I keyed in the last word.

It was frustrating at times like this. Just when we thought we were going to have a good contact, something would happen to spoil it. I was depressed as Curt put away the sextant.

I lay down on my sleeping pad, feeling dejected. Curt looked concerned, but he went ahead and worked out the noon sights. When he had transferred the noon position to the chart, his face lit up. I knew it was good news.

We'd done fifty-five miles in the last twenty-four hours! My mood improved right away, and we treated ourselves to listening in on the UK Maritime net a few minutes longer.

During the night, the wind picked up and the seas became choppy. The boat lurched from side to side, tossing us back and forth,

We built our ocean rowboat *Excalibur* in an old barn in Rhode Island throughout the summer and fall and into the winter of 1980–81. Here Curt is placing batters on the boat frame.

After the hull was completed, Ed Montesi, the boat's designer, recommended an ocean trial on Mount Hope Bay with a hundred gallons of water to simulate the boat fully laden. She passed with flying colors. Shown: Ed Montesi, me, and Peter Wilhelm.

Peter Wilhelm, Ed Montesi, and me rowing during the ocean trial.

Following *Excalibur*'s successful bare hull ocean trial, we began to work on the rest of the boat through the summer and into the winter of 1981.

As an unpaid rowing coach for my alma mater's women's crew team in the fall of 1980, I had the team rowing practices at 6 a.m. Curt drove the launch for me every morning.

In early February 1981, the boat was complete and ready to be driven to Baltimore, Maryland, where we would travel with her onboard the Yugoslavian passenger freighter *Zvir* to Casablanca, Morocco.

Several shots of *Excalibur* leaving Casablanca harbor at the start of our Atlantic row, on March 18, 1981.

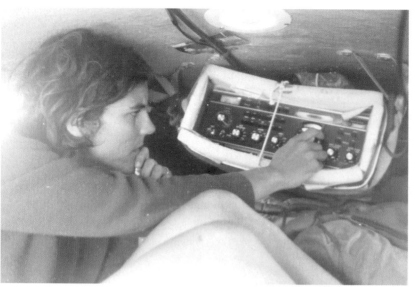

Tuning the ham radio so we can listen for the maritime ham operators we checked in with on a daily basis.

Curt working out his stars sights in the cramped bow cabin.

Excerpt from Curt's Atlantic ro* navigation log.

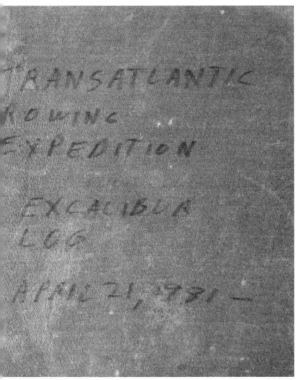

An excerpt from Curt's Atlantic row logbook with comments by me, together with the logbook's cover, below.

Making a pot of macaroni and cheese with local Moroccan ingredients. See the plastic water pump with the red handle beside my knee that we used to pump fresh water from below deck.

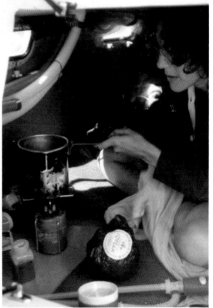

Above: Curt developing film on the deck of the rowboat in the middle of the Atlantic Ocean.

Curt being a good sport while I cut his hair on the windy deck of *Excalibur*.

Making ham radio contact with the Wilhelms in Morse code.

Melting rope ends for the sea anchors.

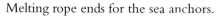

Rowing on the Atlantic in a photograph that Curt took with his remote camera device, which included a plastic box housing the Nikon. He tied a rope to the box and pulled it to the top of the radar reflector. With a quick flick of his wrist, he took the photo by pulling off a clothespin he had somehow attached to the shutter release.

Finishing the Atlantic row. *Photograph by Lynn Saville*

Rowing into English Harbor, Antigua, to end the Atlantic Ocean row on June 10, 1981. *Photograph by Lynn Saville*

until Curt woke abruptly with his face pushed up against the cabin wall. He reached over to see if I was awake. "Let's try to wedge ourselves against each other to stop from moving so much."

He put one leg out straight over me and propped his foot on the opposite wall. I locked my legs around his bent knee while each of us gripped the other's arms and tried to keep from sliding around on the cabin floor. This was much better, though it was a strange position to sleep in.

At last, the wind died down and the waves became less choppy. We fell asleep for almost one and a half hours before I woke up and looked at the watch. It was 0500 local time. It was still dark and cool out there. My body wanted more sleep, but my mind knew it was time to get going. We dressed quickly and went out on deck. The sun was not yet up; the horizon remained obscured by dark clouds. The deck was wet from a recent rain shower.

I thought about our fresh water supplies for a minute and then asked Curt how much he thought remained. We had left the Canaries with a hundred gallons in flexible 2.5- and 5-gallon containers, all stored below deck. We used about one gallon per day between the two of us. It was nearly twenty days since we left Hierro. We had at least eighty gallons left.

The conversation ended and we rowed. Slanting lines of rain moved off in the distance. The cumulus clouds on the horizon turned orange and pink. I commented that sometimes I could see green in the clouds as well.

Curt was feeling obstinate, or maybe he wanted to egg me on. There was no green at sea, he declared. "The only green out here is the green slime growing in your foot well." We had first noticed the slimy growth in the foot well of the stern rowing station a week ago. It was spreading from the little drain hole to the corners of the foot well. My favorite color was green, but not that shade of slime.

Curt's log: May 11

The rain was coming closer as we rowed. Kathleen goaded me. "If it starts raining, I'm going in the cabin."

"You can't stop rowing just because it's raining."

"Oh, yes, I can. There's no reason why I should have to row in the rain!"

But when the rain caught up with us, I realized that Kathleen was just getting me back for what I had said about the green slime. Without a word, she continued to row. The surface of the swells became rippled by the breeze created by the pressure of the rain on the water. Our bodies became shiny with the fresh rain from the sky. We did not stop and stretch out a sheet of plastic to catch the rain, though we had brought plastic for this purpose. Making progress west and the Big Push seemed more important.

We were rowing again before dawn. The wind had changed from northeast Force 3 to 4 the previous evening to an east wind blowing at Force 3. The waves were only two to three feet high, but they were now coming in different directions. I had learned that we couldn't cover as many miles without the larger, constant waves to surf along.

At 1130 GMT, we had a radio call scheduled with Norberto in Casablanca. As we rowed farther and farther away from Africa, it was becoming increasingly difficult to contact him. We kept switching to different frequencies to hear each other clearly. A lot of battery power had been used when, finally, he said that he would try again at 1730. We were reluctant to use more battery power for this extra contact, but he had signed off before I had been able to transmit our position and he might have important news for us. The propagation was much better at 1730, and we learned that a friend of his was going to the States the next day and would take news of our progress to families and friends.

When Curt checked the batteries later in the day, they were showing less than three-fourths power, the lowest since leaving Hierro. It was a good idea to curtail our power consumption and even limit our radio schedule. When Curt suggested we even cut it out completely, I protested. Our families would be worried when they didn't hear from us.

The noon sights were another source of concern. Our mileage was getting slower: we had come only thirty-eight miles in the last twenty-four hours. At this rate, it could take us well into July to arrive at the West Indies. The little choppy waves coming from different directions weren't helping us at all. As a matter of fact, they were only throwing the balance of the boat off and making it difficult to get an efficient stroke with the oars.

To make matters worse, I wasn't feeling well. I hadn't eaten much the last few days and fell asleep almost right after the oars were put away. My stomach hurt, and the top of my foot felt numb. Could I have unknowingly stepped on a loose spine of the blowfish I had caught the other day? I had been sitting on deck, in between rowing sessions, with the hand line trailing behind the boat. I was lost in thought when suddenly the line went taut, startling me out of my reverie. I called to Curt to help me keep the fish in the water until I could get the bucket under him.

As it came out of the water, small with a round stomach and its body covered with spines, the blue and white blowfish started to puff itself up with an ugly hissing noise. Its spines stuck straight up, all around its body. It was hard to get the hook out of its mouth without getting touched by the spines. Every time Curt stuck the knife in its mouth to cut the hook out, the blowfish jumped around on deck and made more hissing sounds. Finally, with the hook extracted, he scooped it up with the bucket and dumped it into the sea. It floated away on its back, looking very dead.

We rowed through much of the afternoon and on into the gray dusk of the early evening. By then, we were in a sort of stupor. We hadn't eaten much at all. The long workouts were wearing us down.

Suddenly, the fishing pole we always left tied to the stern cabin in the mornings now bent way over. It nearly went overboard, because I had put only one half hitch around it so we'd be able to get at it quickly if there was a fish. I started to reel it in. "It feels like a shark," I told Curt, though I had never caught one before.

"It does! Let me see the pole," and he came and took it from me.

I leaned over to get a glimpse of the fish as he drew it closer to the boat in the diminishing light of the day. A sudden jerking motion almost pulled Curt out of the boat. I reached over and put my arms around his waist and leaned against the aft cabin to steady him. "He's a real fighter," Curt managed to say, breathing hard and sweating heavily.

I could see, as it came closer to the boat, that it was about four or five feet long. "An eel!" Sure enough, it had a wide, flat mouth and a long, tapering tail. It rode tiredly in the water beside the boat at the end of the hook.

"Is it any good to eat? Did your grandmother teach you any Portuguese eel recipes?" I didn't know if our specimen was good to eat, but I was going to check the fish book first. As I turned to go into the cabin, Curt stopped me.

"Hey, wait a minute." He started to lift the line out of the water. The "eel" dangling off the end of the hook was a long, ragged piece of polyethylene plastic! Curt started laughing so hard he had to lean against the back cabin. When I saw what we had caught, I started laughing too, so hard that I began to cry and had to sit down on deck.

CHAPTER 20

A Mid-Ocean Celebration

Mid-May 1981

Wᴇ ᴄᴏɴᴛɪɴᴜᴇᴅ ᴛʜᴇ Bɪɢ Pᴜꜱʜ westward, taking advantage of the trade winds and rolling waves. The radio remained silent, and we used only candlelight in the cabin at night. The strong tropical sun did its work too. With the sun shining on the solar panels mounted on the roof of the forward cabin, the batteries built up to near full capacity. On May 14 and 15, we covered sixty-seven and sixty-four miles respectively in the fine surfing conditions.

We were feeling good about our progress, so to celebrate, I made a special lunch of spaghetti with garlic and onion tomato sauce. "We should have brought more Italian food with us," I commented as we ate.

Curt reminded me of why we had only brought a few cans of tomato sauce. "We thought it was more of a cold-weather food than something we would eat in the tropics." I remembered the times we would go with Peter Wilhelm to the Old Venice in Warren, Rhode Island, to have a $1.99 spaghetti dinner and warm up after working on the boat in Tony's drafty old barn in the winter.

"A can of beer would be good too. We should have brought a few with us."

As we rowed along in the afternoon, the sky became overcast and there were several brief rain showers. But they didn't bother us, because the fresh-water showers were a pleasant break from the monotony of rowing.

The wind increased to Force 5 out of the east. Occasionally, waves broke over the side of the boat, draining quickly through the scuppers and foot wells. Slimy blades of green grass in my foot well floated back and forth with the boat's motion. It was obvious I needed to do a little mowing, or I would be sprouting green grass on my soles one of these days.

At 1800 GMT I tuned the radio to the right frequency. The batteries were now showing between three-fourths and fully charged. The new fuses Curt put in on the lines also helped; the batteries were charging more efficiently.

"KA1GIN MM, *Excalibur*, this is Steve, do you copy?"

"This is *Excalibur*, we copy you loud and clear."

"Wow! You have a really strong signal; you guys just about knocked me off my seat. We were worried that we didn't hear from you. How *are* you doing?"

Curt and I smiled at each other. It was so nice to be back on frequency. I reported we were just fine and had, in fact, been saving battery power. Our position at noon today was 20 degrees 4 minutes north and 36 degrees 57 minutes west. We were moving right along.

"John in Rhode Island says he heard a report that you were halfway across. That's great!"

We looked at each other in disbelief. Where had that information come from? John, who was on frequency as well, confirmed that a woman had called him, saying that she had been in touch with us the day before via Morse code and I (Kathleen) had told her that we had not used electricity or the radio and that we still had over two hundred miles to go before we reached the halfway point. I responded to John and Steve and told them that we hadn't been on the radio for a few days and the girl was lying. Having clarified that, I signed off.

Who would do such a thing? It was nothing more than a cruel hoax. And it wasn't a safe thing to do either. If people got the wrong idea about where we were and something went wrong, they wouldn't know where to look for us.

At least the hoax gave us something to talk about while we were rowing. First we vented our frustrations by thinking of things to say about the mysterious perpetrator of such falsehoods. Then we began wondering if the information could simply have become garbled as it was passed from person to person. The "what-ifs" went on for a long time. All we knew was that we wanted to get to the halfway point as soon as possible.

Curt's log: May 17
I was beginning to lose confidence in the latitude calculation of the noon sight. Our southern progress and the sun's northern march toward the summer solstice were making the sun appear nearly straight overhead at noon. In fact, the highest point it reached in the sky as measured by the sextant at noon, May 17 was 89 degrees 57.7 minutes north! (when corrected for the sun's semi-diameter). Normally I had to swing the sextant in a short arc to get the sun to just kiss the horizon. Now I had to swing the sextant in a large sweep parallel to the horizon and try to gauge when the rim of the sun touched the horizon in the southern sky. To double-check these by now suspect measurements, we decided to do evening sights as well. At dusk, I shot Jupiter, Sirius, Capella, and Arcturus. These sights showed us to be at 19 degrees 16 minutes north and 39 degrees 5 minutes west. [About ten miles farther south than the imprecise latitude the noon sight had shown.]

I told Kathleen that we'd made more progress than I thought and she asked if that could be right. She seemed to be tired from the long hours of rowing. The new position meant we were close to the New-York-to-Cape-Town shipping lane. I pulled out the Great Circle chart. I gave one end to Kathleen to hold while I tried to find out where the shipping lane would intersect our course.

The chart filled the entire cabin. Only Kathleen's eyes, the top of her head, and her fingers showed above her end of the chart. I took the dividers and located our position on the chart. I saw Kathleen's eyes widen as she told me to be careful of points of the dividers because her leg was right under the paper. She was remembering the time on the Moroccan coast when the dividers had slipped out of my hand and stuck into my foot. When I finished taking a few measurements, we folded up the Great Circle chart. With the numbers I had gotten, I marked the shipping lane on the North Atlantic Ocean Southern Sheet where I was plotting our course. We were only twenty-seven miles from the shipping lane; it looked like we might enter it during the night before dawn.

During the night, we took turns sitting out on deck watching for ships. We thought it would be better than leaving on the anchor light and would save electric power. At about 0500 GMT by my watch, I thought I saw a light on the horizon in front of us. The air was cool and fresh, a relief from the stuffiness of the cabin. The full moon hanging low in the western sky had floated in and out from behind the trade-wind clouds during the long night.

When Curt came out on deck with the boat light to signal the ship, he had his doubts that the light was really a ship. Maybe it was a star setting, though it would have set in the time we had been watching it. He got out the VHF and called, but to no avail. How disappointing! Didn't they monitor Channel 16 as all ships are supposed to do?

Dawn of May 18 brought us into the New-York-to-Cape-Town shipping lane, which was the halfway point of our row across the Atlantic Ocean, according to Curt's calculations. We were now at 39 degrees 39 minutes west, a few miles east of the midway point of 40 degrees. It looked like it was going to take us more than twenty-six days to finish the first half, giving us a good chance of beating Samuelson and Harbo's record of fifty-five days.

There was also a good chance that we could complete the row by June 15 if we were lucky, not hit by storms, stayed healthy, and kept up the rowing. With those thoughts in mind, we returned to the deck and rowed for another hour, eager as we were to reach the middle of the ocean.

We saw more and more sargassum, the floating sea plant that was yellowish in color with irregular thin branches and berry-like balls. Large clumps, some as big as basketballs, drifted by the boat's gunwales. Our school of pilot fish swam out to investigate, always interested in any new diversion. They had to hurry to catch up with us as we rowed along.

The Sargasso Sea was hundreds of miles to the northwest of us, but somehow the plants had drifted over to where we were. The sargassum clumps formed breeding grounds for the flying fish and even for some kinds of eels that swim up the rivers into freshwater lakes in the United States.

At noonday the sun grew so hot we had to go into the cabin to cool off. The sargassum was forgotten for the moment.

Food was becoming monotonous and repetitive. We searched for ways to spice it up. For lunch, we ate macaroni and cheese with chopped-up garlic and onion. Then we found, by accident, part of a cracker in the tea bag. I had thought all of the crackers had been eaten up weeks ago. We had quite a ceremony of dividing this delicacy. Its damp and flexible shape cut nicely into two half-inch squares with the knife.

These days we were reading Jack London's *Sea Wolf*, with Humphrey van Weyden entertaining us with his exploits in dealing with Wolf Larsen while we lounged on the sleeping bag. I could relate to van Weyden and the Wolf in their trials and tribulations. The sea required a person to be tough, but one had to know what they were doing as well. *Sea Wolf* was like a seaman's bible to us as we traveled along the ocean's waves.

In the evening, after Curt had shot the stars at nautical twilight and calculated them out, we found that we had reached the middle of the ocean. We were halfway toward our goal of rowing the Atlantic Ocean. If we had had a telephone on board, we would have called our families to share in our excitement. Instead, we planned the celebrations for the next morning since we were exhausted after a full day's rowing.

On May 19 we gave ourselves a modified rowing schedule, with a few hours in the morning amid choppy waves and a brisk wind taking care of our rowing obligations. The sun was shining, and we were feeling very happy.

As we rowed, we planned the meal. Long conversations about food were popular on *Excalibur*, especially when we had something exciting to celebrate. Curt suggested we open the can of Spanish pork that Fritz and Kerrie had given us. I agreed and added that potatoes fried up with rosemary would go along splendidly. A can of pineapples would round off the menu with the bottle of champagne given to us by Narragansett Boat Club friends.

While I was cooking, Curt raised all our flags on the mast. At the top was the Stars and Stripes, which we always flew. Then came the Moroccan flag, the Explorers Club flag, and the Société Nautique de Casablanca pennant.

Before leaving Rhode Island, Peter Wilhelm had humorously given us an empty bottle to use as an auxiliary communication device in case all other systems failed. His written instructions with the bottle read: "1). remove cork 2). remove paper 3). remove writing utensil 4). write message 5). replace cork and toss into the sea." We wrote our messages in English and Spanish and threw the bottle into the sea with colorful streamers attached. Our messages were the same in both languages: "This is the ocean rowboat *Excalibur* crossing the Atlantic Ocean from Casablanca, Morocco to Antigua. Today, May 19, 1981 we are at the half-way point in our row." Though we offered a reward for the return of the bottle, we never saw it again.

It was time for the radio call to the Wilhelms. The contact was the best yet. We told them of our celebration, the different species of flying fish we had seen, and that we hoped to arrive in Antigua before the middle of June. They wished us luck for the rest of the voyage and reminded us to continue taking lots of photographs.

"Are you ready for the champagne?" Curt asked after we switched off the radio and prepared to eat. He had attempted to chill the bottle by putting it into a bucket of cool seawater and drap-ing it with a damp white towel. As he started to untwist the wire cap, I positioned myself in the cabin hatch with the camera. The cork exploded outward in a fountain of bubbly champagne. Nearly a quarter of the bottle sprayed over *Excalibur* and the sea before we could get our cups under it. It was appropriate, though, that the sea and *Excalibur* should join in the festivities, having safely delivered us to the middle of the Atlantic.

"To *Excalibur*!" Curt yelled, raising his cup.

"To the sea!"

CHAPTER 21

A Navigation Mystery

May 20, 1981

I LOOKED UP FROM MY BREAKFAST bowl of oatmeal and leftover Spanish pork. "I'm sorry you don't like the combination, but we have to use up the pork before it goes bad."

Curt was complaining about breakfast. I didn't see the problem. Oatmeal was one of the few nutritious foods we had an abundance of in the storage areas.

"We could have had it with grits. *Pork* and oatmeal?? Come onnn."

I was irritated. From the adventure books I had read before our row, it seemed people always complained about expedition food, but here there wasn't much choice. We had to eat what was available on the boat and that included a lot of affordable starches like rice, potato flakes, and oatmeal. Occasionally we were lucky to supplement the diet with canned meats or fresh fish.

We were coming down from the high of having made it halfway. We had as far to go again, and whether the food lasted was not the only concern. There were hurricanes and the problem of making it to land.

Curt changed the subject abruptly. "That was a good session with the Wilhelms yesterday, wasn't it? Except for all those other hams trying to break in."

I had to agree—the people trying to break in so that they could say they had contacted a rowboat in the middle of the Atlantic were really annoying. I thought my ear for Morse code must be improving, though, as I had little trouble picking out the Wilhelms' touches at the key among all the interlopers.

The dawn of May 21 brought rough sea conditions. *Excalibur* was riding wildly up and down. Curt said he couldn't sleep and went out to row. I wasn't sure how practical it was to row in these conditions, so I decided to stay in the cabin for a while. I handed Curt his safety harness before he left the cabin.

The sky was beginning to lighten. Waves were breaking frequently into the deck area, forcing Curt to wait until it was safe to open the hatch door. When the waves slowed down for a few minutes, he crawled out quickly and reached back to shut the hatch behind him.

I lay in the cabin and looked out the plexiglass cabin window. Curt was standing in the stern part of the deck, holding onto safety lines along both sides of the boat. He was watching the waves coming toward us from the stern. He would brace himself when one was about to break over the back cabin. The breaking waves caused seawater to flow over the cabin top and his legs. Between the waves, he reached down and began untying the oars. But he kept glancing astern to watch for other big waves.

It took him about ten minutes to get to his oars and to get the rowing seat out of the stern cabin. He had taken a few strokes when another wave splashed over the port side of the back cabin, causing the boat to tip over to the top of the gunwale. His whole oar, including the handle, was submerged in the foaming wave. I was glad that I had decided to remain in the cabin.

I reached across the cabin and took the blue felt pen stored in the plastic cup mounted on the cabin wall and marked the date on the wall, as I did every morning. Otherwise, I was sure we would forget the date. If the radio pooped out, we would have nothing to tell us what day we were living.

As I wrote 5/21, I realized that we had been at sea for a month since leaving Hierro and we had not seen another person in all that time. Zoran Lukin had warned us that in the latter half of the sea voyage, we could have problems, as May could be a bad month at sea. He told us that it was possible that we could be at our lowest point mentally and physically. We had to be careful not to relax our guard.

I heard another wave crash on the deck. I looked out and saw that Curt had been totally pushed off his seat. He was looking back at me, grinning. I couldn't be in the cabin any longer and just watch. I dug out my harness and went on deck to try my hand at rowing in these conditions.

"You know, I wouldn't be out here if this were the first part of the trip." I yelled so he could hear me above the wind and boiling sea while carefully putting my oars out in between the breaking waves. Curt nodded his head, not wanting to break his concentration. If we could master these wave conditions, they could give us a huge boost that would translate into a lot of mileage.

It was hell to keep our oars from getting fouled when the waves broke on the boat. Just when we had a good rhythm going, the waves would throw us off. If the oar handles happened to be passing over our legs when the boat was suddenly jerked to one side, we were in for a painful jab when the scull hit a knee or shin.

Learning to pause at the end of the stroke and push the oars away quickly was a skill to master. Curt was rowing in the stern because he had come out first. It was hard for me to keep an eye on the waves and Curt at the same time. When he decided to pause at the end of a stroke for a wave he didn't like, I sometimes hit him in the back with the oar because I hadn't paused in time. We started rowing again, and then I had an idea that would result in a less painful situation for him. "Why don't you say, 'Weigh enough!' when you want to stop for a wave?"

"Weigh enough!" and we stopped rowing to let a wave foam by. This was much better. It gave us more coordination in what we were attempting to do. To get the hull speed going with an oncoming wave, we would row quickly and then surf with it. It was exhilarating.

When we stopped for lunch, the big waves were still rolling out of the east-northeast. In the bow cabin, I dried myself off and handed the towel to Curt when he came in. "I found five or six little flying fish this morning on the back deck. They were too little to eat so I put them in the bait can."

"That's great," I told him. "With all these waves splashing over the boat, we're bound to get a lot of them."

"If that were the case, Kathleen, we would have seen more of them when we stopped rowing. They're attracted by the candlelight at night."

"Then how come we only see them when the waves are rough?" I thought I had him with that rebuttal, but he only shook his head.

In the calming seas of the afternoon, I went on deck to fish from my favorite spot. Curt joined me to shoot the sun and handed me the notebook to record the sights. He had hoped the sun had gone far enough north to be able to get an accurate sight by measuring its altitude above the horizon in that direction instead of the south. But he grew frustrated with the waves and the angle of the sun, which was still almost straight overhead.

"Damn shit," he said in disgust. "It's no damn good." He opened the hatch and threw the sextant into the cabin. I watched with some alarm because we had only one sextant. When I asked what his problem was, he turned around and went into the cabin. I turned the other way and went back to my fishing.

Curt's log: May 21

I sat in the cabin with my head in my hands. Nothing frustrated me more than trying to do something and not being able to do it. There must be some way to get a noon sight when the sun is straight overhead. I couldn't figure how to do it. I would have to just keep doing evening star and planet sights until the sun moved far enough north to get an accurate measurement above the horizon. I hated to do that because it wasted electric power at night when I worked out the sights.

I looked over to where the sextant lay. I picked it up and examined it carefully. We would be in trouble if it broke. Though an extra sextant was on the supply list, I had left it out at the last minute to save space. Fortunately, the Davis sextant was a plastic one and it was perfectly fine. I pushed the button on the handle. The electric LED still worked. It was certainly a durable instrument.

"Hey, Curt, I've got something!!" There was a hard tug on the fishing line. I pulled it in, and there was a nine-inch fish beside the gunwales. Curt was standing there ready to scoop up the silver-yellow pompano dolphin with the net. It glowed in the sunlight. Though it was smallish, it would make a good dinner.

A little while later, Curt returned with the camera and Davis handheld wind gauge. He thought the windy conditions made it a good time to document its use at sea. I held up the wind gauge, with the wind whipping around me, and saw that the gauge registered a twenty-mile-per-hour gust. Earlier in the row, I would have been anxious about a wind that strong, but now it felt commonplace.

I stood by the stern cabin while Curt tried to compose the photograph in the viewfinder. He took his hand off the safety line to steady the camera. Suddenly, the image in the viewfinder swung up to the sky as a wave hit the boat. As he started to fall backward, he reached out to grab anything and only succeeded in grabbing a clump of my hair from the back of my head. I screamed as he went down on the rowing tracks. He had made sure to hold the camera against his stomach to protect it, but he came down hard on his elbow on one of the tracks.

Rubbing the sore spot where he had pulled out my hair, I put out a hand to help him up. I saw that he still had a few hairs in his hand, while it was obvious his elbow pained him.

The waves were choppy the next day. The wind had shifted to east-southeast, but there were still remnants of the northeast waves. As we sat finishing breakfast, we would occasionally look out the hatch windows.

The wave's roar at the last minute warned us. The wave rose above the port side of the boat, arched over the deck, and threw hundreds of gallons of cold seawater into the deck area and over the top of the entire boat. Both of us were thrown onto the wall on my side of the cabin. The stove went flying, though fortunately it had been turned off. When the wave had passed, I looked over at Curt; his eyes were wide open in amazement.

"It's not even rough out there today."

In the afternoon, after lunch, when we both lay crammed in the bow cabin, we had a conversation about our lives after the Atlantic row. There was never any doubt that we would be successful, but our concern, or mine, was about the future. What would we do next?

The conversation began lightly with jokes about becoming famous celebrities, and then it took a dark turn. According to Curt, I would have to become more outgoing than I was because something was "lacking in my personality." It wasn't enough for me to have rowed across the Atlantic. When we finished, I would have to learn to speak up and share our experiences publicly, like Curt, who was at ease with speaking in front of a crowd.

I looked at him, only inches from away from me as we lay propped up on our elbows facing each other. Where was this coming from? I wondered out loud. "Why are you telling me this?" I started to feel uncomfortable with the vibe of criticism I was getting from him.

"Like I said, you need to learn how to get along with others. It's not enough to just row this boat. Do you understand?"

I looked back at him, completely understanding what was going on, but feeling threatened at the same time. He was more than ready for, and in fact craved, fame as a successful explorer. He just wasn't sure about me and if I would want to go down the same path as him, I thought. I decided now was a good time for my afternoon row, because it was clear that more physical space between us was needed.

I thought about our talk as I pulled hard at the oars for a couple of hours. I rolled my seat up and down the tracks and relived a conversation we had had in 1978, the year before we got married and I graduated from college. We were visiting his parents in northern Vermont, where I would meet relatives and family friends for the first time. I asked him to go for a hike in the woods surrounding his parents' summer camp, so I could show him the primitive tables I'd artfully constructed earlier in the day with small sticks and twine, following the simple directions from a 1960s woodcraft book I'd found in a bookcase. We stood looking at one while I told him how nervous

I was to be meeting all these new people for the first time. He told me not to worry and that I would do fine. But he added something I never really understood for a long time. "Just remember," he said, "that when you become successful in anything you do, don't forget me or your family, the people who helped you get ahead."

At the time I was flattered that he, a guy ten years older than me, thought I had a chance to become famous. I couldn't imagine what my success would come from, since I was an average student with a low GPA because rowing was more important to me than my studies.

I thought back to that moment and wondered if there was some connection to our conversation in the bow cabin. Did Curt suspect I might have other ideas for how we should live our lives after the row? After all, we had to think about making a living again, since we had no savings left. Was he afraid that, as someone ten years younger, I would no longer want to pursue a life of exploration with him?

It was a lot to figure out, and rowing in choppy seas and having stressful conversations made me extra tired. But I also realized that the fatigue wasn't just from the weather or Curt but also the incessant rocking motion of the boat. To hold on or even to move about took a lot of energy.

I went into the cabin, where Curt glanced at me briefly with a small smile and said he was switching on the radio for our schedule with the UK net people. I knew the power was getting low, but I also looked forward to this evening's visit. However, Curt had no more than given our position when the transmitter went dead.

"Roger, roger. I have copied your position and understand you are saving power, *Excalibur*. Hope everything is going well. Do we have anyone else to check for the net?"

"Damn it, how come they always assume we're saving power when the transmitter goes dead? What is it? The wires?"

Curt was feeling too tired to check into those things, so we sat back and listened for other people to check into the net.

"Well, we have pretty bad weather up here, too. We have gales blowing along the coast. It's wet and miserable," our friend Steve replied to a ham in Barbados. Soon they signed off, the business of the maritime net concluded.

The wind blew hard during the night, with rain showers and building seas. I awoke abruptly at about 0300 local time when I heard Curt yell, "Quick! Water's coming in!" I switched on the light and saw Curt screwing shut the port windows, which had been left open for ventilation.

"Here's a towel, let's try to mop up." Afterward, we threw the wet towels into one of the hatches below and settled back for the rest of the night. It was hot and stifling lying on the cabin floor, our sleeping pads wet from the water that had come in. The skin on our backs made a wet sucking sound as we were jostled back and forth on the floor and against the cabin walls.

"I've been having pains in my hip joints lately," I complained, as we lay in the darkness, unable to sleep. "I think it's from the rowing seats. We sit down too much and we haven't been able to walk in weeks."

Curt agreed. His hips had been bothering him as well. But he changed the subject, realizing it didn't do us any good to dwell on our discomforts. "The rain on the roof sounds like it does on the roof of a cabin in Vermont, doesn't it?" It did sound like that.

That night Curt shot six stars to fix our position. The star sight calculations showed us to be a full degree farther west than we expected to be. Every way he worked it out, the new position showed us at 46 degrees 10 minutes west instead of 45 degrees 10 minutes. It was impossible for us to have covered that much distance. The only explanation seemed to be a time error, though the watches we used to record the sights were not off by four minutes, a whole degree of 60 minutes. We always set the watches by the radio time signals.

I turned on the radio—whose wires Curt and Fritz had repaired in the Canaries and yet had subsequently needed even more electrical tape to secure them against the saltwater—and tuned in the time signal. We watched the luminescent hands on our Rolex Oyster watches closely as the ticking of the time signal approached the hour. The announcer gave the time. The watches were accurate.

Curt went over all the calculations again. But every way he worked them, the numbers showed us to be farther west than 46 degrees. He could find no explanation to account for the missing degree.

CHAPTER 22

Knee Injury

May 24, 1981

To satisfy himself that we had not been carried an extra sixty miles west by a freak current or anomaly of compass deviation resulting from the relative closeness of the Sargasso Sea, Curt shot the sun on the morning of the 24th to get another longitude check. It showed that we had a ways to go to reach 46 degrees. We were still east of where the star sights of the night before had indicated. It was unnerving to have a problem like that creep into the navigation. We would have to be sure of where we were in order to steer an accurate course to Antigua, our intended ending point for the Atlantic row.

We were rowing in the middle of the morning in choppy seas when the hand line tied to a block of oak suddenly jerked. It was pulled from under a spare set of oars and would have gone overboard had I not grabbed it.

Curt leaned over the gunwale and scooped up the fish as I pulled it in. "This is the biggest one yet," he said as he put it on deck. It was another pompano, sixteen inches long. I put another flying fish from the bait can on the hook, and trolled the line again. Soon we caught another one, but not as large. There seemed to be a whole school of pompanos following us. They were clever and soon learned how to get the bait off the hook. They would attack the bait the second it hit the water in a wild frenzy of splashing. One of them grabbed the bait so hard he took the hook right off. The book had been right when it said: "a prized fighting fish, pompanos are known to race at the hook and put up a fight."

The fish had stolen all the bait before lunch, so I cooked what we had already caught. I fried one fish and made a New England–style milk chowder with the other one. There had been so many of them beside the boat, it was a pity we couldn't have caught more to sun dry and salt. We had brought a container of rock salt to preserve some of the fish we caught. At the rate we were catching them, though, I doubted we would even need it.

Early in the evening, when we had finished rowing for the day, we went into the cabin to have dinner. I turned on the radio, hoping the retaped wires would hold, to see if there was any interesting news on the UK net. The first we heard was a ship calling in weather information: "and the barometer has been falling sharply. It's gone down 12 millibars in the last hour."

Curt, who had been slumped in the corner of the cabin, looked over at me with eyes wide. "Where is that guy?" he asked.

I adjusted the dial so that I could hear more clearly. The ship mentioned the Balearic Islands. Breathing a sigh of relief, I said to Curt, "The Med." Our nerves were on edge because of our concerns about the weather. We tended to assume the worst whenever we heard anything on the radio or observed something unusual about the clouds, wind, or waves.

The next morning, May 25, I sat out on the deck in the sun. It was a beautiful day, with a moderate breeze. I was reading Henry David Thoreau's account of his first visit to Cape Cod in 1849. On his way there, he heard the news of a frigate, *St John*, from Galway, Ireland, having wrecked outside of Cohasset Harbor, Massachusetts. He and his companion went to investigate, along with hundreds of other curious New Englanders.

A wave splashed over the page and I wiped it off with my hand. Thoreau's conclusion was that the dead people were going to as fine a port as the one they were bound for on Cape Cod. Another wave splashed over the page. I put the book in the cabin.

I couldn't say I agreed with Thoreau, being on the sea and hoping to make landfall myself. But I thought about land and whether it really was preferable to sea. My convictions all along had been that land was the place I wanted to be the most. But what of it? We listened to the news about the hunger strikes in Ireland, terrorist activities, and the hostile accusations flying between countries. There was very little peace anywhere in the world now.

Some people thought we were foolish to undertake the task of putting together the expedition and building a boat so we could attempt to investigate on our own the wilderness and vastness of an ocean. But I knew there were a lot of people out there who wanted to do the same. Rowing an ocean was not an exercise in living close to the edge, in taking unreasonable chances with one's life. That was only a shallow interpretation. It was an exercise in complex problem-solving that required we carefully consider every decision before it was implemented.

I thought about our conversation of a few days ago and wondered if there had been something I had missed over the days. Was there anything I had said to Curt and forgotten about in the monotony of our lives that made him doubt my commitment to our marriage? I decided to let it go. In a space as small as *Excalibur*, neither of us could afford to stay mad at each other for long. Besides, we had long ago agreed it was better not to be alone on the rowboat at sea.

Later in the afternoon, we went back to rowing. The wind was blowing at about Force 5 out of the east-northeast but the waves were not consistent. Some of them came out of the northeast and others out of the southeast. The result was many choppy, pointed waves that made rowing tiring and surfing practically impossible. I watched the waves come rolling by and break along the gunwales. They were ceaseless, no end to them, to the booming, the hills and valleys and the white foam that accompanied it all. Day after day, week after week. It was a long time to be living so close to the ocean's surface. There was no escape or diversion from the sound and motion of the waves.

Curt's log: May 26

The day began humid and hot. It was particularly stuffy in the cabin because we had closed all of the ports during the night. I had not slept well. A stickiness of salt and sweat covered my whole body. The salt sores I was afraid would plague us had appeared. There was a rash of red sores along my lower back that constantly itched. Scratching didn't do any good; it only made the sores worse. I had to get out of the cabin.

I crawled out onto the deck and untied the yellow plastic bucket. I put the little green ball, our pet, into the foot well. Some of the crustaceans had dried and fallen off. The crab had long since died and been used as bait. There was still some slime on the ball, but the slime seemed to have migrated to the foot wells, where it was growing and thriving.

I threw a bucket of seawater over my body to cool off. Then I took out a pair of oars and began rowing. For over an hour, I sat there, pulling the oars through the water, not thinking about much of anything. Except about how hot it had gotten to be, and the unpleasant sensation of my heels slipping on the slime in the foot well. Our heels would wear holes in it but the slime would still grow back.

When Kathleen called to say breakfast was ready, it was already oppressively hot in the sun even though it had been up for less than two hours.

I sat in the corner of the cabin, my skin sticking against the wall. Kathleen passed me a bowl containing my breakfast. I looked down into the shiny black mass. "Pudding for breakfast?" I asked incredulously.

"Curt, you're lucky I make breakfast for you," she said, with an edge to her voice.

"Oh, you're so nice to go to the trouble of making instant pudding." I couldn't resist egging her on. Instant pudding for breakfast was the end-all.

Kathleen didn't say anything. I watched her take a couple of bites of her pudding. I could tell she thought it left something to be desired, because she reached down into the hatch and came up with a Ziploc bag with a green paper bag containing the last of the almonds and walnuts we had bought in Casablanca. She reached in and pulled out a small handful of nuts. I watched as she went through them carefully, sorting out the black bugs. These she crushed between her thumb and forefinger and wiped on her gym shorts. Then she crushed the nuts and put them in her pudding. She stirred the pudding and started eating again.

"Well, are you going to give me any?" I asked her.

"Bugs or nuts?"

"Nuts to you," I said grabbing the bag. I repeated the same process. I was never sure if the bugs in the nuts came from the flowers or the souk in Casablanca.

Kathleen turned on the radio for the weekly schedule with the Wilhelms after breakfast, but she didn't have much luck. She would pick up a signal that sounded like them, but then it would fade out. After spending a quarter of an hour on the 10-meter band, she switched to the 15-meter band that was part of the backup plan if the first band failed. Again and again she called but could not pick them up. I sat beside her, waiting for the contact. When it didn't come, I felt very depressed. Our expectations for this high point of the day were shattered. I put the sextant that I had used earlier away in its box as Kathleen reached over to turn the radio off.

But before she switched it off, we heard a signal coming in loud and clear. KA1GIN MM de W2BXA k (k = over to you).

Since the guy was coming in really strong, I told her to answer him. Not a good idea because she said since it was not the Wilhelms, we couldn't afford the power, and turned off the radio.

"Wait!" I said, "They may be in touch with the Wilhelms." The ham repeated his call to *Excalibur*. "Hurry up and answer them!" I insisted.

I was pushing my luck and being obnoxious but I wanted to make that contact. "I can't believe you, they could help us."

"Shut up! I'm the radio operator, not you!" She was mad.

I banged the sextant box down on the floor and stormed out of the cabin. It made me so mad. Since I was captain of the boat, I should be able to say whom we made contact with. I stood holding the hand straps on the cabin top, trying to cool down in the breeze.

Curt's presumptive attitude had really irritated me. Who did he think he was? We were both running this boat, making decisions about how we would live our lives on board. I thought about the ham who was still trying to reach me. What IF he had something important to tell us?

I answered him and was glad I did. I called Curt in after W2BXA and I finished our chat. He looked a little contrite, but mostly he was interested in the substance of my contact. W2BXA was a friend of his Uncle Charlie's in New Jersey, I told him. Charlie had wanted to contact us himself, but his rig couldn't put out a strong enough signal to reach us. I sent our position and said we hoped to reach Antigua before June 15. Ben, W2BXA, responded with a promise to pass the information along to Charlie and our families. He added that he would be listening in on a regular basis and would help us in any way he could.

Curt's cranky mood improved. The new contact helped him forget about his salt sores and strange breakfasts. It made us friends again.

That evening when he went out on deck to shoot the stars, he was plagued by the choppy waves that kept splashing over the sides and making the deck wet. He leaned against the forward cabin, trying to brace himself. But when it came time to bring the star down on the horizon, he had to have both hands on the sextant.

In the middle of taking the last sight, he slipped and fell to the deck. The sextant was not damaged, but his right knee banged into one of the rowing tracks. He knew he had hit it hard when he tried to stand and a pain shot through his kneecap.

The next morning when he woke and tried to crawl out on deck, it bothered him. I looked over from my sleeping spot and saw that his knee had swollen up. He could hardly bend it, never mind crawl on it. Until this happened, neither of us realized how important knees were for getting around *Excalibur*. When going into the cabin from the deck especially, the technique was to put both hands through the hatch onto the cabin floor, which was three inches below deck, then swing the right leg in and put the knee on the floor. The left leg couldn't go in that way since the hatch hinges were on that side. Since Curt couldn't put pressure on his right knee, he had to press his head to the cabin floor for support. For some reason, I found this very funny. Whenever Curt came in the cabin, half standing on his head, I started giggling. At least there was some comic relief, albeit at Curt's expense!

If I didn't give him much sympathy, I did have an idea of how to treat the injury. "You need an ice pack from the Norton medical kit that Ed gave us." I went to the back cabin and rummaged around for a cold pack. Curt watched with interest as I pulled out the compress and activated it by squeezing it with both hands and shaking up its contents. I strapped it on his knee by wrapping a roll of gauze bandage around the compress and knee. It was a perfect substitute for ice, the nearest supply of which was hundreds of miles away as we floated on the tropical sea.

As I rowed in the late-morning sun while Curt rested in the cabin, I thought of how serious a major injury could be on a voyage like this. Though we had a copy of the special DH MEDICO code for emergency medical advice by radio, we were very much on our own.

CHAPTER 23

Voyaging among the Stars

May 28, 1981

I LEFT CURT LYING IN THE cabin with his knee wrapped in gauze with the cold pack, and went out to row. It was a windy day with shifting northeast and southeast winds. As the rowboat progressed south and west toward the Leeward Islands of the Caribbean Sea, the winds had become noticeably finicky, as the pilot chart indicated: we had entered a quadrant of winds from different directions. On the far end of the quadrant, we would leave the prevailing northeast trades for the southeast trade winds that blew from the direction of southwest Africa.

I thought about Curt lying in the cabin. Was his knee so badly hurt that he really couldn't row? Surely he was using his knee as an excuse to laze about, drink coffee, and read while I did the rowing. I took a few strokes. The sun was hot, and the boat was very heavy.

There had been so much study in preparation for the Atlantic row. I learned how to use Morse code and acquired my ham radio license, along with learning how to recognize international navigation lights and buoys. I'd also been in charge of finding us transportation to Casablanca and contacting companies for sponsorship. Curt had studied celestial navigation and put together the electrical systems on the boat. He had worked with Peter Wilhelm and Ed Montesi on the boat design. Together we built the boat. But one thing

I hadn't bothered to learn was navigation, trusting—naively—that Curt would be able to navigate us across the Atlantic without any problems. It did not seem possible that he would ever be injured or unable to carry out his job.

I thought about this as I rowed along. It was unreasonable and immature to put the responsibility for two lives on just one person in a situation as unusual as rowing a small boat across an ocean. I resolved to ask Curt to teach me one of his methods of navigation so I could share in it.

But first, I took a break from rowing and sat on one of the cabin tops. Settling myself in between the narrow space between the solar panels, I stared down into the green waters rushing by the red hull of *Excalibur*. I saw the purple pilot fish swimming along, under the bow of the boat. I was sure that I recognized Alpha from the group that trailed after him. For the others I started a naming game to amuse myself. "Charlie, Delta, Echo, and Foxtrot . . ." I dangled my feet off the bow in the cool seawater, feeling pleasantly relaxed. An occasional wave sent the water as high as my knees. A couple of the pilot fish swam up to look at my toes, contemplating their novelty in the life around the rowboat. It occurred to me they might want a nibble, and I jerked my feet up.

I levered myself off the bow cabin and made my way to the back cabin while holding onto the safety lines. I found a flat spot on the aft cabin roof just forward of the tiller and climbed on to enjoy the gentle wind on my face. Over the weeks since we had gone to sea, I had grown to love the feel of the wind on my face and body. Sometimes the air drifted softly over us while we lay in the cabin at night with the hatch door open, settling on us like a veil of soft silk.

It wasn't long before I saw a very large brown fish swimming by *Excalibur*, going in the opposite direction. It was at least five feet long and barely below the surface of the water. It was as though we were passing each other on a conveyor belt or an airport moving sidewalk.

I watched the sea for a long time, mesmerized by the patterns of waves forming and dissolving around the boat. Just as I began to feel hungry, the forward cabin hatch opened and Curt stuck his head out. It was time for lunch, and Curt had prepared a good one.

Over a lunch of chili beans (where had he found them?), I told Curt of my desire to learn a basic method for navigating the boat. I could tell he was pleased I was taking an interest in learning. In retrospect, it seems obvious that we should both have learned celestial navigation, since it was such an important aspect of travel in a slow-moving ocean rowboat. But it wasn't until the 1984–1985 Pacific Row that I participated fully in the navigation of *Excalibur*. Perhaps by then I began to accept the real possibility of one of us not making it.

After lunch, Curt began his lecture on how to obtain an approximate position using the sun and stars without a sextant. I scribbled notes as he talked.

"All you need is *The Nautical Almanac* and your watch set for Greenwich Mean Time. First, you find the North Star at night and estimate how many degrees it is above the horizon. You can do this pretty accurately by visualizing that 90 degrees is straight ahead, 45 degrees is halfway between the horizon and the point in the sky directly overhead, until you get your estimate of how many degrees the North Star is above the horizon. That measurement tells you your latitude.

"Next, you measure the approximate time in Greenwich Mean Time of the sunrise or sunset. The official time of sunrise or sunset is when the sun is two-thirds of its diameter above the horizon."

He opened *The Nautical Almanac* to the page that showed the day's date. He showed me where the times of sunrise and sunset were listed. "The sun rises and sets at different times, depending upon your latitude. Look in the column for your latitude, which you got from the North Star, and write down the difference in minutes between that time in the book and the GMT time you measured by looking at the sun." I glanced over to the faded orange, water-stained *Nautical Almanac* with the year 1981 stamped on the front lying beside Curt. He went on, "Since four minutes of time is equal to one degree of longitude, all you have to do is divide four into the difference in minutes between the GMT and local time of sunrise and sunset. That figure tells you how many degrees you have for longitude."

"That's all there is to it? How accurate is all of this?"

"It gives you an approximate position. Depending on how accurate your estimates are, you could be right to within sixty or a hundred miles. That could help you find your way to a chain of islands. Like the Leewards. Even a shipping lane."

We woke up several times during the night to spot for ships, since we were now crossing the New-York-to-South-America shipping lanes. When the horizon began to lighten, Curt went out and shot Nunki, Alpheratz, Denab, Fomalhaut, and Vega through breaks in the clouds. High gray cumulus clouds moved quickly across the dawn skies, making it difficult to pick out, identify, and bring the stars down to the horizon before clouds once again covered them.

Curt decided to try rowing, since the swelling in his knee had gone down. He could only partially bend his knee, so he began with half-strokes. I joined in, and we rowed together, Curt in the bow and me in the stern. As the sun emerged from below the horizon, I stopped rowing so I could try out his emergency method of navigation and check my figures against his morning star sights. As I did my sun sights, he double-checked the bearing of the compass against the bearing of the sunrise, since it hadn't been done lately.

Later, after we had stopped for breakfast, I got out the *Almanac* and worked on my calculations. I passed Curt the notebook to check what I had come up with. According to Curt, the estimate looked a bit too far north and west, but he was impressed. When he worked out the stars later, we found I was off by 125 miles. Our position was actually 17 degrees 38 minutes north and 49 degrees 25 minutes west.

His own measurements of the bearing of the sunrise showed only a small deviation in the accuracy of the compass, over and above the 18 degrees west variation shown on the chart. That deviation could easily have been caused by the difficulty in keeping the compass pointed straight while we were lurching around in the waves. Generally, we had been steering by observing the row of Xs showing our previous position on the chart and correcting the autopilot settings as needed.

During the night, the wind and waves died down and the seas became gentler in their motion. I blew out the candle and opened the hatch. "It's so beautiful out here, you should see the stars."

We lay on our stomachs, our arms propped up on pillows at the edge of the cabin hatch, the wind blowing softly over us. The sky was crystal clear, and the stars and planets were reflected in the ocean's surface, giving the impression we were floating in space with no earth below us.

I rolled over onto my back and looked up. Curt did the same. All we could see was space filled with billions of stars and planets. It was awe-inspiring. We could imagine ourselves floating in a capsule among the stars, wondering what would it be like to pass by one. How perfect the moment was, floating on the peaceful sea that night.

CHAPTER 24

Atlantic Encounters

May 31, 1981

I AN, A HAM RADIO OPERATOR we'd been in touch with lately, had advice and information for us about Antigua. Over the past couple of weeks, we had discussed the best place to make landfall. Fine-tuning *Excalibur's* course was becoming essential as the rowboat drew closer to the Caribbean side of the Atlantic.

"8P6HZ, this is KA1GIN MM. Do you copy?"

Ian copied us and was delighted to reestablish contact. Like so many of the hams out there, he was more than willing to be of assistance. He sent the following message: "If you're going to Antigua, then English Harbour is a good place to land." I located it on the chart as he was talking. "It's a good port because it's enclosed from the sea but it has a good breeze. But it has no buoys or lights, which is surprising, considering it is an official port of entry. So don't come in at night." I looked at Curt, and he nodded. A night landing was definitely something we would avoid; we'd put out the sea anchor and slow our progress toward Antigua if our approach was untimely.

Ian went on, "As you come in from the east, which I'm assuming you will, you'll pass south of Green Island, across from the Bay of Nonesuch. Go right toward South Point. You'll almost be past the Point when you see the entrance to English Harbour; it's at the very southern end of Antigua. You go in through the Pillars of Hercules, around the Harbor, and to the White Admiral's Inn. That'll be a good place for you to drop anchor."

Antigua was sounding more and more like a reality as we listened to Ian and plotted a course along the south coast of the island according to his advice. We needed to adjust the present course and make *Excalibur*'s line of position straighter. When Curt worked out the star sights that night, he was startled by the results. We had drifted farther north of our intended course: the boat was now at 17 degrees 48 minutes north and 52 degrees 54 minutes west. Either the autopilot, which had hardly ever been turned off, had wandered off course, or the weather had blown us off course. This was the point in the voyage when we needed to steer the most accurate course, without altering, until we caught sight of land. Curt went out to the aft cabin, where the autopilot ceaselessly steered *Excalibur*, and adjusted the course to 265 degrees true.

On June 1, in the half-light of early evening, I caught a triggerfish. Since we were both tired, it didn't matter that the triggerfish was an ugly-looking fish. We were hungry and needed the fresh food.

While Curt was cooking it with the last of the fresh onions and Moroccan olive oil, I saw a light out my port window. As we drew closer to the Caribbean Sea, the likelihood of seeing ships and even being run down had increased. I grabbed the spotlight off the hook on Curt's side and went on deck to plug it in, to let the ship know we were there. Curt turned on the anchor light from the inside and came out and stood beside me. With the VHF radio, he tried hailing the ship as I trained the spotlight straight at it. The ship was only half a mile away. But no one answered our calls. We were surprised not to get a response, and also disappointed, because Curt wanted a position check to confirm our approach to land.

I unplugged the spotlight, and we went back into the cabin. The triggerfish meal was also a disappointment: the meat was bitter and tough. I threw the contents of the frying pan overboard because we didn't want to take a chance with fish poisoning. The pilot fish, however, were delighted with the morsels as they dropped overboard.

It was a rough night. Wind and waves shifted from a comfortable northeast motion to a rougher east-southeast, creating confused seas with breaking crests from different directions. We were jolted around from side to side all night, making sleep for more than ten minutes impossible.

The wind and waves were part of the easterlies, the storm systems that blow from east to west through the trade wind belt and fuel tropical storms and hurricanes. Dark clouds raced across the sky with sudden rain squalls.

Curt's log: June 2
Getting up at 0800 hours GMT, in the dark, to prepare for morning star sights was difficult. I pulled on a pair of shorts and a sweatshirt and braced myself to crawl out onto the wet deck. The scene that greeted me was gray and dark with tall menacing seas of whitecaps. The wind shrieked through the safety lines as I reached down to get the sextant from Kathleen in the cabin. She quickly closed the hatch door to avoid blowing spray and turned on the electric light to record the time and angle of the star sights that I would call out.

On deck, I was trying hard to keep my balance as I brought the sextant up to my eye. When I found Nunki in the telescope of the sextant, I worked the index to bring the star down to the horizon. Or *was* it the horizon? The true horizon was only visible for a brief second when *Excalibur* was at the top of a large wave. Before I could double-check, a cloud covered Nunki.

I wasn't discouraged, though. I tried another star. "Get ready," I told Kathleen, "I'm going to try Formalhaut." Kathleen recorded the data: 0828:44. I tried and got Vega and Deneb. I thought we would have something to advance our position with, though the horizons were somewhat questionable in the stormy conditions.

Too tired to row and unwilling to face the stormy conditions, I went back to the cabin and tried to get more sleep. I had nightmares about the triggerfish Kathleen had caught the night before. Its ugly face and wide staring eyes kept swimming by. Then, suddenly, as I watched in horror, it jumped up at me.

When I woke up again, we were surrounded by the gray light of early morning. I shifted my weight on the sleeping mat. Salt sores on my skin itched and burned. My head ached and my mind felt dull and groggy. Perhaps if I took a bath, I would feel better, more alert. I took care not to awaken Kathleen as I crawled past her. Standing amidships, I poured buckets of cold seawater over my body to rinse the saltwater soap from my body.

To the north of the boat was a gathering of dark clouds. The wind suddenly picked up and hard drops of rain began pelting against my skin. I stood up, holding on to the safety lines, and laughed out loud at the prospect of being rinsed off by fresh water. The rain turned into a torrential downpour.

Very quickly the wind came in violent gusts. The rain changed to hail and the sweet feeling of fresh water became sharp stinging arrows. I had never seen anything like it. The sea was whipped into impossibly steep peaks. All around the boat, waves broke over the gunwales and gushed around me. I felt powerless to do anything as I crouched by the back cabin holding on to the safety lines with all my might.

David and Goliath: *Excalibur* versus *Atlántico*, June 3, 1981

As quickly as it started, the morning's squall ended. The wind died down, and the solid gray clouds flew off to the west. Though the waves were still choppy, it was possible to row. Curt joined me on deck as I leaned down to untie my oars.

By midday we had rowed two hours in clearing skies and settling seas. As we ended the rowing in the gathering heat of the day, a white object appeared in the distance. When we both strained to see what it was, Curt took out the sextant and sighted it through the telescope. It was a ship!

I brought out the VHF and tried communicating but to no avail. It continued along its course, less than a half mile from us. Then I remembered the mirror trick we had used with *Jangada* in the Canaries. I took it out and began moving it back and forth to catch the sun's reflection.

To my amazement, the ship turned toward us and passed port to port about two hundred yards away. I gave Curt the VHF to call, but before he could say a word, the radio crackled to life. In rapid Spanish we heard, "*Que problema? Que quieres?*"

We were stunned at our success in contacting another boat after so many failures in the past, but Curt recovered first and answered in Spanish. "This is *Excalibur*, the transatlantic rowboat, forty-three days out of Hierro. Can you tell us what our position is? We're having trouble getting accurate fixes in these seas."

The letters on the freighter's hull were now clearly visible: *Atlántico*. The captain of the ship, Louis Platensuelo, radioed a position that was 17 degrees 27 minutes north, 56 degrees 14 minutes west. Later, when we compared these figures with Curt's calculations, we found we were only five miles off the ship's computed position.

"Apart from the position, is there anything else you need?" the captain added.

Curt answered in the negative, but I couldn't resist. Couldn't we get something, since these people were our first live human contact in well over a month? I asked for something sweet.

At the same time the captain asked, "Perhaps there is something you desire? Maybe we could give you fresh fruit, *salada?*"

It was hard to resist such an offer. Curt accepted but asked that they not come any closer to us for safety reasons. Was there a way they could get the parcel of goodies to us?

"Certainly," Captain Louis answered. "Don't worry, we will put it so you can get it."

Atlántico motored around us several times, laying down a circle of motor oil to calm the seas. We had not seen people in forty-three days, and now a huge steel freighter was circling us. From the freighter, we could hear the sounds of a hammer banging away, drifting on the wind. I looked at Curt and said, "You can smell the ship. It's our first smell of civilization in over six weeks." He wrinkled his nose, taking in the smells of grease, oil, and paint. It was almost overwhelming.

Soon the result of the hammering appeared and the seamen lowered a wooden raft topped with a large, heavily tied plastic package. *Atlántico* was visibly pitching and rolling in the seas as she attempted to tow the raft of supplies to us with a long rope. Unfortunately, as the raft hit the open water, the rope broke in the tremendous action of the waves and the raft broke away.

The raft with its load of precious provisions was about a hundred yards upwind from *Excalibur*. We could see it as it floated to the top of the waves, and frantically rowed toward it, though the boat was being blown downwind much more rapidly than the raft. Even with the tiller hard over and rowing with all our strength, it was impossible to head directly into the wind in the rough conditions. After five minutes, we were about three hundred yards from the raft and almost even with it relative to the wind. We came about by backing the oars on one side and rowing forward on the other. Some headway was lost in the maneuver, but cutting across on the other tack brought us much closer to the raft. Curt was certain we could reach the raft, but I wasn't so sure.

We were on the verge of making our turn when *Atlántico* altered course and came straight for us. Apparently they thought the rowers would not be able to reach the raft without some assistance, so they joined in the chase. Within seconds, our rowboat was directly below the hulk of the freighter's bow. We needed no further encouragement to row faster. The freighter's bulb-shaped bow came closer, rising out of the water like a torpedo. We hung on tightly to the safety lines as the oars became ineffectual with the rowboat's precarious list to port.

Now in the lee of the freighter, we were completely cut off from the wind, a strange feeling after so many weeks of constant wind on our bodies. We could hear *Atlántico*'s seamen above us talking excitedly. They threw lines down to us. Their engines were turned off as *Atlántico* rolled silently in the waves. Curt grabbed one of the ropes and called up in Spanish, "What are we going to do?"

"Tie the rope to your stern."

As he tried to find an end in the tangled rope on our deck, we both saw the mess of our deck with the eyes of strangers, all of whom were avidly watching us from high above. Loose rope lay in a jumble by the aft cabin with a torn sea anchor tossed on top. These were the ropes used to tie off the sea anchor or the rubber inner tube that we had used for taking photos away from the boat, but when we looked at them anew, it was a shock to see the boat's deck in such disarray. Finally, Curt found a rope end and tied it to the *Atlántico*'s rope.

Still ten feet from *Atlántico,* the near miss fresh in our minds, we wondered what their next move was going to be. Within seconds the ship, rolling broadside to the wind and waves, drifted down to *Excalibur.* I rowed hard to keep us a safe distance away, but the freighter drifted closer and my oar blades caught between the two hulls. I jumped to my feet and joined in pushing against the steel hull that rose and fell in the waves besides us. We pushed with our hands, feet, and the boat hook, with all our strength. Even so, the freighter rolled down against *Excalibur.* There was a terrible crunch of fiberglass against steel.

A confusion of Spanish and wild gesticulation broke out above. Pulling on the rope, the seamen began dragging the rowboat toward *Atlántico*'s stern. They planned to tow us to the raft. Near the stern, the curvature of the hull arched above our heads, rolling down onto the oar mast, bending the navigation light to one side. I screamed and waved my arms. We crouched down in the boat and held our hands on the steep and slimy hull to protect ourselves.

Astern was the gigantic steel propeller rising slowly out of the water. Foamy white water poured off it with the sound of a waterfall. For an instant, the huge prop blade paused in the air above the water like an old rusting guillotine.

With a burst of sudden clarity, we saw how stupid it was to let the *Atlántico*'s sailors pull us toward the stern. There was no way we could avoid being chopped to bits by the sharp blades of the prop.

"No! Stop! *Muy peligroso!*" I screamed, raising my voice in a way I hadn't in weeks. We were almost at the end of our row across the Atlantic, and here, at this moment, we were about to lose it all: the boat and maybe our lives.

"No, stop! Stop!" we screamed in unison, and at this sound, the Spaniards focused on our faces and realized we were not waving in agreement. We were scared to death of what was about to happen.

Excalibur stopped moving and tension on the rope lessened enough for Curt to reach over and untie it quickly before the sailors regained their enthusiasm for towing us to the raft. Together, we pulled ourselves along the hull, back to midship, where the ship's bilge suddenly began spewing gray water onto the deck of *Excalibur*. *Can it get any worse?* I thought. Would this ever end? Another oar in the bow station caught between the hull and the gunwales of *Excalibur* and cracked bit by bit. The broken pieces sank into the ocean.

There was a shout from above, and we looked up from fending off the ship. A seaman had a plank in his hands that he wanted to send down to us as an aid. I started yelling, "No, no!" when he reached over to drop it to us horizontally. Fortunately, another seaman told him to lower it down to us in a vertical position so we could grab it safely. As we rose to the top of a wave, Curt grabbed the plank and used it to lever our boat away.

High above on the bridge, the captain could see it was impossible to tow us to the raft. I watched him as he called down through cupped hands, "*Un momento*, I'll send a new package to you."

"*Gracias, gracias*, Captain." Still shaking from the close encounter with the stern of *Atlántico*, we waited. On the lee side of the ship, the full force of the tropical heat surrounded us. Sweat poured down our faces.

In a few minutes, the seamen lowered another large plastic-covered box of stores. Curt reached up and carefully guided it to the deck. We waved our thanks and I began putting the newly acquired stores into the bow cabin.

We pushed ourselves along the hull with wet hands toward the bow, where we would break loose from the suction created between the *Excalibur* and *Atlántico*. The infamous bulb-shaped bow, riding up and down in the waves, nearly hoisted us out of the sea. With one final lunge, Curt pushed the boat away with the plank, slipping and falling on the deck. I dug in deeply with the oars and rowed hard to clear us of the freighter.

After we were a safe distance from the *Atlántico*, with trembling hands, I passed Curt the VHF. With equally shaking hands, he held the radio and thanked Captain Platensuelo and the crew for their kindness and generosity. We stood on the deck and waved goodbye as the *Atlántico* disappeared over the horizon.

Then, eagerly and without further ado, we reached into the cabin to inspect our hard-earned cache. I cut open the obscenely large package. It was full of fresh food, including four liters of fresh milk still cold from the refrigerator. We split one on the spot. There were also cans of fruit juices, pineapples in syrup, jams, and dozens of Valencia oranges. There were several pounds of white sugar, presumably to fill my request for sweets. A bottle of Johnny Walker Red, two cartons of American cigarettes, fresh salad materials, and a dozen bottles of spring water from Andorra rounded out our package.

After an elegant dinner that night that included a large salad of lettuce and tomato for each of us, with white asparagus tips, we sat on deck resting. We were not only feeling revived from the meal's fresh vitamins, but we were still jazzed up from the encounter with *Atlántico*'s crew. It had been a traumatic day, one that we had been lucky to survive. For the next few days, I continued to feel unsettled, though I couldn't tell if this was due to the impending landfall or our encounter with *Atlántico*.

At the same time, the food and human contact from *Atlántico* had recharged us, pulling us out of the lethargy that had settled over the expedition. Perhaps it had come from the monotonous diet of dried foods or the daily routine of rowing hour after hour. Now we awoke each day feeling refreshed and renewed, and we began doing some of the chores we had neglected.

The food supplies in the bow cabin needed reorganizing. With more space in the compartments below deck, it was now possible to move the flour and canned goods from the stern cabin, above deck, to the hatches below deck in the bow cabin. The boat rode noticeably better with more weight below deck.

Curt worked on the boat lines by the aft cabin that had caused us such embarrassment with their general disarray. It was hard to believe the degree of neglect of the ropes. Curt decided to break out a new sea anchor from the supply of extra odds and ends in the back cabin. The old one was torn around the grommet holes, causing it to stream behind the boat unevenly. He stuffed it below deck in the back cabin.

Curt's log: June 4

I looked in the aft cabin hatches to check for water. There was a little water in the bottom of the side compartment. The bilge pump could not suck up the last drops so I used a sponge to wipe out the last of the water. I found the plastic container with the medicines and the major medical supply. It was full of seawater from the flooded aft cabin that had occurred the day we had met the *Atlántico*. I dumped the water out and wiped off each medicine bottle carefully.

The wind had been increasing steadily all morning. I didn't like the look of the seas. Waves were now coming along and pushing us off course, allowing other waves to hit us broadside. It looked like the wind and waves could push us too far north. Rather than wait, I decided to put out the new sea anchor to slow the adverse drift. With the parachute-shaped sea anchor deployed off the stern, I went to the bow and pulled up the forward dagger board so we could ride more smoothly on the waves. Right away Kathleen opened the hatch and looked out when the motion of the boat changed. She saw that the dagger board had been pulled up and the slot situated in front of the hatch opening was open to the sea. "Look!" She pointed to the slot. "There are little fish in there." Five or six little goldfish-sized fish were riding up and down in the slot, the suction created by the rolling waves transporting them. "Oh, man, they make me sick, watching them go up and down like that."

I put the dagger board back in and we put out the oars.

A curious element had entered our seemingly timeless days of life at sea. As the boat was drawing closer to land, the idea of schedules and organizing life with other people in mind was hard to imagine. Out here, we decided who to interact with, and when. *Excalibur* had become our private world. We weren't sure we were ready for re-entry to "earth" proper.

A radio call with Peter Wilhelm was equally frustrating. The signal kept fading in and out as I copied something about, "TV . . . QTH . . . parents . . . to come . . . Antigua but Lynn . . ." We were eager to know who was coming to Antigua to see us arrive, so Curt suggested I send a list of names and ask him to answer yes or no after each one. I thought that was a good idea and sent the message. I ended with "Are these people coming to Antigua, C or N?" (In Morse code shorthand, C means yes and N means no.)

But Peter did not understand I was using shorthand. His last message before he faded for good was, "*Corn??*"

We looked at each other and started laughing. Peter's last contact with the rowboat at sea was a simple word with no apparent meaning. I could imagine him telling the local TV people who were at his QTH (home) what our last exchange was as we dropped out for good. "Corn?" the television journalist would ask in consternation. "Is that code for 'See you later'?"

The noon sights showed us rowing closer to Antigua. The wave directions were changing all the time. We practiced rowing at various angles to them, something we figured would be useful as we came closer to landfall in Antigua and English Harbour.

We had been thinking about the clothes we would wear on land, a seemingly unimportant area of concern. But it wasn't. It was actually an example of the anxiety we were beginning to feel as land approached. We were looking forward to seeing our families and friends, and to being on land, but what lay ahead for us after the row was uncertain.

We had come to a point where, with every stroke, we expected to see land. But with the thick haze spreading over all of the sky, it was doubtful land would be visible from a distance. By local noon, the sky above was blue, but the thick haze still hung over the water. When Curt worked out the noon sight, he saw that we were only seventy-eight miles from Antigua.

Curt's log: June 8
After I told Kathleen that we were 78 miles from land, I readjusted the autopilot to put us on a course of 271 degrees true.

I did not tell her I was concerned about our latitude. Getting a precise measurement in the haze was difficult, but looking back over the last few sights, I thought I detected a gradual southward drift. We were already off course, and about two miles south of the latitude of the island.

That evening when we tuned in to the UK net, we thought it might be our last contact. We took the opportunity to thank Steve, John, and other hams on the net who had worked hard to keep track of us during the voyage. They had added a measure of safety and companionship to our lives at sea.

They relayed another message to us. A representative from the Explorers Club would be meeting us in English Harbour. His name was supposedly Colonel Byrd. "I guess you know that's quite an honor. Congratulations." We thanked them and sent our best 73s and signed off.

"Who's Colonel Byrd?" I asked Kathleen. We had never heard of such an individual and doubted he even existed since his grand-father would have had to be the famous Antarctica explorer Robert Byrd. We guessed someone had gotten the name wrong.

We went out to row later in the evening. As the sun set in the western sky, the haze became a rose-colored smudge across the horizon. We peered intently for signs of land, lights or dark mounds on the distant horizon, but there was nothing, nothing yet.

CHAPTER 25

Landfall—Antigua

June 10, 1981

Dᴜʀɪɴɢ ᴛʜᴇ ɴɪɢʜᴛ ᴏꜰ Jᴜɴᴇ 8, we kept a close lookout for land. Perhaps the haze would lift enough to let us see lights from the shore as we approached, but the gray cloud cover and haze remained dense.

Early the next morning, Curt woke me up for "Norberto time." It would be our last contact with the French Moroccan. I pulled out my notebook and pencil, ready to record any last-minute information he might have for us.

Soon Norberto's cheerful tones were on frequency: "KA1GIN MM, hello *Excalibur*, this is CN8 Atlantico Pacifico in Casablanca. *Me copia? Cambio.*"

"*Si, si, Norberto, buenas días.* We copy you loud and clear. I think we will reach land today. *Cambio.*" And so it went with Norberto until we ended our last transmission with, "*Excalibur* sending best 73s and signing off."

"73s, *ciao, ciao, Excalibur.*"

Though we tried, we could not fall asleep again, so intense was our anticipation about seeing land. I made a breakfast of oranges, hot chocolate, and fruit juices, with a packet of instant soup for myself. Afterward, we went out to row as the sun rose and the remaining clouds blew away to the southwest. Four-foot ocean swells rolled along with the northeast wind, broken by choppy waves that were an indication of the proximity of land. By 8:00 a. m. local time, Curt thought it would be possible to get a sun sight. I went into the cabin, handed out the sextant, and took out my notebook and pen so I could record the sights.

Later, as he worked out the three measurements of the sun, I rested quietly on my side of the cabin reading Willa Cather's *My Ántonia* for the third time. I was timing it so that I would finish just as we completed the row. I thought it was a wonderful book, with its highly visual imagery of life in the early-twentieth-century American Midwest.

"We're less than fifty miles from land. But I can only guess at the latitude." I looked at Curt and out my port window. We were close, but we couldn't be entirely certain that Antigua was over the horizon.

The sun was very hot on my back and shoulders when I went out to row on June 9. For the first time in weeks, I put on a shirt. The fishing had fallen off in the last week, but I still hoped to hook one last pompano as the end of the Atlantic row drew near. I baited the hook and dropped it over the gunwale of the boat. The pilot fish swam up to investigate and then darted back under the boat. Did they sense we were approaching land?

The sound of voices drifted over to me and I wondered who was talking. Was it Curt? I looked over at the bow cabin and saw he was gesticulating madly for me to come in. He had turned the radio on and found someone who was calling for *Excalibur*.

Guy was an American ham radio operator living on Antigua. Lynn, Curt's sister, who was a professional photographer from New York City, was with Guy as he transmitted his message to us.

"Lynn wants to fly out in a plane and take photographs of you guys as you row into English Harbour. What's your present QTH?" I couldn't give them an exact position because it was now time for the noon sight. Curt was pointing to his watch and already had the sextant in his hand. I promised Guy and Lynn that we'd have a position check for them in a few hours.

"I can't believe it! We've been blown way off course!" Curt had a shocked look on his face. Then he said, "What time is it?" When I told him it was 1450 GMT and not local time, he looked sheepish.

We had gotten the times mixed up. There was still another hour before it was time to do the noon sight. "I guess we're getting a little jumpy about approaching land."

The hams on the UK net were discussing our arrival and Lynn's airplane ride when we tuned in later in the morning. We broke in to give our updated position, and the information was relayed to the pilot of Lynn's plane, which was already in the air.

It was time to dress up and put on our special arrival-to-Antigua clothes we had discussed only last week. The prospect of people flying overhead was exhilarating and overwhelming at the same time. Curt kept the flare gun and sighting compass with its mirror beside him as we rowed. At the first sign of the plane, he fired the flare gun's red meteor flare into the sky.

As I watched, a strange feeling came over me. The ocean was not ours anymore, I thought, and I doubted our lives would ever be the same.

The sound of a plane drifted into our world. Curt took the mirror and flashed it around, but the plane had disappeared. The only effect the flashing mirror had was to attract a large school of fish. I grabbed the Nikonos and stuck it below the water to photograph them. Later, when the film was developed, I saw that the school was filled with dorado.

We rowed on to the Pillars of Hercules, Antigua the entrance to English Harbour.

The course into the harbor was shaped like a dogleg and required one of us to steer facing forward and the other to row. I elected to row, as I wasn't prepared to face the hordes of people waiting on the distant docks. Curt was happy to stand by the aft cabin and hand-steer the rudder. A few small rubber dinghies escorted us as I rowed up to the dock. It was overwhelming seeing so many people cheering and waving as *Excalibur* pulled up alongside the quay.

Both of us saw our family members at the same time, and that is what saved me from pushing away from the dock and rowing in the opposite direction from the crowds. My father stood there smiling proudly at me, while Curt's sister clicked away with her camera. Guy, the ham radio operator stepped up and welcomed us. Other people we did not know came forward and congratulated us, but the welcoming experience quickly became an overwhelming blur of visual stimulus and noise from too many voices speaking at once. At one point, a Galley Bay resort representative stepped out of the crowd and handed me a brochure and offered us a free couple of nights. No one from the Explorers Club was there to meet us in Antigua, but weeks after that, when we and *Excalibur* arrived in Miami by way of a sailboat tow between Antigua and St. Thomas in the US Virgin Islands, followed by a complimentary Norwegian Cruise Line trip from St. Thomas, a fellow of the Explorers Club welcomed us to his home in Homestead, Florida.

Later, after all the congratulations, hugs, and handshakes dockside, as I walked away from the boat, dazed, unsteady on my feet, and holding on to my father's arm, I saw a pack of strange-looking dogs. When I pointed them out—"Oh, look at the dogs!"—my father laughed and said they were goats! To him and anyone who had heard me, my observation was amusing evidence of our long time at sea. But to me, it was evidence of how far I had transplanted myself from the experience of being mostly at sea for the eighty-three days of the expedition.

When Curt and I were finally alone in our room at the Galley Bay Resort, where we had gratefully accepted the complimentary room and board for ourselves and my father and Lynn, we lay together in silence with our bodies still feeling the motion of *Excalibur*. I said to Curt, "Does this feel right? Shouldn't we go out and check to see if everything is tied down?"

He was quiet for a while. No, he couldn't do that and neither could I. Before either of us had fully realized what was happening when our boat touched the dock, we had been whisked away to the other side of the island, away from *Excalibur*, to spend the next two nights in this beautiful resort. We could only hope that Guy, as promised, was watching out for our boat.

The next day I climbed by myself up a trail away from the resort. I settled cross-legged on a grassy promontory high above the sea and overlooking the sugar-white beach and aquamarine waters of Galley Bay. The Atlantic row had ended so quickly dockside, but I knew the experience would be with me for the rest of my life, not only because we had set world records by becoming the first Americans to row from east to west across the Atlantic and because I had become the first woman to row across the Atlantic. There was something more to think about. After the excitement of completing the Atlantic row and meeting new people, I needed solitude, not unlike the isolation of *Excalibur* at sea, from the overwhelming reentry to civilization, because after nearly fifty days from the Canaries and eighty-three from Casablanca, I had changed. Our adventure had changed me, and I needed to absorb that and understand it. It wasn't just about being reluctant to embrace the crowd at dockside in English Harbour. Unlike Curt, who reveled in the attention from the local Antigua reporters and was later so eager to share his experiences with the press in Miami that had been set up by the Explorers Club, I was not ready to share. It would feel like an invasion of privacy until I had processed everything I had learned over the past year.

I remembered how much time and effort it had taken us to get to this point of a successful landfall in Antigua, the year we had spent building the boat and preparing for the row as well as the months at sea. We had begun our planning with a wealth of mostly Thoreauvian notions of independence and self-sufficiency and a modest bank account. In our year and a half of marriage from 1979 to March 1981, when we set off in Casablanca, we lived mostly on our income and savings from our New York jobs, as well as Curt's from before we met, and small monetary gifts from Curt's parents. Curt had also turned to his good friend and climbing buddy George Van Cochran to learn how to gain membership for himself at the Explorers Club in New York and then how to apply for the travel grant that we eventually received.

The amount of cash we had lived on was small, and much of it went to purchases of boat-building materials, living supplies, and paying a boat builder for a short time in the summer of 1980. Our good friends from the Narragansett Boat Club, including Peter Wilhelm and Ed Montesi who designed *Excalibur*, often came down to the barn to give of their free time to help with the building. We also spent money on rent for the barn where *Excalibur* was built, gas for the Pinto station wagon, and the big-ticket item of $600 for the one-way passenger and freight ticket on the *Zvir*. Since our cash was so limited, we'd tried and found that we could get sponsors for expedition products we would eventually need, like food, bottled water, and foul weather gear. It was possible to mount an expedition like this by living frugally, depending to some degree on supporters, and relying on sponsors to partially fund it.

Though we were successful in obtaining a number of small items from sponsors, we never did manage to interest the National Geographic Society in funding us. People had pushed us to solicit their support, as though that in itself would be a validation. In the end, though, after the Atlantic row, we were glad we hadn't received any funding from them, because unlike expeditions who had sold their rights and become known as a National Geographic expedition, we retained all rights to our photographs and written materials. But more importantly and truer to our Thoreauvian ideals, we remained independent, without any corporate logos co-opting the hull space of a boat we had built ourselves and the expedition we had carried out ourselves.

My life had changed forever for sure. It wasn't Antigua's white sand beaches and lush tropical gardens that were now tempting me. It was the realization that whatever had pushed me to suggest we row a boat across the Atlantic Ocean was still inside me. An intense desire to explore the world and maybe understand what it meant to be human on this planet had been awakened in me and was just as avid as before we had started.

I stared at the blue ocean, whose substance I had intimately known for more than eighty days, since our departure from Morocco. Her various moods had alternately thrilled and scared me. One day I had sat cross-legged on the deck during a meditative fishing session, gazing at the sea in the warmth of the midday sun, lost in thought, when a different sort of sound revealed a whale as it broke the surface. Startled only slightly, for waves had been breaking gently around the boat, the thought came to me that what I was living that day, and every day of the voyage, was the most incredible experience a person could ever have. That realization was almost mystical, as I recognized the uniqueness of my journey in that moment. Perhaps it was there that I first understood what I reaffirmed later on the Antigua promontory, that my journey was only just beginning.

PART III

SOUTH PACIFIC OCEAN

CHAPTER 26

Preparing and Starting the Row

1984

I T WAS IN 1982 ON a rowing and sailing trip along the northern coast of Labrador, the summer after the Atlantic row, that we began thinking about rowing across the Pacific Ocean. Though we didn't know exactly where we'd begin, we knew it would be some coast facing the South Pacific, an ocean with hundreds of islands across thousands of miles. Curt wanted the challenge of navigating *Excalibur* across the largest ocean in the world, from the South American continent to Australia. As for me, not only did I love the idea of traveling for a longer period of time, the prospect of visiting remote islands in the middle of an ocean was exhilarating.

Others had tried to row across the Pacific before us. A Swedish-born, naturalized New Zealand citizen by the name of Anders Svedlund made an unsuccessful attempt in 1974, three years after his successful row across the Indian Ocean. Svedlund had rowed due west from Huasco, Chile, toward the setting sun. He made it as far as the Society Islands, where he picked up new food supplies that ultimately gave him an unrelenting case of chronic colic. He aborted the row at Apia, Western Samoa, in late 1974.

A British couple, John Fairfax and Sylvia Cooke, rowed in the early 1970s from California to Australia, making landfall on an island where they were picked up and brought to the mainland. Peter Bird, another Brit, made two attempts from California. On the first, he lost his boat on a reef in Hawaii, and on the second he made it to the Great Barrier Reef, where his boat was wrecked and he had to be rescued by the Australian Navy.

We wanted to row an even longer distance—10,000 miles across the South Pacific Ocean, a feat that no rower had attempted before— but our motivation was largely fueled by our love of nature and not solely by the desire to achieve a new first and set a record. Anders Svedlund had rowed his oceans with the same intent, to seek the peace of mind one could encounter in the solitude of a vast ocean environment.

What made us think we could do it? A crossing of that distance could last six months or even a year. Though we planned to stop at islands along the way, wasn't twelve months of sharing *Excalibur*'s nine-foot deck and sleeping in its six-foot-three-inch cabin, whose widest point was three feet and narrowest six inches, pushing it? Our successful Atlantic row in 1981 proved we could get along for an extended period, though during that row there had been moments of tension and grief as we struggled to cope with life at sea both indi- vidually and as a married couple. We loved each other and enjoyed spending time together, but even so, we knew that sharing the con- fined living and sleeping space for up to twelve months was going to challenge us mentally and physically.

The route we chose, from South America to Australia, a distance more than three times that of our Atlantic row, was a natural one, for the Humboldt Current flowed north and the South Equatorial Current, which we would encounter at the Galápagos Islands, flowed from east to west. We also imagined the weather in this area of the South Pacific to be more stable than what Fairfax, Cook, and Bird had encountered on the West Coast of the United States and later as they crossed the Equator. Besides, the multitude of islands sprinkled across the South Pacific Ocean would offer shelter, rest, and resupply, and were home to cultures we were eager to explore. After leaving South America in July, the winter season, when the Humboldt Cur- rent was at its strongest, we planned to stop at the Galápagos Islands, the Marquesas Islands, American Samoa, and then straight on to the east coast of Australia.

To get in shape, we decided to row down the Mississippi River during the summer of 1983. We had seen far-off places in the world but very little of the United States by boat. What better way to see America than drifting down the Mississippi, from its headwaters at Lake Itasca in northern Minnesota to New Orleans, in a rowboat? Besides, rowing the length of this vast river would be excellent physical training for the long row across an expanse far wider than the North Atlantic. The row down the Mississippi River would also give us the opportunity to revisit our boat-building expertise and put our boat-handling skills to the test in the sudden severe weather that, we read, would regularly roll out of the Midwest summer skies.

Because many dams would have to be portaged in the upper river, we decided to build a light river-rowing boat. Curt sketched out a plan for one eighteen feet long with a forty-two-inch beam that would be quick and inexpensive to make, and strong and stable enough to endure the row from the headwaters to the Gulf of Mexico. We built *Guinevere*, as we christened her, in the backyard of Curt's parents' summer house in Morgan, Vermont. After a series of tests on nearby Seymour Lake, we were happy with her stability and speed with two people rowing. She had ample space for all the camping gear we would take and two rowing stations with sliding seats.

Through June and July, we rowed and portaged *Guinevere* around fourteen dams north of Minneapolis/St. Paul and through twenty-eight locks and dams south to St. Louis, then along the great, wide expanses of the last thousand miles of the Lower Mississippi to the Gulf of Mexico. We encountered severe line winds and thunderstorms in the upper and middle reaches of the river and Civil War history on the Catfish Front by Vicksburg and Natchez; we shared the Lower Mississippi river channel with tows pushing sixty or more barges in fast-moving currents.

When we returned from New Orleans in late August, we put together our latest educational slide show on the Mississippi row to supplement our other offerings on the Atlantic and Labrador rows.

Ever since returning from Antigua in June 1981, we had made a modest living giving one-hour slide lectures at private schools and boat clubs in New England and the Middle Atlantic States as part of an informal, self-managed lecture series. I had learned to enjoy speaking to large audiences with Curt, who reveled in his new role as a celebrity explorer. To supplement the lecture fees, beginning in the fall of 1981, we displayed *Excalibur* at the Philadelphia and Norwalk boat shows sponsored by the National Marine Manufacturers' Association and spoke to hundreds of people about our adventures. In between our school lectures and boat show appearances, we accepted the Kalmar Nycel Award, named for the seventeenth-century Dutch trading ship that had successfully crossed the North Atlantic to set up a Swedish colony in present-day Wilmington, Delaware. We returned to the Explorers Club with the flags we'd been given to carry on the Atlantic and Labrador trips and gave lectures at their headquarters.

We restarted our efforts to gain sponsors with the publication of an essay about the Atlantic row in *Smithsonian* magazine in 1982 and other articles in smaller publications, hoping to develop interest in funding and supplying the upcoming South Pacific expedition. As with the Atlantic sponsors, we offered to acknowledge their equipment donation or free transportation (there were never any cash donations) in our lectures and articles we published. In late fall 1983, we attended the Explorers Club annual dinner made famous by the exotic and unusual delicacies served and then rode the subway to Lower Manhattan to purchase charts of the South Pacific from New York Nautical.

We spent the winter of 1983–84 house-sitting a family friend's home in Morgan, Vermont. When the weather warmed up enough during the daytime in March to begin re-outfitting *Excalibur* for the tropical South Pacific environment, we had to dig the boat out of the deep snow in the driveway at the Saville family summer camp, where she had been parked. We began to work intensively for several months preparing for the expedition. We installed tinted ports and extra air vents and gave the interior of the cabins a new coat of white paint. We repainted the hull a bright orange with a neon-yellow stripe at the gunwales, figuring that since we would be out at sea for such a long stretch, we might be in need of a rescue sometime and a bright orange boat would attract attention more easily. We cleaned up the solar panels, and resettled them into fresh beds of silicone gel to protect the connecting wires. We contacted our old ham radio and Narragansett Boat Club friends, Kurt and Peter Wilhelm, for advice on an alternate antenna setup on the boat. Curt had fiberglassed in place a handy little shelf in the bow cabin where the TR-7 transceiver now rested. To make things more efficient with our communications, we wanted a better arrangement than the precarious dipole antenna we had on the Atlantic that had been tied to a sweep oar shaft. The Wilhelms recommended a taller set of whip antennas than we carried on the Atlantic and that screwed into a metal ball bolted into the roof of the bow cabin. The Wilhelms gave us a spare collection.

When the preparations were finished, we rechristened the boat *Excalibur Pacific* and got ready to ship her and ourselves south to Ecuador, where we had decided to begin the row. Leaving from Guayaquil, Ecuador, at the head of the Gulf of Guayaquil, would make for a straight shot to the Galápagos Islands, our first intended port of call after departure. After a send-off by our friends and families, we boarded the *Santa Paula*, of the soon-to-be defunct Delta Steamship Company, for a complimentary passage from Philadelphia to Ecuador. *Excalibur Pacific* rode below deck in a shipping container while we lived the good life above deck as *Santa Paula* steamed through the Caribbean islands and transited the Panama Canal. On June 16, 1984, we and our boat were deposited on the docks in the port of Guayaquil, Ecuador. From there, it would be only six hundred miles to the first island stop: San Cristóbal, Galápagos.

Pirates in Gulf of Guayaquil and Points South

Within hours of our arrival, we were informed that leaving from the Gulf of Guayaquil was a bad idea because of serious problems with pirates. A local shipping agent told us that highly organized groups using small motorized speedboats and automatic weapons were preying on unsuspecting boats in the gulf and on the coast.

While we contemplated the possibility that the row could end before it had even begun, the local shipping agent suggested we go into the city and meet with the director of maritime transportation, who might be able to advise us. Part of Captain Naranjo's remit as the longtime director of maritime transportation was rescue operations between the coast and the Galápagos Islands. The captain advised us to set off instead from Callao, Peru, for a couple of reasons: the piracy problem was not as bad there as in Ecuador, and starting from farther south on a longer trajectory (twelve hundred miles versus six hundred) would put us in a more advantageous position to row with the currents.

"Whatever you do, don't try to reach the Galápagos from the east," he said. "You could get caught in a branch of the Humboldt Current that flows north toward Panama. That's what happened to the balsa raft expedition. They had to be towed so they could reach the Galápagos."

He pointed to a large chart of the region on the wall of his office and said the *Excalibur Pacific* would do best to begin the row by going due west from Callao. The current would carry us north, and hopefully we'd arrive at a point south of the Galápagos where we could safely make a final approach to San Cristóbal Island.

The Galápagos are a possession of Ecuador, and special permission is required to go there in a private boat. Though we had sent repeated inquiries to Ecuador's embassy in Washington, DC, nothing in the way of a permit had come. But happily, Captain Naranjo gave us a letter from his office with the all-important stamps stating we had applied for the permit. In the end, the letter served the same function as the permit, which never did arrive.

Peruvian Bureaucracy

We were lucky. In a few days, the small feeder ship *Strider Fearless* en route to Callao, Peru, arrived in port to take on cargo from *Santa Paula*. The British captain agreed to take our boat and us to Callao. Once there, however, we faced a customs strike and possibly the worst bureaucracy in the world. Everyone was afraid to allow anything to leave the port. Noticeable anti-American sentiments and a Soviet presence didn't help. We spent twelve days doing nothing but paper-work, unable to gain access to our boat, which remained locked in its shipping container. It was fortunate that we had packed *Excalibur Pacific* with almost everything we needed, including the navigation and radio supplies, a couple of 35 mm cameras and a VHS camcorder housed in a special Airex protective fiberglass box that Curt had fash-ioned, a fishing kit, clothing, reading and writing materials, tools kits and extra supplies for radio, the Autohelm, a kitchen stove, water pump, material for rowing equipment repairs, and the bulk of our dried and canned food store. There was even a small handgun stuffed under deck in the bow that we had bought for security in port like the many yachts we had read about that sailed in international waters. While aboard *Strider Fearless*, we had also loaded sixty gallons of fresh water into her hull below deck. All we needed was a little fresh pro-duce from the local market. In addition, Santiago Woll, a Peruvian-based shipping agent whose company handled *Strider Fearless* and our newest patron, convinced us to take a live chicken on board for the eggs she would lay and the meal she would eventually provide.

The one problem we could do nothing about was the boat's batteries. After weeks in a shipping container where no light could reach the solar panels to recharge them, they were nearly flat. We could only hope that, after a few days at sea, the sunshine would recharge them enough so we could contact the ham radio operators who would be listening for us.

CHAPTER 27

To the Galápagos

July 7, 1984

Rock pinnacles towered black and menacing along the Peruvian coast in the dimness of the moonlight. *Excalibur Pacific* bounced around in the crazy agitated waves, and though we had been rowing hard on and off for hours since leaving Callao, there was no question of putting down the oars. We were drifting into the maelstrom of the treacherous Grupos de Hormigas and possibly the Huaras within our first week at sea. Unless we kept going, *Excalibur Pacific* would join the legions of boats and ships that had crashed and broken up on Peru's perilous rocky coastline.

Pinpoints of green bioluminescence lit up our oar blades with each stroke we took. Curt called out, and I squinted my eyes in the darkness. Sliding under the boat was the startling sight of an enormous snake-like greenish-white luminescence. I stopped and stared as the glow slid smoothly under the starboard to the port side of the boat, not unlike the bioluminescent sea creature we'd encountered on the North African coast in 1981.

In the near distance, what looked like the spotlight from a ship flashed brightly, but as we rowed closer, I saw the shining whiteness was really a warning light positioned atop a large, shadowy rock tower. Curt grabbed the navigation chart and in the yellow glow of a flashlight, he searched for an *hormiga* with a blinking light. If he located it, we would know where we were on this treacherous coastline north of Callao.

Several days before this, our first night at sea was strange and surreal because our departure had been so abrupt. At four in the afternoon on July 4, the Peruvian port authorities finally gave us grudging permission to depart. Perhaps the $200 had changed their minds.

Gray rain clouds, a harbinger of the Peruvian winter, hung heavy over the port as I stored fresh food supplies below deck and Curt hooked up the radio antenna. I craned my neck upward to look at the cement quay where new friends, port officials, and a police corporal grimly looked down at us. The policeman had been assigned to accompany us on the *Excalibur Pacific* to Peru's two-hundred-mile limit in order to prevent us from selling the boat before we left the territorial waters, but no one had ever told us or the obviously frightened policeman how he would get back to land once we reached mile two hundred. For a week, we had haggled with Peruvian police, customs officials, and port authorities over their insane demand. When we made an official protest to the US embassy, the Peruvians backed off. Now we just craved the peace and quiet of our rowboat.

A flock of brown pelicans lining the edges of the quay watched solemnly as I turned away and put our oars and rowing seats in place. Curt tied the squawking wild Indian chicken, a gift from Santiago, to the water pump in the stern. With a nod to the quay, we sat down to begin rowing out of port. Our lugubrious departure party waved a cheerless goodbye while the corporal smiled broadly.

The row west toward the entrance of Callao port was slow, as the boat wallowed in its weight of months of supplies. There was a sizable number of oddly rigged Soviet-flagged fishing trawlers with revolving radar antennas throughout the anchorage. Peruvian fishing boats putted by, their aft decks outfitted with simple winches and woven nets. In the watery light of the setting sun, the high-security prison island of El Frontón sat as a dark smudge against the western horizon. A friend had told us that a tunnel ran from the mainland to the prison island's cell blocks. As I rowed in the gathering dusk of the port, I imagined prisoners splashing their way toward us as they attempted to break free.

While I kept up the stroke, Curt took a break to make a stew of fresh vegetables and dried llama meat we had bought from the local market. Within an hour of eating it, he developed a terrible headache and felt sick to his stomach. In the middle of the night, unbeknownst to me, he woke up and didn't know where he was when he crawled out on deck without a safety harness, shouting and lunging for the gunwale. Just as he started going overboard, the sight of the black ocean water brought him to his senses and he remembered he was out at sea on *Excalibur Pacific*.

Curt's log: July 6, 1984
One of the reasons we want to row across the South Pacific is to spend a long time in a very wild place, to experience the planet in its rawest, most primitive state. In a slow-moving rowboat, close to the water, we can meet the sea on its own terms and for a time be in control of our own destinies. We think it will take about six months to row across the SP.

The second day out from Callao, we rowed into a huge area of floating debris. Everything from plastic bottles to plastic bags, bits of wood, slime, and lumps of tar or sewage covered the surface of the sea. Clearly we would have to row farther to find those ocean regions beyond the influence of man. We collected samples of the plastic floating in the sea and put them into bottles with formalin as part of an informal ocean study of the influence of pollution on the marine environment that we are contributing to gratis for Harvard University.

The masses of floating debris seemed to be caught between two currents, because within a few hours we entered a region of clear sea water and rolling three-foot waves that would foam when they broke against the side of the boat. I told Kathleen that we must have left the Peru Coastal Currents behind and the water temperature might start to feel colder.

The Humboldt Current that flows north along the South American coast is a cold-water current that is rich in marine life. It is distinguished from the Peru Coastal Current, which extends irregularly out from shore and is more influenced by tides and the effects of the continental land mass. Getting into the Humboldt Current as soon as possible would be good because we'll be free from the immediate dangers of the coastline and can expect a more constant northward drift. I felt no difference in the surface sea temperature though when I put my hand in the water by the port gunwale earlier today.

The hazy, overcast conditions, though typical of this region, are frustrating. We can't see the coast for compass bearings, and the sun, moon, and stars are impossible to see for sights with the sextant. We're concerned about the Hormigas de Afuera, a group of dangerous, rocky islets about 35 miles west of Callao. Captain Hitchen of *Strider Fearless* told us, "If you row due west, I'm quite sure the current will carry you far enough north to miss the Hormigas and Huaras." Still we're uneasy.

July 7: Surviving the Grupos de Hormigas and Huaras

"Can you tell where we are?" I yelled to Curt over the crashing sound of breakers too close for comfort.

"Yeah, I think it's number four, Hormiga Quatro. We're only about thirty miles north of Callao"—the wind swallowing the last of his words.

"Shit, this is a nightmare. We've got to go west before we get sucked in any further." I began pulling hard on the starboard oar to swing the bow around. "Come on, let's row together." Curt tossed the chart into the bow cabin.

Green bioluminescence flashed in a synchronized dance of light as I changed course and pointed the bow westward, away from the Hormigas rock towers. All around the boat, the sea had taken on a luminous iridescent green color. Thousands of pinpoints of light flickered. We were in a sea alive with bioluminescence, billions of microscopic organisms giving off their own light as the waves carrying them rushed toward the rocks.

"My God!" I shouted as the realization suddenly dawned. "We're in the middle of the rocks already!"

Curt hastily sat down at his rowing station, and together we started rowing at an angle away from the lighthouse, our eyes becoming more adjusted to the darkness. Every time a wave broke by the boat, it sent a shower of green fire across the surface of the sea that glowed for a second and faded to blackness. Each time our oars dipped into the sea, it was as though they were scooping the green fire. Even the contours of the sea floor a few feet below the boat were apparent.

Though at any moment we could hit a rock, tear a hole in the boat, and be swamped or become food for sharks, there was a fantastic beauty about the glowing reef that night.

We talked briefly of anchoring and waiting for daylight to find our way safely through, but the tide, Curt reasoned, could force the boat further onto the reef. The sound of breaking waves came with greater intensity off the bow.

Curt stopped rowing and stood up to look around. The waves were breaking with a green froth of bioluminescence across our bow. But the green fire was appearing in the same places, while other areas remained dark and free of the breakers.

"Hit it on the port, Kathleen," he shouted. If we could stay in the dark areas, we might avoid the rocks. Just then we saw a thick mass of diffuse green light coming toward us in a circuitous course from the side. Another enormous fish was disturbing the bioluminescent organisms and leaving a glowing trail in the water. As it passed beneath the boat, we could see it was leaving a trail that was longer and wider than the boat!

The light given off by the sea was so bright we were able to cross the line of breakers and row into an area of darker, deeper water. Still, we were cautious and kept rowing into the dawn until, in the distance, the rock pinnacles stood dimly in the mist, several miles off the stern. That was the only land visible and was our last sight of South America.

Curt crawled into the cabin and brought out the compass to take a bearing off the rocks and then shot the morning sun with the sextant when it emerged briefly from the clouds. From this information, it was apparent that we had left behind the Hormigas and only just missed the Huaras. There was still a ways to go before entering the north-flowing Humboldt Current.

Later in the morning, I made a big breakfast of fried potatoes, Colombian coffee, and eggs. We ate on deck, enjoying the sunshine and chatting about the near miss of the evening before. Even Callao, as we had named our little Peruvian chicken, was feeling better. She had taken to perching on the handles of the spare oars at the edge of the deck to sun herself and dry the dampness of the night from her ragged feathers. She survived on a diet of bulgur grain from a half bag that was given to us by the dockworkers in the Peruvian port. On the front of the mesh bag was stamped in red and blue letters: GIFT OF THE PEOPLE OF THE UNITED STATES OF AMERICA. I silently thanked my fellow Americans.

As the horrors of the Hormigas and Huaras faded into the southeast horizon, the wind picked up. With a brisk wind behind us after breakfast, we rowed west-northwest farther out to sea. By mid-afternoon, we pulled in the oars for a break.

Whoosh! I looked around and saw the shiny black back of a whale sinking into the sea off the starboard beam. We were surrounded by a pod of humpback whales. After Labrador, where we had seen small minke whales, we hoped to see more whales in their natural habitat, but when the humpbacks swam right up to the boat, we were scared. The whales weren't aggressive, though, and seemed only to be curious about the boat.

To Curt, this was an invitation to go for a swim and get a better view from underwater. "You're crazy to go in the water, you don't know what they might do!" I said to him as he pulled out his mask, snorkel, and fins from the compartment below the bow rowing station.

"If I don't swim with them, I'll regret it later." he retorted and slipped overboard, the Nikonos 35 mm underwater camera in hand.

Curt's log: July 8

On the South American coast. From under the water, the whales seemed bigger and more awesome. The sight of a 65-foot humpback whale appearing out of the pale blue distance, its gray mass growing bigger and bigger as it swam toward me, was unforgettable. Just when I was about five feet away, it changed course and swam under me, so close I could have touched it. I saw a great smiling mouth, four feet across, and a big eye staring up at me.

I could see its skin was rough and covered with scars and a few remoras. There were also barnacles and a whole school of fish swimming alongside it. I wondered if some of the humpback's pilot fish would become our pilot fish. I hoped so.

I had my own story to tell Curt as well. While I was standing on the forward deck, looking down into the sea as he snorkeled below, I heard another whooshing sound off the bow. I looked over and saw a whale had stuck its head out of the water again, less than half the boat's length away, and fixed its eye on me before it slid back into the sea. The sight riveted me. I didn't know where to look for the next one: under the boat or the spot where the whale had surfaced.

While Curt was in the water, he had seen that *Excalibur Pacific* had its own entourage of followers—three small purple-and-black-striped pilot fish swimming under the hull, along with a few barnacles growing by the dagger board slots. In the late afternoon, while we rowed, Curt saw a newcomer—a shark whose fin cut sharply through the water a short distance off the stern.

The Humboldt Current

By July 8, four days after leaving Callao, we had entered a region of the Humboldt Current rich in marine life. One sunny morning after Curt had done the morning star sights, a splashing beside the boat startled us. A bewhiskered sea lion came to the surface beside the gunwale to breathe. Then it dove and splashed playfully around the boat and stayed with us all day. Often the sea lion came right up to the edge of the boat, cocking its head at us as if to say hello.

A few days later, a large green sea turtle that was four feet across with a pointed head the size of a coconut replaced the sea lion. It swam behind the boat as we rowed, occasionally splashing the water with its finlike feet. Its presence made me think of Darwin and other sailors who had overfished the hard-shell chelonians, using them for food on their long voyages.

Every day we were visited by birds, some of them circling the boat and looking for small fish that might be following us. They would swoop down, dive in the water, and shoot upward with fish in their beaks. Daily, we photographed red- and blue-footed boobies, frigate birds, jaegers, and petrels.

Occasionally, a booby or gull would land on the stern of the boat, only a few feet away from Callao, the hen. She seemed unaware of these visitors and more concerned with her reflection in the Lexan port of the aft cabin hatch. When it was sunny, she could see her reflection so well that she thought another chicken was on board. For hours, Callao would peck at her reflection, ruffled feathers waving madly in the wind.

Life on the rowboat, we had always found, was very different from life on land. Our navigation and living routines established on the Atlantic Ocean started up again on the South Pacific, as though there had been no gap in time. Surrounding the boat, as on the Atlantic, was a wilderness of ocean, sky, and creatures few people had experienced in such intimate detail. In the Humboldt Current, we saw only two ships, and they were too far away to see us.

It was a lonely world, made lonelier by our lack of radio contact with others. The skies were overcast so much of the time that the solar panels on the roof of the bow cabin couldn't charge the batteries enough for successful radio contacts. We could listen to the TR-7 transceiver radio for time signals to set the watches by for navigation, but our inability to contact the outside world concerned us. If we had an emergency, such as sickness or damage to the rowboat, we were totally on our own. Also, we knew our families and friends would become worried when our amateur radio and boat-building friend, Peter Wilhelm, continued to report: "No contact today."

The worst thing about the lack of radio contact was not having another person to converse with. It was a psychological thing. We had each other, but it wasn't enough after so long away from the sea.

Kathleen's log: July 12, 1985
The sun came out early today but it's disappeared now. Clouds over the whole sky as usual. Barometer 1023 millibars. We are rowing a

290-degree course with easterly winds. Last night was calmer and I found it a little easier to sleep. It's rocky one night and calm the next. We had the fishing line out, but caught nothing. During the rowing session in the middle of the day, it's still quite cool. The cold current, I suspect. I wear the red sweatshirt to row in that I got from *Strider Fearless*. I wish I were on that boat now instead of this one!

My new seasickness pills are working. It's better than the Atlantic when I had nothing. Should be able to go off of them in a day or so.

Getting used to one another on the rowboat again was something that took time and patience. Though we had spent enormous amounts of time together since getting married six years before, we always managed to find our own space to be alone. *Excalibur Pacific* obviously had limited space, but we knew from the Atlantic row where each of us liked to sit on the boat and be alone. My favorite spot was on the port side of the deck and later on the bench that Curt built with an Ecuadoran carpenter in the Galápagos. Curt's place of solitude was the bow cabin where he worked on the navigation and read his books, away from the sun. It was a matter of reestablishing those boundaries again. It was also a matter of accepting responsibility for once again setting ourselves adrift at sea, which sounded crazy and heroic at the same time. But this part of the expedition was in some ways the most difficult. Curt got into the business of survival right away. It was a role he couldn't wait to take on. I, on the other hand, though always intrigued with the idea of playing the intrepid explorer, tended to adopt a look-and-see approach in the beginning. It took a while for me to warm up to the idea of expedition living.

For the most part, on both the Atlantic and Pacific Oceans, we rowed a mixture of separately and together, each putting in at least six hours a day at the oars. The best time for Curt to row was first thing in the morning. He would shoot the stars at dawn if it was clear enough and then row a couple of hours. I would take over after breakfast when he would work out the star sights. We'd get together to talk over lunch and do the noon sun sights, weather permitting. I would then put in another couple of hours in the middle of the day, and Curt would do his two hours in the late afternoon. Usually, we'd put in one more rowing session in the early evening together before dark.

Rowing separately gave each of us a chance to stretch out in the little bow cabin. Because living on the rowboat could be confining, it was vital to have this time to relax alone. Writing in logbooks, working out navigation sights, cooking meals, reading, or listening to my Moody Blues or Curt's classical music tapes played on a small cassette recorder were things we looked forward to doing.

It was on a rowing-together session that I talked about my new feelings about the voyage. "I don't know what it is, maybe it's about the length of the trip, or the loneliness of the environment, but I'm finding I really want to be off this boat. Maybe I'll fly home when we get to the Galápagos."

This revelation came as a shock to Curt. "But look, we worked hard to put this expedition together. You wanted to see South America, the Pacific, the South Pacific islands. You wanted a significant ocean-rowing first," he pointed out.

I thought a moment and said, "Well, no one else has rowed the Humboldt Current from Peru to the Galápagos. That's a significant ocean-rowing first. Besides, I miss our friends and life on land, and I'm tired of living in a cramped boat day after day."

"You know what people would say, don't you?" he countered. "They'd say we failed. We said we would row across the Pacific; we got all that equipment and support from our parents; so we just have to keep at it. You'll feel better after a few days in the Galápagos."

We rowed for a while, and then I said, "Well, you could go on with the row, and I could go back. I could line up some hams with really good antennas to contact you. I could keep the sponsors informed about your progress."

"No way I'm doing this row alone. I'd have to find another crew member, maybe advertise, 'Wanted: oarsman or oarswoman to continue Pacific row.'"

"No way you're taking this boat out with another woman!" I yelled.

And that was the end of the discussion for a while. Still, Curt knew I wasn't happy with how the voyage was going. Progress was slow. The Humboldt Current was proving to be weaker than usual, perhaps because of the lingering effects of El Niño.

Then, too, we were different people in some respects. Curt tended to want to bash ahead and finish something regardless of adversity. I was more practical, I thought. If the ocean currents were messed up and conditions were not as our research indicated, I had nothing against playing it safe and getting out.

Late on the night of July 18, long after we had taken in the oars and squeezed into the bow cabin to sleep, we had a strange visitor. An odd rasping noise on the hull woke us. Curt went out and saw, with the aid of the hand-held spotlight, that a nine-foot shark was rubbing against the hull. There was a remora on his back; perhaps he was trying to get it off. The shark, which we thought was a blue, continued to follow us for three days.

At night, we would stay awake talking or listening to music as long as possible to keep the shark away. But without fail, when the boat was quiet and we were asleep, the shark would return.

On the second night, the shark's behavior was more aggressive as it banged into the boat and pushed at the hull with its snout. It was hard to sleep with less than two inches separating us from this predator, for the thickness of the boat hull was made up only of thin Airex foam and fiberglass on either side.

By now we had noticed that whenever we heard the clicks from a pair of thirty-foot whales, the shark would pay us a visit. For some reason, the shark and the whales traveled together. Or perhaps the rowboat was attracting a larger community of marine life besides the three purple pilot fish.

Curt's log: July 20

I suited up this afternoon and went overboard to check the hull for damage. We hadn't seen the shark all morning, so around noon when visibility under water was best, I decided to go in. I wore my three-quarter wet suit for protection from the cold current and carried a knife in case. Kathleen kept a lookout for a shark fin.

The hull was in horrible condition, not from anything the shark had done but from the barnacles. A forest of marine growth and many hard shells an inch or two long covered the bottom of the boat. No wonder progress has been so slow! The resistance to the water of these barnacles must have cut our speed in half. All afternoon, I scraped off the shells with the knife. The job on the hull made the boat row much more easily, even though it had been impossible to remove all the growth.

That night we heard the whales outside the boat. Then the shark made the most violent attack yet. It banged into both dagger boards. Each dagger board runs through the hull in a slot on the deck. I was afraid the repeated blows from the shark could damage the hull. The rudder was next. It runs through a similar slot in the back and we had no spare. The shark banged against it and it felt like the rudder had been bent.

I finally had to kill the shark with the small semi-automatic that fired .22 long rifle shells. The bullets left a luminescent trail in the water that led to the middle of the shark's body. The first shot did nothing more than incense the shark. It banged the boat even more violently, nearly throwing me off balance. As it surfaced next to the boat, I leaned over and shot it in the head at point-blank range. Blood and saltwater splashed and the shark went limp and sank slowly under the boat. It didn't bother us again.

Rowing in the Humboldt Current to the Galápagos Islands

Day after day, I watched Callao, the wild Indian chicken tied to the deck in front of me, while I rowed. I visualized her legs in a frying pan with Peruvian olive oil and fresh rosemary sprigs, her breasts, back, and wings in a pot of chicken stew with dumplings. And then I would think what a horrible fantasy I had conjured up because Callao was such a nice bird.

Every day I watched as she sat on the aft dagger board, drying out her bedraggled feathers. When she closed her eyes and fell asleep, her eyelids rolled upward and she would weave back and forth like a drunken sailor in the boat's motion. At night, she helped Curt to dispose of the potato and carrot peelings. She ate most anything, even barnacles from a piece of wood found floating in the sea days before.

According to Curt's latest sights, which he had managed to snatch from small openings in the night and dawn skies when they cleared long enough, our position was 5 degrees south, 87 degrees west with only 290 miles to San Cristóbal Island in the Galápagos. Each X Curt marked on the navigation chart showing our northward progress meant Callao's demise was close, because we couldn't take foreign livestock into the Galápagos Islands.

On July 29, it was time to have Callao for dinner.

"I can't watch you do it," I told Curt. "I'm staying in the cabin. Let me know when you're done," I said, handing out the frying pan. I shut the hatch and pushed the "on" button to the tape deck. I grabbed a paperback and tried to read as the Moody Blues sang about white nights in the background.

With a quick snap of Curt's wrist, Callao was no more, but in his nervousness Curt twisted too hard and her head came off in his hand in a disgusting mess. A few minutes later, the hatch opened and the frying pan was handed in with the skinny featherless legs and breasts of Callao. I looked down at our former pet, gulped, and turned away to start the Optimus stove. We were so starved for the fresh vitamins that Callao would give, helping us to row through the maze of intersecting currents of the Galápagos archipelago.

The early dawn sky was clear on July 31 when Curt measured the morning stars with the plastic Davis sextant. We worked as a team: Curt calling out the star's name and the word "Mark" when he brought it down to the horizon. My job was to record the time and altitude measurement as he read it from the sextant. It was important to know our position exactly as the islands drew closer, because the Galápagos currents tended to diverge, one branch flowing north and east of the islands and the other flowing west and becoming part of the South Equatorial Current system. We had to be right in the middle to catch San Cristóbal Island. On the morning of the 31st, after we shot four stars, as Curt turned to hand me the sextant to put away, he saw land off the bow of the boat.

"Kathleen! Come look! It's land!" I stuck my head out of the cabin with the camera and saw it was Española Island, the southernmost island in the Galápagos.

"Wow! I can't believe we're so close! We'll practically drift into port."

He nodded. "I don't think I need to work out the sights. Let's eat breakfast and then start rowing."

"Sounds good to me," I said, happy the islands were so close after nearly four weeks at sea.

It turned out that the sights should have been worked out because we were already in the South Equatorial Current and slipping westward much faster than we knew. We should have neglected the extra cups of coffee and leisurely conversation about our imminent successful arrival, which Curt was ready to film with the camcorder, and jumped right on the oars. It was while we sat on deck chatting that I noticed the angle of Española Island to the rowboat had changed.

"Hey! There's something wrong here. Look at Española!" Curt looked over my shoulder and jumped to his feet.

"Shit, I think we're moving past it! The current is carrying us too far west!"

In a controlled panic, adrenaline flowing hard, we tossed the dregs of our coffees overboard and shoved the oars out.

"Hard on the port!" he called, and we pulled hard on the right side of boat with more power than the left. The boat needed to point east of Española so we could counteract the effect of the current.

In the noonday heat, a huge black-and-white frigate bird swooped out of the sky and nearly dug its talons into Curt's scalp, but he managed to duck in time. Española was only twelve miles away now, yet after rowing the rest of the day and into the evening, we had gained only four and half miles and were slipping west all the time.

Overnight, as we lay exhausted from the rowing, *Excalibur* was left to drift on a sea anchor. At dawn we began rowing, but by midmorning it was obvious that we couldn't reach San Cristóbal, only a few miles north of Española. The current was just too strong. On August 1, with the boat on a northwest course, we decided to try for Santa Cruz Island as we slipped between Española and Floreana Islands. The chances were good that with constant pressure on the oars, we could reach Academy Bay at Santa Cruz in a couple of days.

On the night of August 4, in the complete darkness of a marathon rowing session, there was an ominous tinkling sound like glass breaking under the boat. Our curiosity piqued, we both let go of the oars at the same time to listen more closely. Then there was a loud thundering boom as an enormous wave crashed into the sea off the port side of the boat. Stunned into action, we picked up the oars and began rowing in a fast-synchronized stroke when we realized at the same moment that *Excalibur Pacific* was floating on a reef and the next wave would smash directly over us. We kept up the stroke, our adrenaline driving the boat beyond the reef's edge and into calmer waters.

Near midnight, the Southern Cross transited the sky and then dropped gracefully over the horizon while a huge fragmented meteor briefly lit the sky over Santa Cruz Island. A quarter moon reflected on the waves, and the glow of green bioluminescence outlined the shape of our oars, reminiscent of the memorable night among the Hormigas rocks off the Peruvian coast. This time, however, the seas were gentle and the approach to Santa Cruz was straightforward until the navigation lights leading into Academy Bay went black at midnight. Anchored at its entrance, however, was the Ecuadoran supply ship *Iguana*, whose single faint light guided us into port. I rowed up to *Iguana*'s aft deck while Curt stood up and hooted for the crewmen.

"Hey, *caballeros!*" he called out in his best Peace Corps Bolivian Spanish. "Where can we anchor?" Silence, and then heads appeared over the gunwales.

"*Que quieres? Donde estás?*" The night was silent

"*Estamos aqui!*" The crew of *Iguana* looked down at our rowboat, the spotlight in Curt's hand. "Where can we anchor?" he repeated.

The crewmen on deck looked at each other, unsure about this odd-looking boat arriving in the middle of the night.

"You're in the Islas Galápagos, Santa Cruz island." They thought we were lost, and I couldn't blame them, because the orange rowboat resembled an oversized lifeboat. A crewman climbed down a hastily unfurled rope ladder, saying he would show us a spot to anchor. He landed on our deck with a thud, startling us out of our solitary world. I rowed to where he pointed, and before we could figure out how he was going to get back to his ship, *Iguana*'s dinghy pulled up to the gunwales and he climbed in.

"*Muchas gracias, caballero. Adios*," Curt called after him.

Twenty-nine days after leaving Callao, Peru, we had arrived in the Galápagos at 2:30 a.m. on August 3. The anchor went down, and we collapsed on the deck, exhausted but too keyed up to sleep. Curt got out the rum and maple syrup while I scrounged around for the remaining Peruvian limes. We toasted our success at reaching the first island of the rowing expedition by clinking our plastic coffee cups.

A strange silence now surrounded the boat. Gone were the never-ending sounds of the blowing wind and breaking waves. For the first time in nearly a month, the boat was still and the air was sweet smelling with the herbal scent of land.

CHAPTER 28

Puerto Arroyo, Academy Bay, Santa Cruz Island

Curt's log: August 4, 1984

At seven the next morning, we were awakened by a squad of curious motorboats that came to see the human-powered craft that had arrived during the night. Academy Bay was much larger than it appeared in the dark. The waters were a startling mix of emerald green and light blue at the edges. Candelabra cactus and black mangrove trees rimmed the shoreline. Everything about the island appeared exotic. Rough outcrops of volcanic lava rocks jutted into the bay while every boat at anchor seemed to have a brown smooth-skinned seal sunning itself on deck.

A white motor launch putted up to *Excalibur Pacific* and on board was Santa Cruz's port captain, dressed in a pristine Ecuadoran military uniform. We were fortunate to have the permit required of all private boats visiting the Galápagos Islands, as Ecuador is very strict about visitors to the islands. They want to protect the natural habitat for the many endemic species found there. We were given forty-eight hours to stay on the island and resupply the expedition. Then we would have to leave.

Kathleen was very disappointed that we would not be staying longer. She said she'd just been thinking that she would not be flying back to the US because it had been too hard rowing into these islands to quit. But what's the point, she asked, if we had to leave right away?

I showed the port captain, again, the official document from Captain Naranjo's office that we had obtained in Guayaquil. I told him how a shark had damaged our rudder, and that we would have to build a new one before continuing on the voyage.

Happily, he relented and gave us permission to stay two weeks.

There are several sailing yachts anchored throughout the harbor. Close to *Excalibur Pacific* is *Andiamo III*, a forty-two-foot Hans Christian owned by Susan and Andy Kerr, who are sailing around the world. Susan and Andy helped us get settled for our first nights in the Hotel Galápagos, the best hotel in town. Soon we were taking freshwater showers and eating all the fresh foods we could find to get our strength back. We slept at the Hotel Galápagos for two nights, after bringing the rowboat into the mangroves beside the hotel dock where we're going to sleep aboard for the rest of our stay. Forest Nelson, the owner of the hotel, is an American who arrived by boat twenty-four years before and decided to stay. In the workshop at the hotel, Forest introduced us to Efrien, an Ecuadoran Indian who is a talented carpenter. He's going to help me build a spare lightweight rudder, an extra dagger board, and a bench for sitting on deck when no one is rowing.

It was early morning in the harbor, where there was always a light wind. It was almost perfectly silent: some small waves lapping at the edges of the boat while a blue-footed booby calmly flapped past, making a deep-throated noise. It was the third day of our stop at Santa Cruz Island in the Galápagos, and I was on deck while Curt slept quietly in the bow. The fishing boats in Puerto Arroyo had gone out of the harbor, and the splash of seals filled the air. Susan and Andy paddled their dinghy past our rowboat after visiting the bakery on shore. I waved to them and they waved back.

I was sitting on the deck of the rowboat with a cup of Nescafé coffee, looking around the harbor at the extraordinary view of the desert with its cacti and the bottle-green waters of the South Pacific breaking lightly at its edges. It was wonderful. Sylvia Earle once said,

"With every drop of water you drink, every breath you take, you're connected to the sea. No matter where on Earth you live." We were connected to the sea in a way only we could explain. Once a friend said when I told her of our latest plans to row the South Pacific, "Don't you get bored out there? With nothing to see for miles and miles?"

It wasn't "boring," though. "There" had innumerable cloud formations, the different ways waves moved in the wind, and the changing colors, not just with the time of day but through the hours as the sun and clouds shifted positions. In another sense, she was right, because its seeming emptiness took a long time to drag me into it. Sometimes I listened to silence and other times to the rhythmic and constant breaking of waves all around the boat. The irregular lines of waves at sea carried sound all around me.

I was still buoyed in spirits after we had successfully rowed into Puerto Arroyo three days earlier after a mammoth effort of rowing and navigating the treacherous currents of the Galápagos archipelago. The first part of the South Pacific row was completed. All done, twelve hundred miles up the west coast of South America from Peru to Ecuador's Galápagos Islands. Last night, we sat with neighboring yachties and our Ecuadoran beers, and we began a year-long relationship that would continue through calls on the marine radio and on islands we would later visit.

Five minutes earlier, a reddish-colored marine iguana swished its way past the boat not more than five feet from the deck where I sat. They were common creatures everywhere in the islands, swimming in its nutrient-rich waters to feed on algae-covered rocks. On the other side of the harbor, I saw the morning's iguana horde lumbering up the face of volcanic rock to bask in the warmth of the rising sun. I hadn't seen them often in the water, but the first time we went to a harborside restaurant for a meal, there were three or four huge marine iguanas basking in the sun not far from my feet. Though Charles Darwin called them "clumsy disgusting lizards" and "imps of darkness," I thought their uniqueness, as the only iguana in the world to live and forage from the sea, a true marvel of biology. Their brick-red bodies tufted with spikes welcomed me into the environment of Galápagos marshes and mangroves where we eventually beached our boat for two weeks. *Amblyrhynchus cristatus*, the marine iguana, reminded me of the exotic and unconventional nature of our decision to row across the South Pacific.

Leaving the Galápagos Islands

The day before our departure, we went to the port captain's office to officially check out and pay our harbor fees. The Ecuadoran port captain very eloquently told us there would be no fees for us because he admired our courage and bravery to do battle with the sea in such a small boat. We left his office touched by his kindness and sorry to be leaving the Galápagos, whose exquisite beauty we had recorded daily with the camcorder and 35 mm cameras.

Curt's log: August 17

It was a Friday when we planned to leave, though something felt wrong about this departure date. Maybe it was that we were going against the old sailors' superstition never to begin a voyage on a Friday. We ignored it and left on Friday because it was simply time to go. It's late in the season. [Considering how slow we traveled, we expected to be at sea for almost two months. We hoped to be in the Marquesas by early October, the start of the hurricane season.]

The early-morning row out of Academy Bay and into the sea skirted the rock reefs along the Santa Cruz's south coast and headed in a southerly direction. By daybreak, hopefully we'd clear the headland that overlooked the bay. To the west was the breaking shoal where the boat nearly turned turtle on the approach to Academy Bay two weeks earlier. As we rowed, *Excalibur Pacific* rolled side-to-side, the rudder and dagger boards banging softly like a padded pendulum arm of a clock. It was a familiar and comforting sound as the current pushed us south and westward.

All day long we rowed into headwinds and choppy waves, the current only a knot strong and the skies overcast. Inquisitive soft-eyed sea lions swam and played just off the tips of our oar blades.

Blue-footed boobies and albatrosses flew overheard as *Excalibur Pacific* began transiting the Canal Pinzon, a twenty-five-mile channel that separates Santa Cruz from Isabella Island. The north-flowing current increased in strength because of a southeast wind and made it hard rowing all day long. To get sucked into the Canal Pinzon would mean exposing the boat to worse dangers of outlying rocks, unlit islands, and the precipitous east coast of Isabella. It meant getting caught in the east-flowing Equatorial Countercurrent north of Isabella and being forced back toward the South American coast.

By the end of the first day, we were still in the middle of Canal Pinzon. A cold *guara* mist began to fall and darkness settled around us. Together we rowed all night, always pointing the boat south-south-west, the only way to counteract the current and ferry our way across to the south end of Isabella Island and out of the Galápagos.

At moments during the night, I felt like a very small entity in the blackness of space except for an occasional star reflected in the sea or a dim spot of light from a distant shadowy island. We steered by the lights from the village of Santa Maria on Santa Cruz Island. When thick clouds descended over the island, all I saw was a faint glow, and then at midnight the lights went off. After that, we steered by the feel of the wind. When I felt its touch on my left cheek I knew the boat was heading in the right direction.

Every hour I would switch places with Curt, grateful to give up the oars, and crawl into the bow cabin to fall asleep immediately. After a few hours, it wasn't the rowing we minded the most or even the blisters that burst and stung from the saltwater; it was the interruption of our dreams that was the hardest.

Curt's log: August 18
As the day began to lighten, I could see that I was rowing close to Islas Hermanos, islets of steep rock off the southeast coast of Isabella. I called to Kathleen and we both began rowing together. We cleared the rocks and by 9 a.m., *Excalibur Pacific* was off the shore of Tortuga Island. This collapsed crater in the shape of a turtle was the turning point in our row out of the "Galápagos Sea." We stopped and saw we had entered the west-flowing current. Tortuga Island was slowly

slipping by as we traveled west in the current. We tied off the oars and had a hot meal for the first time in two days. Kathleen scrambled fresh eggs with onions, boiled water for coffee, and cut thick slices of Ecuadoran bread. We've christened the new bench that Efrien and I had built in Forest Nelson's workshop by eating breakfast on it and watching Tortuga Island recede to the east. Times like this make it seem all worth the difficulty of ocean rowing. A flock of small black-and-white petrels landed nearby and danced lightly on the surface of the sea, using their delicate feet to attract fish.

Twenty-nine hours after leaving Academy Bay we took a long nap and got up late in the day to row a few more hours. At sunset, *Excalibur Pacific* was about four miles off the south coast of Isabella, so we took in the oars and allowed the boat to drift. We slept well as the boat bobbed along in a light southeast breeze and clear skies.

The next day, with the rising sun and dissipating sea mist, we felt good and optimistic about the row to the Marquesas Islands. We had successfully navigated our way from Peru to the Galápagos Islands, and now were on our way to French Polynesia. Ahead lay the broadest stretch of ocean on the Pacific Ocean. The distance of 3,500 miles was almost as far as our row across the Atlantic.

The beautiful weather of the first two days after leaving Isabella and the Galápagos put us in a good frame of mind, but it was not to last. When land disappeared over the horizon, the weather settled into overcast skies and intermittent rain squalls. The wind and waves consistently hit the boat broadside and made for rocky conditions. With the relentless motion, we had trouble sleeping at night and woke every twenty minutes to move around and stretch our numb limbs.

The weather was surprising because the South Pacific of my imagination was balmy, with steady trade winds. Perhaps it was the time of year, but according to the South Pacific Pilot Chart, which was designed with an overlay of weather-predicting wind roses, we were well within the good-weather season. It could have been that the statistics used to create the pilot charts were recorded by merchant ships whose extreme height above the water's surface gave a very different perception of the ocean environment compared with our meager six feet above the water.

Curt's log: August 29
The bananas from Santa Cruz are all going yellow. The huge stalk that once harbored a cricket who jumped off the boat the first week at sea, is tied on top of the roof of the aft cabin. We see yellow bananas while rowing so we're always taking a break to eat one. Fresh food like this keeps up our strength. The only problem is that they are ripening so fast that we find it hard to keep up. It feels like we are on some kind of banana diet: banana milk, bananas dipped in peanut butter, and banana sourdough bread. Just for variety last night, I put sliced bananas in the frying pan, poured rum on them, and set a match to them. Voilà! Banana flambé.

Even with the fresh food, we often have food dreams that make us hungry. I dreamed we were at a fine French restaurant checking out the menu. I saw all the wonderful entrees to choose from but woke up before I had a chance to order.

On Sunday mornings we make a big breakfast and don't start rowing until 10 a.m. One Sunday, I made crepes for breakfast with jam rolled up inside and maple syrup on top. But even this breakfast doesn't make our food dreams go away.

The bulgur from Peru continues to be in our diet. It once fed Callao and now it feeds us. We add it to soup or bread dough or sometimes make a cereal. The bulgur is better than the stale oatmeal we bought in the Galápagos.

September 5. Today we heard the sailboat *Blue Goose* checking into the ham radio network to report an adverse current. A single-hander named Chuck who owns the sailboat, left the Galápagos for the Marquesas before us. He has encountered an adverse current west of our present position. We've been rowing southwest, trying to counteract the south-southeast wind and row around the region of adverse current. It makes for a choppy ride. Mileage is only 15 miles in the last 24 hours. We may have hit the bad current.

We are near the San Francisco-to-Punta Arenas shipping lanes, so have been looking out for ships. Saw a ship this morning at 0530 but couldn't raise them on the VHF. Strange, because we had the radio checked at Academy Bay and it works perfectly. The ships either aren't listening or don't respond.

Getting used to being at sea again with the bad weather and adverse sea conditions took a toll on our bodies and minds. The fresh food was going fast, and we were eating a lot of instant mashed potatoes and drinking sweetened fruit drink for energy. On September 11, we spotted a large dorado near the boat. We pulled in the oars, and Curt went into the water with the spear that we'd been given by the French couple in the Canaries and that Curt had adapted into a spear gun with the aid of a large rubber band. The water was much warmer than it had been in the Humboldt Current and so blue that it was possible to see to a great depth. He swam down to about thirty-five feet for the encounter with the four-foot dorado and fired the spear gun into the side of the fish, but he couldn't pull it out. The dorado was so large that it pulled him after it for a short distance under the water. Finally, the spear bent enough that it came loose and the dorado sped away. Curt surfaced with the spear gun and a frustrated look on his face.

Later in the day, I was sitting on Benchly (the nickname we gave to the new Galápagos bench) reading when I saw a small grouper and called Curt. He suited up and dove in. This time the spear worked well and we enjoyed a fresh meal of grouper with onions and peppers from Santa Cruz.

CHAPTER 29

Overboard—
Navigating Like a Native

September 13, 1984

T HUMP. SILENCE. THE BOAT DIDN'T feel right; she felt heavier and yet empty. I tilted my head, listening for Curt's voice calling out the next altitude measurement of the star Regulus. But there was nothing but the swishing of waves as they broke beside the boat.

All at once it hit me: the boat's motion felt strange because I was alone. The boat was empty because Curt wasn't where he was supposed to be: on the aft deck, taking measurements of the morning stars. The realization that I was all alone on the rowboat was like a firecracker going off inside of me. With no thought in my mind but to find him, I charged out of the forward cabin without grabbing my glasses. I stumbled barefooted along the crowded nine-foot deck to where he should have been, a million thoughts going through my mind: I know he's attached to the safety harness, so he's probably dragging behind the boat. Does he still have the sextant? Is it on deck? What if I'm too late? What if I'm alone? I scanned both sides of the deck but it wasn't there.

I looked out at the breaking waves to where Curt was dragging behind the boat. Even without my glasses, I saw his flailing arms, and my ears picked up his screams above the wind.

"Sharks! The sharks are going to get me! Pull me in!"

I looked around the deck again for the sextant and then reached out to the safety line that attached Curt to the boat, the lifeline that connected me to the only other human being in this ocean, and began pulling hard.

He was heavy in his soaked cotton sweats. I braced my right foot on the corner of the starboard gunwale so I wouldn't go overboard with his weight.

"Stop screaming! There's no shark out there. Help me to pull you in!" I yelled.

The tautness of the line eased as he tried swimming toward the boat. Hand over hand, I pulled until he was looking up at me from the water, still mumbling nonsensically about the sharks that were coming for him.

"No, it's okay. There's no shark. Just help me now!" I reached down to grab his arms while the boat dipped precariously to the water's edge. "Get your leg on the gunwale. I can't do it if you don't help."

I pulled hard with both hands, hauling his body over the sweep oar that was tied along the side of the gunwale. It was a difficult maneuver with sopping wet cotton sweats. He looked at me, eyes slightly glazed, as he rolled on his back, the hood of his sweatshirt still tied tightly around his white face.

"Where's the sextant?" he asked.

"It's not here, it's not on deck. Did you drop it?"

He thought and shook his head. "I don't remember . . . I think I dropped it. . . . I just remember standing there one minute with the sextant up to my eye and the next . . . I was flying through the air."

I looked at him and then turned away. Our solitary, undisturbed world was shattered because the sextant had been lost. The sea now appeared menacing, and the wind blew uncomfortably hard against the boat, pushing us to where we did not know.

I looked back at Curt, who was sitting up, propped against the cabin hatch, in apparent shock from what had just happened. I turned to look out at the ocean waves breaking with a whooshing sound around the rowboat. Though it was another rough day at sea, the implicit dangers of the rowing voyage loomed greater than they ever had before. I looked hard at the water, willing the sextant to float by. For an absurd moment, I imagined that it was there, a gray shape floating easily beside the gunwales, so close I could just reach out and grab it. But it was only my mind already playing a survival game. I blinked and looked again. The grayness became foam from a wave shattering itself on the ocean's surface. We were rowing a small homemade boat across 3,500 miles of open ocean from the Galápagos Islands to the Marquesas, a small collection of volcanic, mountainous islands. Now with the sextant lost, we had to figure out how to find those islands with only a cheap Casio watch to back up our Rolex Oysters, a ham radio, and navigation tables with star altitudes. We had just thirty days' worth of water and food.

From the moment we lost the sextant, the sole navigational instrument available to us in 1984, we were lost at sea. It took a while to comprehend what this meant. But as Lukin Zoran, the Yugoslavian seaman had once taught us, it was better to take remedial action right away than to stop and lose momentum from a major event like the loss of the sextant. To explain what had happened to an audience he imagined would watch this film in the future, Curt got out the camcorder and gave it to me to operate. I sat hunched against the bow hatch and pushed the small Record button, listening to Curt's recounting of the moment the boat was slammed by a wave and he felt himself cartwheel off the deck into the cold ocean water. When we replayed the recording later with the camera's battery plugged into the solar panels, Curt sounded dazed and looked shocked by what could have happened to him if he had not been wearing his safety harness.

After Curt worked out the star sights that he had been able to get, we pulled out all the eastern South Pacific charts from below deck and spread them on the cabin floor. Our last known position was 5 degrees, 8 minutes south and 108 degrees, 22 minutes west.

Looking at me with a strained expression, he said, "The chance of anyone finding us out here is nil. We're nothing but a speck on the ocean. No one is going to find us."

I stared back, but I was determined not to be discouraged. "What if we built some kind of astrolabe or protractor to try to measure the sun or stars? We could get a general idea of where we are that way, can't we?"

The greatest danger seemed to be the possibility of missing our destination, the Marquesas Islands. If we were more than a few miles off course, the South Equatorial Current could force us into the sparsely settled Tuamotu atolls, an area of thousands of miles of treacherous currents and low-lying coral reefs. Most recently, the atolls of Mururoa and Fangataufa in the southeastern Tuamotu Archipelago had become infamous as a nuclear testing site for France's government under then president François Mitterrand. Our food and water could run out if we didn't land on a populated atoll. The potential dangers mounted as we worked through the possible scenarios.

"Maybe we should stop fighting these south waves and row north toward the Equator." Curt pointed to a chart. "We could pick up the Equatorial Counter Current and row back toward Panama. At least there would be a continent to hit if we went east."

"I don't know, we might be too far west already," I said, remembering that we had already rowed at least a thousand miles since the Galápagos.

"Yeah, you might be right." We studied the chart with its neatly penciled-in Xs marking our progress. Though the weather had been rough and overcast most of the time, *Excalibur Pacific* had covered an impressive amount of mileage. It became obvious that we were too far west to successfully go north to catch the counter current. Oddly, the same day the sextant was lost the winds began to come more out of the east than the southeast. We would be hard pressed to row north with any speed.

Rowing toward French Polynesia

The new course would be 240 degrees south-southwest. The Marquesas were approximately 9 degrees south, about 4 degrees of latitude south of our present position or approximately 276 miles (sixty-nine miles per degree). We decided to keep up our rowing schedule and try to reach the islands.

That evening, as I tied my oars down, I said, "Why don't you try to fix the radio antenna while I make dinner? I think the problem with the radio contacts has something to do with the whip antennas. Maybe they're not high enough to catch a signal. Maybe we could get advice or help for what to do."

Curt's log: 5 p.m:
In the aft cabin, I found the tool kit, the spare dipole antenna we had made for the radio, and some extra wire. Kathleen crawled inside the bow cabin to pass me the ham radio book. I looked up the formula for calculating the length of a dipole antenna for the frequency we needed to reach our sailboat friends in the Galápagos. With cut pieces of wire held together with electrical tape and connected to the coaxial cable, we hoped for the best. I insulated it all with plastic tubing and wrapped string and propped it up with the boat hook. If the waves didn't get too rough, the jury-rig would stay in place long enough to make radio contact.

After dinner, we tried the radio, and to our great relief were able to make contact with *Andiamo III*, who was still in the Galápagos. Between *Andiamo* and *Excalibur Pacific*, we discussed ideas for navigating without a sextant. We talked about different types of astrolabes and after a few trials and errors we came up with a design that worked best for our situation.

Using the hatch cover from the bow cabin navigation compartment, I scribed the degrees of a quarter circle, 90 degrees from a point near one corner of the board. I put in two small finishing nails in line with the 0 degree gradation. To use it, one of us sights along the nails at the horizon to keep the astrolabe level, while the other person reads the degrees marked by the shadow of the sun. Since the boat moves around so much, the person sighting at the horizon says "Mark" the instant the board lines up on the horizon. We record the highest readings at the sun's highest point in the sky for the date of the measurement. After we apply the declination of the sun for the date of measurement, we have a rough idea of our latitude.

The latitude is an important measurement. If we can row south to the latitude of the Marquesas, we can then row west until we reach them. But if we're off by much, we will miss the islands.

In a couple of days, we made another refinement in the astrolabe. As he described for the camcorder, Curt attached a movable pointer with white adhesive tape to the shadow nail to make it easier to see its shadow. The person sighting at the horizon could move the pointer until the shadow was in line with the nail. It became easy to read the sun's altitude when it was close to the horizon in the morning or evening for the longitude check.

Despite the custom-designed astrolabe, a problem beyond our control developed. As the sun rose higher in the sky with the advancement of summer in the southern hemisphere, the shadows at noon became increasingly difficult to distinguish, because the sun was almost directly overhead. The device would be useless by mid-October, just when we needed it most for the final approach to the Marquesas.

Navigating by the Stars

One afternoon when we were rowing together, I said to Curt, "Do you remember Marvin Creamer? We met him a few years ago when we got that Kalmar Nycel Award in Delaware."

"Yeah, of course. He sailed across the Atlantic without instruments, didn't he? I think he was planning to go around the world."

"What if we try to contact him for any ideas?"

Our ham radio friends in Hawaii very quickly tracked Creamer down at a boat show in Connecticut where he was displaying his boat. Within a couple of days, he was on the radio sharing ideas for navigating without instruments. Essentially, Creamer's technique was one used by ancient Polynesian navigators. As he talked, we took copious notes.

"What you should do," he advised, "is pick a star with the same declination as the latitude of the island you are heading for. When the star crosses your meridian, it will be directly overhead if your latitude is right. You can accurately judge the zenith point by tracing imaginary lines in the sky at night with your hands. Draw the lines perpendicular to the horizon at various directions from your boat." The celestial meridian he referred to was the arc that passed through the celestial North and South Poles and the zenith, the highest point in the sky in relation to our position. The meridian divided the sky into east and west. A star whose declination was the same as the latitude of a Marquesas island would act as a guide post for us to follow as we rowed west.

"Perpendicular to the horizon? Can you repeat, Marvin?"

"Yes, once you find your star, get out there on deck, and when it crosses your meridian, draw lines perpendicular to the horizon." I copied his words verbatim. His advice meant the difference between reaching land and saving ourselves or failing—something we would not consider.

"Where the imaginary lines cross will be the zenith point," he continued. "With practice, you'll learn to tell if you are north or south of that star at the meridian transit. Then you'll adjust your course accordingly."

The unique part of Marvin Creamer's technique was that he used his hands and arms as instruments for determining, by physical observation, the zenith point in the sky.

Curt asked him, "Is this technique accurate enough to enable us to find the Marquesas?"

"Yes, it is," he answered.

That night we went to bed more hopeful than we had been in a week. Starting the next day, the rowing schedule was changed to mostly nighttime. The new schedule was not only good for navigation, but it also removed us from direct sunlight during the heat of the day, which was now very hot. Rowing at night would save water because we wouldn't perspire as much and need to drink so much.

We would use the astrolabe as a backup, though. Maybe it was our European ancestry or maybe because the hatch-cover astrolabe was something we could physically hold on to as we determined our fate.

Night Rowing while Navigating

Curt's log: September 21

Rough seas. Each day one of us pumps saltwater in the empty water bottles below deck for extra ballast. We put "S" on the caps so we know which are filled with saltwater and which are fresh.

Rowing at night is wild in these conditions. We wear our storm gear with safety harnesses. Big waves all around us with strong, persistent winds. We row and watch the transit of Eridani in the constellation of Eridanus and Rigel in Orion just as the twilight comes in. Both are guiding stars that will lead us to kappa Orionis. It's hard to tell in these conditions. We make the observations and compare notes. I think we're about 6 or 7 degrees south. We are ultimately aiming for the star kappa Orionis in the constellation of Orion. This star transits its highest point in the sky above Hiva Oa island in the Marquesas, our ultimate destination.

Sometimes we sing while rowing but mostly we row and watch the stars above our heads, craning our necks backward. It's strangely beautiful out here. The dull gray foam of breaking waves. Cold winds when we're wet. The sound of waves coming from nowhere in the dark of the night is scary.

Once I was hit in the face by a flying fish. I didn't know what the hell it was. We both stopped and flashed on the spotlight and saw it was a small flying fish knocked out cold. Kathleen tossed it in the bait can.

It is now the equinox where the sun is over the equator. Shadow observations of the sun are difficult in rough sea conditions but the results agree with the star observations.

I guess the initial scare of going overboard and losing the sextant has worn off. But the experience has left us with greater respect for the sea. Can't let the guard down ever. Even with being tired, run down, wet, and scared. I still don't know where we really are, though longitude estimates put us roughly halfway to the Marquesas. Looks like rougher conditions may be with us for the second half. We've got to keep it together, figure out the latitude, and be careful and methodical about everything.

Rowing in the darkness of night with waves that broke with a certain heaviness and violence fueled my imagination. With every stroke we took, we'd looked upward for the stars we needed. For several nights, we watched the transit of Eridani in the constellation of Eridanus and Rigel in Orion as the twilight came in. At the right moment, we'd leave our oars to trail in the water and get up to go to the fore and aft decks. Like a high priest and priestess in a mystical rite of predicting the future, we searched the skies again for Eridani or kappa Orionis, and then raise our right arms while facing each other and point directly at the transiting star. Together we'd lower our arms directly down to the horizon as we drew imaginary meridian lines.

"I think we're still north of kappa Orionis!" I called to Curt, whom I could barely see at the other end of the deck. He stood like me, legs spread wide for balance on the rolling deck, with one hand holding the safety line while his right arm repeated the meridian line dance.

"Yeah, I think you're right. We'll keep the same course another night." With that, we'd tie down the oars and crawl into the bow cabin to sleep as the fringes of the eastern horizon began to lighten in a fusion of a soft magenta yellow.

On September 25, I made a list of the food stores on the boat and calculated that if we ate two meals a day from now on, the food would last another three to four weeks. And then? When Curt checked the marine batteries, he found one of them was one-fourth charged. The radio schedules would have to be shortened and candlelight replace the light in the cabin.

Eventually, we began feeling light-headed while rowing due to the reduced diet. While Curt was swimming one day in an attempt to spear a five-inch pilot fish for dinner, he shot the port side of the hull instead, allowing a bit of water into the port stern compartment.

On October 6, it seemed that we were finally under the star of kappa Orionis, whose meridian passage was over Hiva Oa in the

Marquesas, our destination. Curt set the compass for 270 degrees due west. It was miserable, however, because the waves were hitting the boat on the beam, in other words, in the middle of its side. We had fought our way against south waves to get far enough south, only to be caught in a region of waves coming out of the north. Now we had to fight not to go too far south. The flopping back-and-forth motion brought back my seasickness.

Swamped at Sea

Late one afternoon, too tired to sleep, I rowed alone in choppy conditions, struggling to pull the oars in and out of the water. Often I paused between strokes to let foaming waves slide under the boat. It was a complete body workout, because as the waves slammed up against the side of the boat I pushed my hands on the oars downward to lift the blades out of the water and at the same time twist my body around so my weight was on the down side.

Then all of a sudden, on the starboard side, there was one wave bigger than all the rest. It was a huge white wave coming right at me. I watched, paralyzed, as it swept toward the gunwales and dumped a seething cauldron of green seawater in my lap and the open deck area. The boat wobbled under the weight and tipped precariously, with the starboard gunwale almost going underwater. I dropped the oars and jumped to the high side, screaming to Curt, who was in the cabin, to close the port windows. He slammed them shut, but it was still too late to prevent gallons of cold seawater from flooding in. Frantically, I bailed out the deck while Curt did the cabin. It was dark when we sponged up the last of the water. Days later, I was still shaking from the experience of almost flipping over.

From that day on, we found ourselves rowing in rain squalls through the heavy night seas that would switch directions from northeast to southeast on the hour. Since the near flip, every wave sounded menacing. Despite the nasty weather, by October 16, we estimated our position to be only 120 miles from Hiva Oa. I hoped the skies would clear so we could see land.

CHAPTER 30

Missing

October 18, 1984

T HE SKY WAS OVERCAST, AND thick stratus clouds lined the horizon when we awoke at dawn on October 18, expecting to see Hiva Oa off the bow. I strained my eyes at the distant horizon and used the lens of the cameras to try to see better, but it wasn't there. By mid-morning, a dark smudge of land appeared through the clouds. We were ready to celebrate after Curt took compass bearings from the distant land and matched its outline with sketches of Hiva Oa in the *Sailing Directions for the Pacific Islands Planning Guide*, published by the US Department of Defense. Relieved and ecstatic, Curt went to the rudder and changed course toward the sight of land.

At the scheduled radio contact time, we reported to the fleet of sailboats that had been following our progress via the ham radio from the Galápagos that we were in sight of Hiva Oa. The yacht *Andiamo III*, who was now near Hiva Oa, sailed to our presumed position but found nothing. By late afternoon in the clearing skies, our worst fears were confirmed: there was no land.

Fear and Despair

A sense of despair and mounting fear hung over the boat. I crawled into the cabin with my safety harness on and flopped onto the sleeping mats, my head spinning with the possibilities. How could we have missed so badly?

After weeks of plotting a course with the astrolabe and the night stars, Hiva Oa was not there! Could it be we were not even near the Marquesas? Were we lost? The thought was too terrible to imagine. Our food stores were strained, while using one gallon of water between the two of us was making it last longer. I couldn't understand, because all our sights had been consistent in their progression. It had been obvious that we were moving west and south.

In the twilight, Curt pulled in his oars and fumbled to tie them to the edge of the deck. He pushed hard and I felt a hard tug on my safety harness.

"Stop it!" I shouted. My safety harness was caught on the oar, and it pissed me off. I looked out at Curt on deck and yelled again to stop what he was doing. He said something back, but I told him to shut up.

That did it. "I did not do it on purpose! How was I supposed to know your fricking safety line was wrapped around the oar? Huh? Huh?" He stomped down on the oar and broke off the blade. I slammed the hatch shut, screaming, "Go to hell!"

Curt's log: October 18 at 8 p.m.
I stood on deck and looked around the horizon one last time before going in the cabin. Nothing. I looked toward the bow cabin and through the Lexan hatch, saw Kathleen light the candle. We were in a very lonely place. If we didn't find land very soon, we would run out of food and water.

I made my way back along the deck toward the dim cabin light after setting a sea anchor [to slow the progress of the boat drifting westward]. Inside the cabin, I saw Kathleen had pulled out the *Sailing Directions* and was sitting hunched over on her side of the cabin. "I'm making a list of islands beyond the Marquesas we might try to reach." I could tell by the tone of her voice that the storm had blown over. It was typical of Kathleen to go on as if nothing had happened. We learned early on that we could not hold grudges. Breaking the oar was like opening a pressure valve. It was time to go on.

I had made a list of islands while Curt spread the chart out on the space between us. With both of us in the cabin, there was about four feet square of open deck space to place a chart.

The Tuamotu archipelago lay beyond the Marquesas. It was a vast group of coral atolls extending over nine hundred miles of longitude. Though they represented the closest land if we had indeed missed the Marquesas, we would have to row five hundred miles south to reach them. Considering the west-flowing current, our weakened physical condition, and dwindling food stores, it was a difficult proposition.

"I've titled this list 'Lost at Sea Strategy' and come up with six possible atolls, including Fakarava, which is the second-largest atoll in the Tuamotus. It has a village called Rotoava in the northeast." Curt looked at the chart and the speck I was pointing to.

"See these arrows?" he said. "The whole archipelago is filled with tricky currents going in different directions. It's like the Galápagos all over again."

We fell silent, remembering the difficulty of reaching Santa Cruz island when we had originally aimed for San Cristóbal to the east of Santa Cruz. The west-flowing currents had carried us right past San Cristóbal. Fortunately, we had been able to catch the next island, but not before encountering the horror of rowing over the barrier reef protecting the harbor entrance. It had been pitch black with only a faint harbor light to row toward when we heard a tinkling sound like broken glass and then the distinctive whoosh of heavy waves pulling back to break forward. We had heard it all on our right side and realized the wave was going to break right over the boat if we didn't make a 90-degree turn to the south and row like hell.

That was over two months ago, but the memory remained strong.

Neither of us slept well that night, with the jerking motion of the boat on the sea anchor. By 6:00 a.m. we couldn't take it any longer, and Curt crawled out on deck. He considered pulling in the sea anchor and rowing. But which way would he row?

Curt's log: October 19

Which way would I row? It was a terrifying question. Instead, I set up the bench that I had made in the Galápagos with Efrien, and sat down and watched the seas. There was a thick haze across the horizon, making it impossible to time the sunrise for longitude. I sat on the bench and watched the waves and sky. When the haze burned off, I still couldn't see land. I sat thinking about the situation, trying to keep down an overwhelming sense of dread.

Suddenly, a scent cut like an arrow through my entire psyche. I jumped up and sniffed the air. There it was again! That unforgettable smell: sweet and herbal. It was land. I called to Kathleen to come out.

She joined me on deck and sniffed the air. No, she didn't smell anything. She looked at me as though I had been imagining things and said, "It must be your athlete's foot medicine you were smelling." With that, she turned around and crawled back into the cabin. "Do you want some breakfast?" she called over her shoulder. It was only going to be oatmeal and coffee, since after sixty-four days our food stores had become extremely limited. We had been eating the buggy Ecuadoran oatmeal for over 2 months now.

While Kathleen was making breakfast, I grabbed my tube of athlete's foot medicine and compared the smells. It wasn't the same! It was distinctly different. I had smelled land.

CHAPTER 31

The Color of Life

October 19, 1984

W E SAT ON DECK EATING oatmeal and sipping watery coffee. Occasionally, one of us would pick out a bug from the oatmeal, flick it into the wind, and continue eating. Curt looked preoccupied, and when we finished, he came out with his plan.

"The wind is coming out of the northeast," he began. "I'm sure I smelled land on the wind this morning, and if I'm right, I smelled Hiva Oa and we missed it by going too far south."

"That sounds logical," I said. So powerful was our need to believe that land was somewhere nearby, it seemed perfectly plausible that we had just missed it by aiming for the smudge on the horizon two days ago. We had neglected to remember the adversity of inter-island currents from our island miss in the Galápagos.

He continued, "We must be somewhere southwest of Hiva Oa, but we could never reach it because we can't row against this current and wind." I nodded. "But Nuka Hiva and Ua Pou islands lie to the northwest of Hiva Oa, and if I've got it right, they lie to the north of our present position. If we row due north, we may just possibly be able to see one of those islands before the current carries us too far to the west. We could get a compass bearing from an island we could identify and radio to the sailboats in the island. One of them could come out and bring us a sextant, food, and water, or maybe tow us to the harbor," He paused for a breath. "What do you think?"

I leaned over to rinse the cups and said, "Well, we did row south for half a day, and I think there's a good chance that land lies north of our present course. Okay, let's do it. Let's row north. There's nothing to lose at this point, right?"

"That's right. It's this or we're heading for the Tuamotus, I figure." I looked at him and nodded again.

Curt pulled in the sea anchor and changed the course to due north by adjusting the rudder and the compass-driven Autohelm. We sat down in our seats and rowed together all that day in a blur of bright sunshine, brisk wind, and spray. Throughout the night we rowed, taking turns to sleep and eat. In the early hours of the morning, we took a break to observe the meridian transit of kappa Orionis and got the impression we were still south of the star, and so still south of Hiva Oa or the more southern Marquesan island of Fatu Hiva.

At dawn we put out the sea anchor and once again ate a meager breakfast of buggy oatmeal in the cabin. We would give up the Marquesas after twenty-four hours if we could not see land.

Curt's log: October 20

I stood on deck and looked out at the sea, striving to see some sign of land. A sickish feeling in my gut warned me that we might be very far from any land. I took compass bearings from clouds far off on the horizon to see if it made any sense for land to be under those clouds. But these clumps of cumulus clouds, sometimes an indication of land, were at random bearings.

I studied the waves, hoping to get information from them. The wind was blowing stronger now out of the east-northeast. There were four- to six-foot waves coming from the direction of the wind. As they rolled by the boat, I noticed two other types of waves, much smaller and subtler in nature. The wave patterns came from the southeast and northeast. Something instinctively told me that these were land waves caused by the bigger waves echoing off the islands. We had been at sea long enough to recognize the differences between ocean waves and land waves, and these waves were different from anything we had seen since leaving the region of the Galápagos more than two months ago. It seemed very clear to me that one group of waves was coming from the direction of Fatu Hiva and the other from Hiva Oa.

When Curt came back into the cabin, we talked about our current situation. We decided to continue rowing north, though it would be difficult after the long hours we put in the previous day and night. The wind, however, was becoming in our favor, as it blew briskly out of the east. Our course was northeast and we regained some of the lost longitude.

By sunset of the 20th, the skies were still clear, but there was no sign of land on the horizon. I was discouraged and very tired. We both retreated into silence and only spoke to each other briefly when we took our shifts at the oars. Fear was beginning to fill us individually as we rowed and struggled with thoughts of the consequences of missing the Marquesas. Images of my family flashed in my mind, and the idea of never seeing them again made me want to cry. I thought of my mother, and all of a sudden I found myself praying to her to help me. It had been many years since, as a little girl, I had asked my mother to help me. In the midst of this horrible situation, it was my mother I asked to come to my aid.

On the morning of the 21st, three days since missing land, Curt went out early to time the sunrise for a longitude check. We would at least know how far we had slipped beyond the Marquesas. He left the cabin as the dawn was breaking over the sea, the same as it had done for sixty-seven days since we had left the Galápagos.

He stood on deck and turned to look over the bow. And there it was, the most beautiful sight ever. "Land! Land!" I heard Curt yell and pushed the hatch open to see. It was Ua Pou! Its great basalt spires rose with incredible steepness out of the sea. I stood mesmerized by its beauty and what it meant to us. We turned to each other and hugged tightly. We were saved, it seemed. Ua Pou was only about thirty miles away, and that meant we could reach land the same day, on our own. I reached into the cabin and pulled out the cameras, and we both recorded our first real sight of land in months.

It took another fourteen hours of rowing to reach the island. In the final approach, we rowed a slightly eastward course to compensate for the west-flowing current. When the island was only five miles away, a strange splashing sound startled us.

"What's that?"

I looked over my shoulder in time to see the tail of a whale disappear below the surface less than fifty feet from the boat. We left the oars trailing in the water and jumped up to get a better view. It was exhilarating to see whales close but a little frightening as well. There must have been fifteen minkes in the pod, all breaching and splashing their tails against the water for food.

By late afternoon, the land was quite close. We started pulling harder at the oars so we could be at anchor by dark. At sunset, we were rowing between Ua Pou and Motu Oa, a sixty-five-foot rock spire off the south coast. Thousands of nesting birds flew above our heads, some of them dipping down to the boat. For a few minutes, we stopped rowing and let the current carry us west and gazed up at the greenery that covered the rock spires of Ua Pou. Never had land been so impressive. In a few minutes it was dark, and we were rowing in the shadow of the great obelisk of Motu Takahe. Its imposing presence silhouetted against the stars of the night acted as a signpost to turn north toward the lee shore of Ua Pou.

By 8 p.m., we were rowing along a quiet dark coastline. In the near distance, a dim cluster of lights appeared. We pointed the boat toward the lights and rowed on. As we rowed the boat closer to shore, there was the sound of hard-breaking surf. Would we be able to anchor here? Curt reached into the bow cabin and grabbed the foghorn from its place above my pillow. He brought the flare gun out for good measure, and while I rowed *Excalibur Pacific* closer, he fired flares and beeped the foghorn. The light from the flares illuminated a steep rocky shoreline lined with coconut palm trees. Flying fish attracted to the light flew into the gunwales of the boat. With all the noise we were making, someone woke up and paddled out of the darkness to greet us with a shy smile but saying nothing. Curt dredged up his high-school French mixed with English and said, "*Nous sommes de la mer. Où ist possible ancler le bateau?*"

The Marquesan seemed to understand and gestured that it would be fine to anchor the boat right where we were. Before we left, he said in French, "I will return tomorrow morning when it is light."

Curt lowered the anchor, and I pulled hard on the oars one more time to set it. For the first time in more than two months, the boat was finally still. Curt sat on the bench, and I leaned against the bow cabin as we absorbed the sweet rich smell of land. We smiled at each other. Curt reached out his hand to me, and I came over and wrapped my arms around him in pure happiness.

Arrival in Ua Pou

As we lay in the cabin of the rowboat early in the morning of the first day, the enticing smell of wood smoke drifted into the port windows. We could hear the little village of Hakatau wake up with the sounds of children calling to each other, dogs barking, and roosters crowing. After two months at sea, it was as though our ears were more acutely attuned to the sounds of life on land than they had ever been before. When Curt crawled out on deck and I followed, the view from the rowboat, at anchor, was fantastically surreal. Everywhere we looked onshore, it was green. Green mountains, green palm trees, and green tropical fruit trees. Ua Pou, shaped like a diamond covering forty-one square miles, is the third largest of the six Marquesan islands. At the center of the island, the volcanic rock spires of Oave, Pouke, and Matahenua rose to more than four thousand feet above sea level behind the village.

Off the starboard bow, we spotted a dugout canoe with an out-rigger heading our way. It was the man we had met the night before. He introduced himself as Charles, the local policeman. There were no French administrators in Hakatau, but he had informed the gendarmes in the small capital of Hakahau by radio of our arrival.

"The gendarmes are on their way down to check you in," he said in French. "They said you are not to leave your boat until they arrive, but since they are coming by motorboat, and won't be here for a few hours, would you like to come to shore and join us for a meal?"

Curt and I smiled and nodded our acceptance of his invitation. We were dying to get off the boat. Carefully, we lowered ourselves into Charles's fifteen-foot canoe with Curt clutching a camera around his neck. Though it was made from a single hollowed-out log and rode close to the water, it was surprisingly stable because of the single outrigger. Charles paddled easily to shore, and when the boat crunched onto the boulder-strewn beach, we jumped out and turned back to help him pull his canoe ashore. Almost at the same time, Curt and I started to keel over from the odd sensation of being on land, a stable surface we weren't used to anymore. Charles quickly reached out to both of us. He held us by our elbows as we stumbled with him up the beach. When we stopped, I sat down to hold my head, as the sensation of being on land was too much after being at sea for so long. Curt couldn't focus his eyes on objects in the middle distance; the idea of a stationary object being fifty feet away seemed dimensionally impossible.

Charles came over to me and gave me his arm again as Curt staggered after us. We became aware of a crowd of Marquesan men dressed in shorts and women in brilliantly printed *pareaus*, a two-meter cloth, staring at us. I smiled at them, but it was difficult to tell what they were saying to me. The problem wasn't the French some were speaking; rather, it was hard to separate out individual voices in a crowd because we had become so accustomed to our own on the rowboat and the tinny voices from the ham radio.

When it seemed as if things were becoming too overwhelming, Charles gestured toward a path that led to his house. We shakily made our way along it, taking in the sights as we walked. Curt snapped photos of the red and yellow bougainvillea bushes lining the way, of the skinny chickens running helter-skelter in front of us, and of the fat pigs resting under a mango tree chomping on dried coconut rinds. I felt as though I was moving through an extremely vivid scene from a 1960s Technicolor film set in the South Pacific. Charles reached up to pick a lime from a tree in his yard and handed it to Curt, who inhaled its citrus fragrance with a look of sensual pleasure. When we reached the porch of Charles's house, a windowless blue prefab structure with a tin roof, Curt asked for a knife. He sliced open the lime and began eating it yellow-green peel and all. Mary Josephine, Charles's wife came out the front door and graciously offered us a breakfast of mangos and crusty baguettes that she had baked in the village beehive oven behind their house.

As Curt ate his lime, I looked around, savoring the new sights and smells of a foreign culture I had never been in before. The village of Hakatau was charming with its bustle of life. From the rowboat, we had been unable to see much of the village because coconut palms and a mountain range obscured it from view. But as we waved goodbye to Mary Josephine and followed Charles back to the main stone pathway, the village unfolded in front of us, extending far into a verdant cleft between steep-sided mountains.

After a short time, we found ourselves tired and overwhelmed by all the new sights and sounds of the village. Curt asked Charles to take us back to the boat. As we sat on the deck of *Excalibur Pacific*, a flotilla of outrigger canoes returned from their morning's fishing. A few of them paddled up to our gunwales and generously gave us gifts of green coconuts, bread, and fish.

In the afternoon, a motorboat arrived with two French gendarmes dressed in their neatly pressed khaki uniforms. While the Marquesan driving the boat held on to our gunwales, the gendarmes handed over arrival forms for us to fill out. When we handed them back, completed and signed with our scratchy signatures, they requested our passports to take back to Hakahau, Ua Pou's capital, for the official stamp for entering their territory of French Polynesia. They then told us that the Marquesas Islands were poorly stocked with the kinds of supplies we would need to continue the row. We should consider going to Tahiti, they advised, to obtain fiberglass and resin to repair the boat and the oar that Curt had broken a week ago. In the well-stocked port of Papeete, we would find wheels and axles to repair a couple of the rowing seats that had also broken in the weeks before we reached the Marquesas.

Considering that the hurricane season had already begun in the western South Pacific, we revised our plans to leave within a few weeks and decided to stay in French Polynesia for at least five months until the good-weather season returned.

CHAPTER 32

Hiking in the Marquesas

November 1984

A MONTH AFTER DROPPING ANCHOR AND meeting up with yachting friends from the Galápagos Islands, we went for a hike into the lush interior of Ua Pou Island for an overnight camping trip. We walked along a dry streambed and climbed over huge volcanic boulders to reach higher into the verdant river valley. With dusk coming on, we made camp in a shallow cave on the banks of the streambed. The depth and height of our niche were perfect: it was easy to crawl into and lay out the sleeping pads, and it was protected from the evening's light drizzle. With raindrops pattering on the broad canopy of pandanus trees outside the cave and the rich scent of wet vegetation, I felt like an explorer deep in the tropical rainforest.

As early evening turned into darkness, we lay on our pads with a solitary candle flickering along the musty interior. We ate our usual Laughing Cow cheese with a shared baguette. Outside, the drizzle continued. We talked expedition matters, our favorite topic, speaking softly and then a little more forcefully as the drizzle came down harder.

"What's that?" I asked. "Can you speak a little louder?"

"I said, we need to plan where to put *Excalibur* . . ." His voice disappeared. I felt dampness around my feet and saw a thin trickle of water seeping around the edges of the floor.

"Look, there's water coming in here. Where do you think . . . from?" My voice faded in and out against a deeper sound above us, above the cave, and it wasn't rain. All at once I knew what it was. We had to evacuate the cave right away because the stream was filling and a flash flood was starting. We grabbed our pads, stuck the snuffed-out candle and food into the backpacks, and scrambled out into the darkness. We had to climb very fast up the valley walls, as far upward through the vegetation as possible.

We climbed blindly upward, hand over hand. Our leather boat shoes made it even more difficult because they had no traction in the slippery mud. We grabbed tree branches, slippery leaves, whatever came to hand. The sound of rushing water came closer, but still we kept going in the dark, until finally there was a niche high enough above the now raging torrent.

For the rest of the night, we sat wedged behind a couple of skinny trees, like a pair of embattled seabirds in a teeming rainstorm. As the stream roared below us, Curt pulled our sleeping pads over us and we huddled closer for warmth. Neither of us could see the stream or even the trees we were wedged behind, it was so dark in the valley. Curt marveled over and over how close we had come to being drowned in the flash flood. And I marveled at our ignorance in setting up camp in a dry streambed, in monsoon weather. It seemed in the short time we had been on land that we'd forgotten to apply our hard-won survival skills learned at sea.

Tahiti Travels

Christmas morning found us baking pies on the sailboat *Sanctuary* for a party that evening. A week earlier, with the last of the sailboats heading south for the hurricane season and *Excalibur Pacific* resting safely in the island doctor's garden, we hitched a ride aboard *Andiamo III* to Rangiroa atoll in the Tuamotus. From there we bought tickets on *Manava Pitti*, a small copra and supply ship to Tahiti. For three days, we shared the crowded stern deck with families from all over French Polynesia and chatted with Manava's crew about weather conditions in this part of the South Pacific. Every day someone would invite us to their corner of the deck and share their stewed chicken in coco-nut sauce or whatever they were eating. In the evenings, we spread out our sleeping mats on deck and fell asleep listening to the nightly patter of soft rainfall and murmur of voices speaking Tuamotuan or Tahitian.

Tahiti, like Ua Pou, is a mountainous, verdant island. The morn-ing *Manava Pitti* motored into the tropical harbor of Papeete, which is protected from the sea by a man-made breakwater, we saw hun-dreds of sailboats lining the quay at Boulevard Pomare with commer-cial vessels anchored around the harbor. *Manava Pitti* motored over to a far wharf and there, like all our new Polynesian friends, we departed the ship by jumping off the bow gunwale. As luck would have it, we ran into a couple we had met in Rangiroa atoll at a Sanito Iglesia conference the week before. Jane and Allen Breckenridge were pick-ing up packages that had been shipped to them from Rangiroa via *Manava Pitti*. They kindly offered to give us a ride to the boat basin, where we planned to stay with sailboat friends from Ua Pou. As we were deposited at a black-pearl store across from the yachts, the sky opened up and a heavy deluge of rain poured down. Everyone was in good spirits as we met up with our sailing friends again.

On Christmas Day, before the party on *Sanctuary*, we planned to share a noontime meal with Jane and Allen, who were missionar-ies from the Reorganized Church of the Latter Day Saints (RLDS). After lunch, we planned to go with them to a leper colony on the east coast of Tahiti. Every year, the Sanitos choir, as the Tahitians called the RLDS, led by Allen, their pastor, sang Christmas carols for the leper colony.

With Allen at the wheel of the car, we arrived at a white build-ing covered with brilliantly colored red and orange bougainvillea. A group of lepers waited for us on the open porch. Jane told us that in the past, the lepers would sit apart from visitors behind glass windows, but now, in 1984, they could sit out with people because research had shown that only open sores were contagious and repeated contact was necessary to contract the disease. Leprosy had once been a seri-ous problem in Polynesia, but sulfa drugs helped to control it, though some of the residents had disfigured hands and faces. It was sad to think that these people had to be incarcerated and cut off from their lives in the outside world.

The Sanitos' Tahitian songs were beautifully melodic, and it was apparent that the lepers enjoyed the music very much. At the end of the performance, a spokesman for the group stood and thanked the Sanitos choir in Tahitian for remembering them as they did every year. A reception line formed, and we and the choir members shook hands with the lepers.

Most of our stay in Tahiti was spent hiking and camping. From time to time we would visit Jane and Allen and spend a few nights with them. They had told us that whenever we wanted a shower and a bed to sleep in, to come by and stay. As the month went on, we stockpiled our new expedition supplies in their back bedroom. Because they had worked with the Tahitians for over twenty years and spoke fluent Tahitian, there was so much they could teach us and share about Tahiti.

One January evening, Curt and I gave a talk about our Pacific row to a congregation in the village of Tirona using the color slides we had had developed in Papeete. We both spoke in English while Allen translated into Tahitian. At the end, there was a funny exchange about the two villages of Hakatau and Hakahau in Ua Pou. It seemed the Tahitians had the impression that the two must be one and the same, because they regarded the Marquesas Islands as remote and primitive as compared to Tahiti and not capable of sustaining development. And because the Tahitians were Polynesians and we were "poppa," or white people, who would know better what the truth was? I wasn't sure who won the argument, but we were given lots of shell leis in appreciation for our talk.

By late February, we became restless with Tahiti and our wayfaring lifestyle. We missed *Excalibur Pacific* and knew it was time to return to Ua Pou and ready the boat for a March departure. Once back on Ua Pou, in between enjoying the Hakahau *cai cais* (feasts) where we sampled the Marquesan *poe* (fermented breadfruit) that was not as sweet as the Tahitian *poe* and the delicious coconut-flavored *poisson cru*, and laughed with the villagers as we watched and Curt filmed the stilt races, we began working. The puncture from Curt's spear gun in the fiberglass hull was repaired, and new food stores were repackaged and stowed below deck along with a bag of new used paperbacks from our yachting friends in Tahiti. A new Weems & Plath metal sextant sent by Curt's father and a new donated spare Davis plastic sextant went into the navigation hatch in the bow. Our friendship with Fred, the island doctor, and his wife, Magali, strengthened as we came to their yard regularly to work on the boat. We shared daily meals with them, and I would babysit their ten-month-old son while Magali, also a doctor, would prepare for her sex education classes at the College de Ua Pou.

When the weather improved, I filmed *Excalibur Pacific* being launched in the harbor at Hakahau with Fred, the gendarmes, and village men helping out Curt, who captained the operation. On the eve of our departure to Hakatau, our original port of entry, where we would continue the row to Samoa, our French friends threw a special *cai cai* in our honor with *écrevisse*, the small Marquesan crayfish, *poisson cru*, and Tahitian *poe*. Jean-François, the teacher who shared the anchorage with us in his sailboat *War Vor Atao,* strummed his guitar and sang about traveling. In his last song, he mused about meeting people and making new friends and the special friendship born out of travel. He concluded by saying there was sadness in those friendships, because when a traveler says goodbye, there is always the possibility that one will never meet again.

Departing Ua Pou for American Samoa

On March 23, 1985, at 11:30, with only one sailboat to say goodbye, we left Hakatau, Ua Pou. Soon, we were out of the shadow of the island and rowing at a good speed with a following sea.

The seas were easy, though the boat's motion was hard to get used to again, as usual when we set out. Sometimes the boat swayed gently side to side as we rowed and drifted easily at night, its motion soothing. At other times the motion was extreme as the boat rocked hard from port to starboard.

Excalibur Pacific was well supplied, but there was little fresh food except for a bag of *citrons*, a few *pamplemousses* (extra-large, sweet grapefruit), and a couple of coconuts. The reason for this was that a strange and awkward episode had put a damper on our fresh food collection. We didn't fully understand what went wrong. A month before, while anchored at the main village of Hakahau, we had ordered several packages of dried bananas from the bank manager, who in turn called her sister in Hakatau, our original port of entry, to relay our order. Everyone was pleased that we wanted to take their bananas on the boat. Unfortunately, the Hakatau villagers dried a kind of banana that was not the sweet one we'd ordered and on top of that, they wanted to charge more money than agreed. When we refused to pay the higher amount, their attitudes changed and hardly anyone in the village would speak to us. Before that, when we arrived back at the village, we made the mistake of not first going to greet Charles. At a religious festival happening at the same time we sat with the town drunk, a schoolteacher, and the sailboat family. These unfortunate missteps made our departure less than congenial.

Curt's log: March 22, 1985
The gendarme came this morning with his speedboat and towed us at high speed southwest to Hakatau in one and a half hours.

In the village, we met Jerome, the village drunk, and a new schoolteacher. We drank wine and ate *poe* with them, while outside of the *fare*, a local open-walled house, there was a religious procession with a child at the head holding a cross. Jerome gestured to us to be quiet as half the village filed past our party, chanting prayers with the priest. The teacher became emotional as he drank more wine and talked about the bomb testing at Mururoa atoll that was taking place on a regular basis in the southern part of the French Polynesian archipelago. I think, in the end, this nuclear bomb testing will cause France to lose this Pacific empire.

March 23. We've left Ua Pou, having purchased only sugar, noodles, beans, rice, matches, and condensed milk from the second store. The first store had nothing but cocoa with the price specially upped for us. We didn't buy there. We bought some fruit too.

I picked up the anchor and sat down to row with Kathleen away from Hakatau at 11:30 a.m. with only the sailboat accompanying us. Charles and Mary Josephine didn't come down to the waterfront. Our last sight of them the day before was odd: they stood at the door of their house, eyes looking glazed, with all their children beside them, staring silently at us. I think there is a certain amount of cousins marrying cousins that contributes to the startling resemblances between most villagers. Only their oldest daughter, Virginia, whom we had met at the high school in the main village of Hakahau and who was visiting for the weekend, came to say goodbye. She seemed to be the only adult in the village not glaring at us and walking crookedly.

As Curt and I rowed away from Ua Pou, the last sight of land was the brownish, dry west coast of Ua Pou, which had looked so green to us when we rowed between Motu Oa and Ua Pou five months earlier.

Despite the pleasant months we'd spent hiking on Ua Pou and socializing with the yachties in port, the wonderful visits to Tahiti and a few of the atolls in the Tuamotus, we were both happy to be out at sea again. None of the parting was hard. For the French who were our friends, their time in Ua Pou was transient as well, as they would be leaving someday too. Curt and I talked about our long discussions at anchor with the French sailor Jean-François and his anti-American sentiments. We never responded in kind to the things he constantly threw out at us, but if we had spent more time together, it would have come out eventually.

Over the months in French Polynesia, we had thought of home, which was so far away. Vermont didn't seem real anymore, though the previous year we had left from there for the Pacific row. But fleeting glimpses came back in flashes: the hilly Echo Lake Road drenched in a late spring shower, the silence of snowflakes falling in winter, and the intense green of the Vermont summer in the Northeast Kingdom.

Before losing sight of land, we caught a forty-pound bluefin tuna with our friend Gigi's fishing rig: a large plastic squid and 200-lb.-test fishing line. Gigi, a schoolteacher on the island, had given us one of his best plastic squids and me an elegant necklace he had threaded together from the yellow green spikes of a sea urchin. With the meat that Curt cut up into small chunks, I made a tasty *poisson cru* snack marinated with soy sauce and lime. I hung the rest on the safety line to dry while listening to Gabilou, the Tahitian singer whose tapes I bought in Papeete. Though the batteries to my tape cassette recorder were fading and the music became softer with time, Gabilou provided fine background music to life at sea again.

A few nights after we had left Ua Pou, Curt rolled out his new handmade hammock and rocked for a while on deck. It was exceptionally quiet that night, and a multitude of stars were visible, especially those far enough away from the quarter moon. Though we were returning to our routine at sea with decided improvements from the last voyage, it took time to relax and adjust to life back on the rowboat. The best way to sleep at night on rolling *Excalibur Pacific*, I decided, was to exhaust myself by rowing a lot. Curt agreed with me and thought that doing his navigation helped him to rest easier once he knew where we were heading.

CHAPTER 33

Forty Days and Forty Nights

March 1985

Two weeks after leaving Ua Pou, there was a first for us: shark baiting. It started with the fishing line that had been out all day without a single bite. Curt was rowing and I was in the cabin reading, waiting for my time at the oars, when I heard, "Kathleen, we've got a bite!" The new fishing line and squid lure that Gigi had given us had scored another strike.

I crawled out on deck to see an eruption of blood and agitated water on the port side of the boat. A bluefin tuna was being eaten alive by a brown shark. Curt gave the line an extra hard jerk and the tuna flew out of the water, landing hard at my feet. I gasped. "Look at that! It looks like an apple eaten around its core!"

Indeed, the shark that now raced up to the gunwales and then disappeared had ravaged the sixty-pound fish. A minute later the boat started rocking violently. The shark was banging the boat's rudder.

"Jesus Christ. The asshole. Let's play tag with it. Like John Fairfax."

"I don't know," I said. "That sounds like a bad idea." Our boat was only twenty-five feet long and the shark was about five feet. The deck we would be "playing" from was only nine feet of crowded space. An image of John Fairfax's bitten arm flashed to mind. He and his girlfriend Sylvia Cooke had been rowing across the Pacific Ocean in the early 1970s when one day John started to fool around with the sharks. A miscalculated grab at the shark with a grappling hook left him with a forearm that looked a lot like our tuna.

I crouched by the bow cabin door while Curt leaned against the stern cabin, looking off the port gunwale. The shark had reappeared beside the boat, and it seemed he wasn't going away.

Curt looked over at me, and I barely nodded my head. It *was* tempting to see what would happen if we dangled a little bit of the tuna over the side. We were bored after just a few long days at sea. The hours could be monotonous: Sunrise. Curt rows. Breakfast. Kathleen rows. Lunch. Curt works out navigation sights and updates the course. Kathleen does boat maintenance and reads on deck. Late afternoon we both row. Dinner. Ham radio contacts. Sunset. Do the evening star sights. Write in our logs. Sleep. The next day, do it all over again. There was a distinct quality of sameness about our existence on the rowboat. Tuna tag was the perfect antidote, but it was very risky.

We started with the innards, which were splayed out on the deck. The tuna was a sorry sight, though no longer alive. The shark gobbled up the offering.

"Let's see the knife," and Curt cut the tuna's head off and threaded a one-inch braided rope through its gills and mouth. He wiped his bloody hands on his shorts and got ready to swing the head over the gunwale.

"Hold it," I yelled, and dove into the bow cabin for the camera. Curt paused and braced himself, right foot on the edge of the gunwale and left foot wedged under the lip of the water pump. I leaned against the bow cabin with the Nikon around my neck, ready to take photographs and grab Curt if the shark tugged a little too hard.

In one fluid motion, he lifted his right arm with the tuna head dangling off the end and flung it like an old mangled softball with a sharp snap of his wrist. Before the tuna even landed in the water, the shark was reaching for it. Bam! It was a strike. Curt grabbed the rope with both hands to stop it from disappearing overboard. I clicked away, caught up with the excitement.

"This is crazy. It's like playing tag with an out-of-control dog," he managed, his arm muscles straining with the violence of the shark's reaction. The port gunwale dipped precariously as Curt

...rt working on the deck of *...calibur* in Vermont as we prepared ...the South Pacific row. We would ...aptize the refitted boat *Excalibur ...ific*.

Repacking *Excalibur Pacific* while on board the Callao, Peru–bound commercial ship *Strider Fearless*, in June 1984.

My blisters show the difficulty of rowing throug the wild Galápagos Islands currents in July 1984.

Curt preparing to take sun sights with the plastic Davis sextant. This photo was taken before he fell overboard one morning and lost that crucial navigational tool. Behind him on the aft cabin is the Autohelm, housed in a plastic bag to protect it from the constant salt spray.

Curt's Pacific navigation logbook would record the stars and timing that Curt "shot" with the sextant When he finished, he calculated our latest position using H.O. 249 tables commonly used by sailors and aviators before satellite navigation and GPS.

Callao, the Peruvian chicken we bought at a market in the port city of that name. She never produced any eggs but was good company as we rowed north in the Humboldt Current to the Galápagos Islands.

After losing the sextant on the Galápagos to Marquesas Islands passage, we came up with several substitutes, including a crude astrolabe that Curt made from the deck hatch in the forward cabin. He is trying to take a shot position with it at noon.

he stress of the g passage from the Galápagos Islands to the rquesas shows Curt's and my faces after fifty ys. The passage ventually took xty-seven days.

When we arrived in the Marquesas Islands after a couple of months navigating like Polynesians, we ordered two new sextants, including this fancy metal one from Plath.

Far left: All our fresh water was kept in the hatches below the nine-foot-long open deck Every day, one us would pump out a gallon for cooking and drinking.

Left: Cooking a omelet on Curt old camping sto in the bow cab

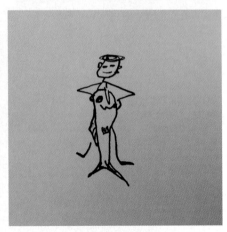

Sketches from my notebook, clockwise from top left: bugs in bananas; Curt climbing; Curt with his tuna catch; me cooking.

Sitting by the aft cabin late in the day on the South Pacific.

We used heavy-duty canvas sea anchors off the stern of the boat to slow us down when the wind and waves were adverse. I made several, including this one I am holding, to handle the challenge of navigating through the Great Barrier Reef in July 1985.

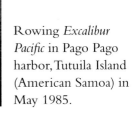

Rowing *Excalibur Pacific* in Pago Pago harbor, Tutuila Island (American Samoa) in May 1985.

Tying up the boat ropes in Cairns, Australia, after successfully completing the Pacific row on July 31, 1985.

The happy couple posing by *Excalibur Pacific* after completing the Pacific row.

By 1986, we had become landowners in northern Vermont. *Excalibur Pacific* rested behind the house in between boat shows and future boat jaunts.

Four-year-old Christopher. After our 1988 row and sail down the Baja California coast, we became interested in using solar panels to power an electrical motor for voyaging. Curt took the model of *Excalibur Pacific* he had built in 1982 and added an *ama*, an outrigger hull, to increase space for extra solar panels.

urt leaving solo on *Solar Eagle* from Casablanca in early 1991. He abandoned the expedition most a month later when the boat was damaged in a storm off the Moroccan coast.

In late summer of 1991, we returned to the US with only a few bags and no rowboat. We are standing at a UK train station on our way to Heathrow with the only gear we were able to salvage from the failed solar electric voyage.

To symbolically complete the *Solar Eagle* ocean crossing, we bought a beautiful handmade wooden electric boat and traveled with her along the coastal waters of North Carolina.

pushed against it with his foot, pulling hard on the rope while the shark kept up the pressure. "You wanna try it?"

I was tempted. When would I ever have such a chance again? "Yeah, this is dangerous. But I want to . . ."

The shark was waiting, and Curt was looking at me. I said no. But then I said, "How are we going to get rid of it? That shark's going to follow us from now on." I imagined it just below the surface when I washed dishes, or even worse, whenever I hung my bottom over the side to pee. Though our last encounter with an aggressive shark was seven months earlier off the South American coast, the fear from its nightly bumping of the hull was still there. I didn't want to go through that again.

"We have to shoot it," I said. "It's not going to go away otherwise." We looked at the dark shape swimming just below the surface. The rope was trailing limply in the water; the tuna head was completely gone. Frayed ends of the rope floated beside the boat and there was blood in the water.

The headless tuna was crosswise on the deck, its blood dripping slowly into the ocean through the drain hole in the stern rowing station. There was no way to clean up the deck without dipping a bucket into the sea, but neither of us was particularly anxious to dip anything into the ocean now.

I crawled into the bow cabin, put the camera away, and reached for the plastic bag with the handgun wrapped in one of Curt's old faded bandannas. I pulled it out and unwrapped it carefully. I had practiced with it only once on land. On the ocean as on land, Curt was the shooter.

Standing against the stern cabin, he braced himself while I stood by the bow cabin watching; the shark was still there. He fired a couple of shots, and then fired again, until the shark faltered, pointed downward, and sank slowly out of sight.

Thunder and Lightning

Curt's log: April 1985

Lately, we've been recording unbelievable mileages of 85 and 60 miles per day respectively. Fast moving squall lines hit the boat and send us flying. The other night it was stormy with the wind dying but with heavy rain. *Excalibur Pacific* wallowed around in lumpy, confused seas. The sea anchor I put out did nothing to smooth our drift. It only hung limply below the boat at the end of its rope.

Kathleen woke me so we could go out and row away from the storm now that the wind had stopped. I didn't want to go out on deck in the rain in the dark. But she pushed me because it was our chance to break out of the low-pressure trough, so we got dressed, clipped on our safety harnesses, and went out on deck.

The night was pitch dark and the rain came down straight in the absence of any wind. The rain had damped down the waves. I untied the oars while Kathleen handed out the rowing seats from the aft cabin. We began rowing but the boat did not surge forward the way she would in following seas. Though there was an absence of any defined direction to the waves or current, the boat plowed through the low waves without a great deal of effort.

Anyone who thinks it is possible to get across an ocean in a rowboat by the flow of the currents alone is mistaken. The currents on the surface are linked to the weather conditions and if we don't row on a regular basis, we will never reach Australia. The other night we also needed to get out from under that low-pressure trough and back into the area of trade winds and good weather. We both wanted to be rowing in the bright sunshine, surfing the boat on following seas and watching for schools of flying fish.

Our minds were half asleep as we rowed the boat through the rainy night until a light cut across the bow. We stopped rowing and jumped up. It was the moon, which was nearly full and so low in the western sky that it emerged from behind thick black clouds into a line of clear sky along the western horizon.

"See?" I said to Kathleen. "We'll be out from under these clouds by breakfast time." She agreed but asked if there was such a thing as a rainbow by moonlight.

I had never heard of a moon bow but when we looked directly off the stern, incredibly, there it was: Much dimmer than a rainbow by sunlight, but plainly visible with the bright moonlight and dark rain clouds. We stood on the deck watching this beautiful sight. Then

Kathleen noticed an even more extraordinary sight: below the moon bow, there was a second one showing as a faint shadow below the first.

At the most unexpected times, the sea shows us a rare scene of primitive beauty such as this. We resumed our rowing, our eyes fixed on the double rainbow by moonlight until it faded away in the light of the day. By the time the sun rose, we were rowing out from under the edge of the clouds. When the sun broke above the clouds, we took in the oars and I made pancakes for breakfast.

April 20. Sea calm and swelly. Clouds on the horizon all around us and things are very slow. I estimate if we continue an average of 42 miles a day to Samoa, it will be about two and a half weeks. We have nicknamed the boat "Slow Boat to Madness."

The Autohelm electronic self-steering device finally gave up the ghost. It had worked so well up to this point of the expedition, but the constant pounding of the waves breaking over it caused the inner electronic components to corrode and stop working. I've tried to fix it by taking it apart several times but the corrosion is too advanced.

It is much more difficult to steer a course while rowing without the Autohelm. We have to tie off the rudder, thus steering by watching the compass attached to the aft cabin bulkhead. We have to pay more attention to the course as we come closer to Tutuila Island in the Samoa Islands.

April 21. There is the tremendous thunderstorm sky astern of *Excalibur Pacific*. Black, deep rumbles, flashes of white lightning, and it is only 4:30 p.m. Kathleen says she is trying to maintain calmness and not give way to extreme feelings of fright. The wind has died out—swallowed up by the thunderstorms to the east, northwest, and southeast for an hour or so. The sky is totally closed down. All the fish have disappeared and there is one bird sitting on the rudder. He just let out a squeak as the thunder rumbled close to the boat.

April 22. The thunderstorm did not come in as bad as predicted. There was rain but it passed to the south of us. Now the sky is completely

overcast and the temperatures are cold. Weather report out of Honolulu this morning indicates a low-pressure trough is moving at 15
miles per hour with four-foot waves, while the thunderstorms bothering us are on a line directly crossing route.

It took forty days to reach the natural harbor of Pago Pago in the
island of Tutuila—better known as American Samoa—from Ua Pou.
During most of the time, the weather was poor and often consisted
of great anvil-shaped towering cloud masses that covered the western
sky in the front of the boat, creating winds so violently strong that the
seas would be flattened around the rowboat for miles. To control the
boat, Curt was constantly throwing out the sea anchor so we could
ride out the storm until the prevailing east wind and clear skies built
back into our region of the South Pacific.

    Three weeks at sea, we decided, was the cut-off point when
fatigue would set in and we would tire easily. One evening on the
last third of the Marquesas-to-Samoa crossing, Curt was on deck
and saw a green flare in the distance. He remembered the stars near
the flare so he was able to get a bearing. That night, we heard on the
ham radio, a warning was being issued for the yacht *Sealestial*, which
we had seen in Tahiti. It was being chartered with a full crew by the
journalist William F. Buckley for a book he was writing on sailing
in the Pacific. When we learned that *Sealestial* was overdue from its
crossing from Tahiti to Hawaii, Curt plotted the course he imagined
it must have taken and discovered that it crossed our course right
where we were.

    What we did next is an example of how rationality can be
eroded on a long voyage in a small boat. For the next two days,
we changed course and rowed toward where he had seen the flare.
We imagined that *Sealestial* must have sunk and we would row to it
and rescue Buckley and company! We rowed many miles off course
before we came to our senses and realized that we had long since
gone over the area of the flare, which had probably been a signal from
a Japanese tuna fishing boat. Again we changed course and got on
route for Samoa. After that, we scrutinized any decisions we made to
guarantee we would arrive in Samoa in a couple of weeks.

The detour almost cost us, though. When we pulled into Pago Pago harbor in a rainstorm, the harbormaster told us that a severe low-pressure system was due to move over the Samoan archipelago imminently.

May 1985: American Samoa—Arrival

In the early evening of May 1, we were on deck, resting from a rowing session, when I saw the faint rounded shape on the western horizon.

"I see land, it's land!" I screamed. "Look, it's over there!" No matter how many times I'd first seen land after a long passage, I still found the approach by boat exciting. Curt turned quickly to see where I pointed: close to the horizon, in a magenta smudge, there was the dark outline of an island.

"There's another one!" He pointed north. "These must be the Manua Islands." The late anthropologist Margaret Mead had done much of her research for *Coming of Age in Samoa* in the Manua Islands, which lie next to American Samoa.

We rowed throughout the night while Curt fine-tuned his navigation by reducing the moon sights he had taken earlier with the sextant. By daybreak, the last of Tau and Ofu islands in the Manuas were off our stern, and Tutuila Island, American Samoa, was not far off. We rowed into the next morning, as the sky began to darken with ominous dark gray clouds that marched in from the southeast. The green mountainous coast of Tutuila was only five miles off the starboard as we rowed alternately in rain and sunshine.

On the final approach to Tutuila, a motorized catamaran fishing boat came up to us. The man, a Samoan, driving the boat called over, "Hey, you guys okay?"

"We're fine. We're just rowing across the Pacific." Curt replied in a cheery tone.

"Oh . . ." He frowned and smiled uncertainly. "Good luck then." The man and his son motored away.

From our rowing seats, we watched a yellow American-style school bus driving along the coastal road of Tutuila. With some trepidation, we passed a wrecked freighter aslant on a nearby reef.

The entrance to Pago Pago slowly appeared between two sloping verdant hills. Red and green navigation buoys guided us into the inner harbor, while fishing trawlers passed by on the way out to sea for an evening's work. Finally, the range lights appeared, a pair of light beacons indicating the safest course through the inner harbor, and we lined up *Excalibur Pacific* by pulling hard on the starboard oars to counteract the current. A long sleek Samoan *amatasi* (Polynesian rowing boat) glided by us, the coxswain calling for the paddlers to switch sides. Cars sped along the single-lane road that rimmed the inner harbor. As the clouds settled in for the night, we reached an anchorage, glad to be off the ocean after forty days from Ua Pou in the Marquesas Islands.

Early the next morning, *Excalibur Pacific* strained at her mooring in near gale-force winds. Inside the bow cabin, we snuggled together inside the sleeping bag, thankful we were not at sea in this weather. Later in the morning, though, we reluctantly got dressed and went to check in with customs and immigration. In Pago Pago, we read in the guidebook, officials do not come out to newly arrived boats. One had to notify them by radio and then paddle to shore.

In the strong winds and choppy waves, Curt took out the dinghy from the aft cabin and pumped it up while I held on to it as it flopped madly in the wind. With our passports and papers in a waterproof bag, I rowed the dinghy over to the small boat dock and we went to huddle in a nearby shelter, waiting for the harbor officials. A friendly Samoan who was fishing off the dock's edge cheerfully informed us the US officials did not like to come out in the rain and would most likely wait until the weather calmed down.

Eventually, we cleared customs and began a month-long stay. There were several jobs we had to accomplish, like renewing my passport. Though it expired in a month and a half, I didn't want to take any chances arriving in Australia with an out-of-date passport. With a little legwork and red tape, Samoan style, I sent off my passport through the proper offices to Hawaii, where they promptly returned the new passport with the canceled old one in only one week.

CHAPTER 34

Pregnant or Not?

May 1985

I WAS SITTING ON THE WINDY deck of *Excalibur Pacific* when I made up my mind. I would go to the island hospital and get a pregnancy test. My body was different; for a few weeks it had felt bloated and heavy. I suspected that we had had a little too much fun on the "Slow Boat to Madness" from the Marquesas, perhaps influenced by the child-centered cultures we had encountered throughout French Polynesia. It seemed wherever we traveled, there were children laughing and playing while the adults looked on with indulgent smiles. Sometimes families, our missionary friends Jane and Allan in Tahiti told us, would send a child to live with their grandparents to keep them company and help them with their lives. For the first time, I began to imagine what it might be like to have a child.

Curt, who had plans to work on the Autohelm that had died en route to Samoa, paddled me to shore where I would catch the local bus to the hospital. What would I do if the answer were a positive? Would we continue the row? I put those thoughts aside to climb on board the American-style public bus when it pulled up in front of me. I looked out the windows as we traveled through winding, rain-slick roads that led inland from a promontory and tried to imagine living on Tutuila. It was a lush, overgrown garden of tropical beauty, but we had been told that most of the villages on Tutuila were off-limits to foreigners, including Americans. Without permission from the village headman, you couldn't even visit a village. Could we, I wondered, even find jobs in this American welfare state?

In the horribly crowded women's section in the whitewashed hospital, a nurse told me to take off my clothes and wrap myself in the large cotton sheet that she handed me.

"But I'm only here for a pregnancy test!" I protested. Her response was an unsympathetic "Sorry, this is the way we do it." I undressed and joined a crowd of huge half-naked Samoan women milling around the examination rooms. My turn would come, the nurse told me.

It was noisy and chaotic as I waited, and I began to doubt that I really needed to be there. Perhaps the challenging conditions of living on the rowboat had caused my period to be late. In a few minutes, before I changed my mind, I heard "Kathleen Saville" called over the confusion of Samoan and English. I walked over to the nurse, who asked me why I was there. "A pregnancy test," I said, and was given a plastic cup with a top to pee in. She didn't appear to notice that I was wrapped up in a bedsheet just to pee in a cup. In fact, there was a line at the bathroom, so I wasn't alone in this bizarre ritual of peeing while wrapped in swaths of white sheeting.

I handed the sample to yet another nurse and fled. Outside in the pouring rain, I caught a bus back to the harbor and thought about what I had just been through and what it could mean if I were really pregnant. The idea didn't hold any reality for me. It was more of a fantasy. At the harbor, I called over to *Excalibur Pacific*.

Curt popped his head out of the bow cabin, and I waved at him to come get me. He climbed into the little dinghy and paddled over. While I squeezed into the bow cabin and mopped my face from the rain, we had a good laugh over the images I created of myself draped in a bedsheet, jostling for service amid a mob of healthy Samoan women getting gynecological checkups. It was funny in retrospect, though the consequences of the results sat quietly in the back of my mind. Would I continue the row or not? Neither of us talked about it.

In the meantime, we told no one about the private side of our visit to Samoa and went on with boat repairs and yachting parties. The harbor smelled alternately of smoke and sour fish. The smoke drifted from the Sunday *umu* dinners that Samoan families prepared every weekend. *Umu*s were the meals slow-cooked in a subterranean oven pit, and at our anchorage we were in direct line of the smoke. Years later, visiting my Azorean grandparents' island of San Miguel, I was reminded of the Samoan *umus* when I encountered the Azorean specialty of *cozido*, which was cooked in the steaming vents of the subterranean volcanoes of that island.

The scent of Sunday smoke in Pago Pago was pleasant in comparison to the sour fish smell coming from the north end. A StarKist tuna factory regularly dumped their sewage in the harbor, causing much of the boat anchorage to be filled with a putrid, oily tuna smell. The harbor water was foul, too; the bottom of our dinghy turned a bright purple color that could not be washed off. Little barnacles started growing there within days of our arrival. There was a lot of life in the harbor, and not all of it was pleasant.

In a few days, it was time to call the hospital for the test results. The weather was windy the morning we paddled to shore so I could use the public phone near the marine shop. The dinghy oars were flimsy, but with a series of little short strokes, Curt rowed directly to the dock without too much sideways slippage.

In my backpack, I found a dime and the slip of paper with the number of the lab. I dialed and asked the American who answered for my results. He began laughing because his office was accounts and not the lab. I was in a testy mood and spoke to him sharply, asking him to transfer me. Chastened, he apologized and transferred the call right away, but it took a few minutes for the clerk to find the results. In my mind's eye, I imagined the hundreds of rumpled slips of pregnancy results he was sifting through to find mine. When he came back, he reported the results as negative.

I thanked him and put down the phone. I walked over to a nearby bench and sat down. I felt curiously deflated, because I knew instinctively that my body was different. If I were pregnant, it would only be about two or two and a half months, and perhaps it was too soon for any signs.

Curt's log: Pago Pago, May 30, late evening
After 27 days at anchor, we made final plans to leave for the final leg of the journey to Australia. On May 30, I pulled the dinghy out of the water for the final time. When I looked down at the slimy purple bottom that was covered with barnacles, I swore that I would never eat tuna fish again.

Kathleen didn't want to leave Samoa so soon, and she protested by pointing out the sun dog halo around the sun. I looked up and saw the high choppy cirrus clouds and knew she was right: bad weather was coming in. But I wanted to leave Samoa because we'd lose the momentum of the voyage if we didn't go now. And besides, with Kathleen possibly pregnant, we might never finish the row. I told her that the most recent meteorology report said the weather at sea would be good for 48 hours, but she only shook her head.

High tide was approaching and we were ready. Yacht dinghies motored beside us as we rowed toward the harbor entrance. The crew from *Iron Butterfly* gave us a set of classical tapes they had thoughtfully recorded for us. *Annie Laurie* blew whistles and shouted good luck. Earlier in the day we had crammed, below deck, a long narrow plastic tube filled with the latest additions to our book collection: *Berlin Game* by Len Deighton, a couple of murder mysteries by Lawrence Sanders, Stephen King's *Cujo*, and a few books by Australian authors Nene Gare (*The Fringe Dwellers*), Colleen McCullough (*The Thorn Birds*), and Nevil Shute (*A Town Like Alice* and *On The Beach*). Our friend Beth Ruze and her friends waved from *Taloa*. There was a commotion as Beth was motored up in a dinghy driven by Verne. "Here, these are for you," She gave me two shell leis. "Good luck!" And at the same time Verne handed us two cold beers and said, "Bon voyage."

Kathleen and I smiled at everyone but the same thought was going on behind our show of bravado: "I wish that was me on *Taloa*, watching someone else row out to sea."

It is getting harder to make these departures into the unknown.

CHAPTER 35

Heavy Weather
and Crash Landings

May 30–June 1985

I WISH I WAS DRINKING THAT beer on land," Curt commented as the beer bottles rolled back and forth on deck while we rowed.

I gave him a dirty look and said, "Well, who was it that wanted to leave before June first?" He ignored me and stared straight ahead as he rowed. The weather was beginning to look uncertain, a fact he didn't want to discuss.

Excalibur Pacific rolled with the coastal chop. The lights of Tutuila came on in the evening, one speck at a time. It was a beautiful island to watch from a distance. I pulled in my oars. "I think I'll go lie down." The motion of the sea was bothering me, as it always did the first week, but now I couldn't keep down the seasickness pills and I suspected the negative pregnancy test results might have been wrong after all.

By 8:30 p.m., the boat was off the island airport and on the outer fringes of the barrier reef surrounding Tutuila. To a certain extent, we counted on the coastal currents to push us away from land, but rowing was necessary to guide the boat in the right direction. The wind speed picked up.

At 10 p.m., we were in a full gale with winds from the northwest. The wind had completely veered to the opposite direction and we were in danger of crashing onto the reefs. With a safety harness on, Curt went out on deck to put out the sea anchor. The height of the sea had risen to twenty feet in just a short time. The wind blew so hard the tops of the waves were pure spray. Hopefully the sea anchor would slow our progress north.

Throughout the night we took turns looking out the Lexan port to sight for fishing trawlers. The wind switched briefly to the west and then came back to the north and the northeast. We had learned on the Marquesas-to-Samoa row to expect bad weather when the wind blew from the northeast.

In the early hours of June 1, I woke Curt to say conditions had calmed down. The wind was a mere Force 3 from the east. It was still overcast, but the seas were rowable. As I made a light breakfast, Curt rowed with the rudder set in a westerly direction. From bearings taken off of distant Tutuila, we gathered that a north-flowing current was affecting *Excalibur Pacific*. The news was both good and bad. To the north lay Western Samoa, and in between Tutuila and Western Samoa was a channel with a strong north-setting current.

By noon of the next day, Western Samoa was twenty miles off our starboard. We thought of Beth, who had said she would visit Western Samoa at this time. Later she told us of a moderately strong earthquake that hit Samoa the night we had the gale-force winds. We had experienced the earthquake in the form of heavy weather as we rowed hard to pull *Excalibur Pacific* away from the gravitational force generated by the north flowing tide of the channel.

In the early evening, as I sat on the bench peeling a taro root and carrots for a stew, I saw a strange east–west shelf cloud, outlined against the completely overcast sky, passing almost directly above the boat. It was too quiet for the ocean, I thought. A slight breeze blew. I called to Curt, who came out with the cameras and photographed the phenomenon. The western South Pacific, we were quickly figuring out, had a very different weather system from the eastern side.

Curt's log: June 4

Overcast and very windy today. Force 5 to 6 and winds out of the south-southeast. Too many squalls with the wind right on the beam making the boat rock back and forth heavily.

We are 190 miles from Tutuila as the crow flies. Nearest land is 75 miles south-southeast. Tonga Islands? Perhaps this is why the waves are so miserable and hard hitting. It's like having a freight train racing at the boat and bam! When it hits, it hits hard. The small dagger board in the bow [built with Efrien in the Galápagos] is helping to maintain our course.

The new Autohelm ordered in Samoa appeared to be in trouble this morning but I checked the power supply and found loose connections. It's okay now.

Our diet is pretty good with cucumbers, onions, potatoes, and taro. The taro was good with tomato sauce last night but it was heavy and gave us a stomachache.

The wind of a couple of nights ago came from the northwest, which isn't good. These winds last for hours and blow very hard with tremendous downfalls. The amount of rain that comes down is astonishing.

We had been at sea for a miserable week after leaving American Samoa. The sky was a relentless shade of dark gray and rough seas whipped up by high winds constantly blew cold spray into our faces as we rowed. One night, after Curt threw out the sea anchor again to slow the boat's drift to the south, he confessed he was depressed about the dangerous weather conditions. I looked up from my book, the words swimming on the page with the rocking and rolling of the boat. "What? What's the matter?"

"I said this weather is getting me down. I wonder if we should keep going with this expedition."

I looked at him, surprised. Though I knew he wasn't happy with the lousy conditions, I didn't think he wanted to quit. Then I realized we had done a reversal of roles from the beginning of the South Pacific row when I was depressed about leaving South America. Though nowadays, I wasn't happy with the weather either, and most likely being pregnant on the rowboat was making my life uncomfortable, I was all for continuing the row to the end. I didn't want to give up at this point, but a part of me knew that I really didn't want to leave Curt on his own. He was tired and run-down, and he wanted to be done with the trip. Or maybe he was feeling guilty for pushing to leave Samoa with the possibility of pregnancy hanging over the expedition. It might not be just the two of us on the boat anymore.

"What are the possibilities for finishing this trip?" he asked another day as *Excalibur Pacific* rolled around. The boat felt like a marine version of a Bobo doll with the waves pushing us this way and that way all day long. I looked closely at him and asked, "Do you mean stopping at an island in the Fijis?" He nodded. The Fijis consist of hundreds of islands and atolls. They were approximately a hundred miles south of our present course.

"Well," I said, and reached for the *Sailing Directions for the Pacific Islands Planning Guide*. "There are quite a few islands listed in this book. Are you thinking of a deserted island?" I sounded like a tourist agent: "Need an island to crash-land on? Let's see what we can find."

"It depends on whether there are inhabited ones nearby."

I scanned the descriptions closely. After spending several months on sparsely populated Polynesian islands, we had a fair idea of what life on an island was like.

"Remember Ahe and Rangiroa in the Tuamotus?" I asked. We had spent a rainy week trudging from one end of Rangiroa to the other, fighting flies and a sense of claustrophobia. It was odd we felt that way on land when our rowboat was only twenty-five feet long. Curt's enthusiasm for an island hideaway dwindled for the day, and we went out to row.

A couple of days later we took up the conversation about quitting again. "How would we land at one of these islands?" I asked. Figuring out how to land on an island was a fun exercise in strategizing, something we enjoyed doing together. Our conversations now considered what it meant to quit the expedition when we were more than two-thirds of the way across the South Pacific. We considered how we would lose face if we just rowed into any port announcing the end of the row because we wanted to be done with it. Or was a possible pregnancy a good excuse?

"We could crash-land unless we navigate into a lagoon at slack water." Time was passing and, despite the bad weather, the Fijis were slipping behind us. One Sunday we had awakened to the alluring smell of smoke from a distant cook fire. At once we were reminded of the Samoas, and knew the Fiji Islands were not far off.

"A crash-landing's dangerous, and we'll need the boat to get off the island at a later point." Already there were reasons not to quit.

"What about Futuna or Wallis Island? They're not too far west of our course." I grabbed the *Sailing Directions* and thumbed the pages to find both islands.

"It says they're a territory of France, though they're on the western fringes of French Polynesia. . . . Wallis is surrounded by a barrier reef with an opening about at 176 degrees west. We'd have to negotiate a pretty tricky tidal flow to get in there." I looked up at Curt, who nodded. "Futuna hasn't got the barrier reef like Wallis, but the best ports are in the south and west, and you have to negotiate a narrow passage between it and Alofi Island."

"That sounds like a lot of effort to get into those islands."

"Yeah, I agree. It's a lot of effort, in this boat, to get into any port."

For the rest of the week, as the Fijis slipped by, we talked of one scenario after another until we compromised and plotted a course to Efate Island in the western Melanesian archipelago of Vanuatu. Port Vila, Efate would be a good stopover to reassess how I was feeling and buy last-minute fresh food supplies before going into the Coral Sea and through the Great Barrier Reef, though it was risky for us to stop at any island. In Samoa, we had bought enough supplies to last until Australia, to avoid having to stop. After all, when we rowed from Peru to the Galápagos, we hadn't been successful in reaching San Cristóbal. Adverse currents and winds caused us to miss the island and instead land at Santa Cruz. On the second leg to the Marquesas, our original port of call was Hiva Oa and not Ua Pou. As a matter of fact, Pago Pago was the first island we reached as initially planned.

Role-playing worst-case scenarios had been good for us psychologically, besides giving us a cheap form of entertainment as we imagined challenging crash landings on remote Fijian atolls. In our ham radio contacts with yachts we'd met earlier in the row and maritime nets, we never shared our thoughts about quitting. But just figuring out how we could quit the row, oddly enough, made us stronger in our resolve to follow the expedition to the end.

Sea Snakes and Pumice

Curt's log: June 25

According to my calculations, we are approximately 100 miles from Efate. It's important to approach the island properly because of the numerous islands and outlying reefs in the Vanuatu archipelago.

The other night we were sitting on deck eating a spaghetti dinner as the seas continued to flatten out. The silence was eerie. The north wind had died down to a whisper. All of a sudden we heard "Swishhh, swishhhh," and I said, "What's that?" Both of us turned in unison at the sound.

"There it is!" Kathleen pointed off the aft cabin, at a large yellow sea snake swimming on the surface of the water. It was so quiet that we could hear the movement of its tail swishing back and forth as it moved along away from the boat. Kathleen recalled reading that a bite from such a sea snake could mean death. I wondered out loud why the snake had suddenly appeared off the stern. And then we realized the snake had probably been on the boat! [According to the *Sailing Directions for the Pacific Planning Guide*, sea snakes are mostly found in coastal areas and rarely far out at sea.]

A few days later, we heard a tinkling sound against the hull when we woke in the early morning. The sound wasn't coming from under the hull but beside the boat, at the waterline. There wasn't anything out there until one afternoon, when I was rowing, I saw a gray skein of floating rocks nearby. I looked closer and saw it was pumice: small irregular lumps of gray pumice shot full of holes from the submarine volcano that had spewed them into the seawater. I felt my skin prickling when I recognized them. When we looked at the samples that I had scooped from the sea beside *Excalibur Pacific*, we felt a sense of awe for what was happening in the ocean below us. It was frightening to think that, beneath *Excalibur Pacific*, somewhere on the ocean's bottom, there could be an active volcano.

As we drew closer to the archipelago of Vanuatu and the island of Efate, the wind blew in stronger gusts from the north and then the northwest. The sky to the west took on a menacing look, becoming darker than the oncoming night. Thunder rumbled around the boat, and lightning flashed intermittently off in the distance. One day I took down the dipole radio antenna that we had been using to supplement the whip antennas, disconnected the radio wires, and stuffed them into a plastic bag behind the starboard oars. We tried to sleep, but by 2 a.m., the wind and waves were too strong to ignore.

"How are the sea anchors?" Curt asked. The day before, I had spent the afternoon untangling the ropes that led from the swivel to the grommet holes in the sea anchors. Though the swivel was supposed to prevent fouling of the lines, the boat's jerky motion and hard thrust from the waves caused the ropes to twist around each other and sometimes even unravel their braid.

"They're okay," I answered. "But I'm not sure you should put on your safety harness in this lightning when you go on deck." The metal clips on the front of the harness worried me.

Curt agreed and tied a plain rope around his waist instead. Thunder and lightning are the most frightening occurrences imaginable in a small boat. In our minds, lightning was apt to strike metal anywhere, including the safety harness.

The motion of the boat smoothed out noticeably with the sea anchor deployed from the stern. *Excalibur Pacific* slowed her southeast drift, and we were able to sleep easier. But in the morning Curt found the sea anchor had torn and was dangling by two ropes, side by side. I wondered how far south the boat had gone overnight. With Efate so near, what if we missed it and went into the Coral Sea?

One evening, as *Excalibur Pacific* drifted in calm seas, we were suddenly awakened by the sound of thousands of tiny pumice stones hitting the boat. It was startling, and we both fought for the chance to get out of the cabin first to see this phenomenon. For as far as the eye could see, a gray blanket of pumice floated on the nearly flat surface of the sea. It was an eerie scene, as we floated in the middle of it all in our orange rowboat. I fell back to sleep that night listening to the tinkling sounds of pumice as the boat drifted along.

June 27, 1985: A Quick Turnaround
in Efate Island, Vanuatu

Groggily, I opened my eyes after a fitful night's sleep. Something was different; the boat wasn't doing its usual back-and-forth dance through the waves. Curt got up on his knees and pushed the hatch door open. "Shit! Kathleen, get up! We've got to row!"

I pushed my way past him and saw to the northwest, less than a couple of miles away, the wooded shores of an island, which we assumed was Efate. Without a word, I knew what had to be done. Curt stumbled over the rowing stations to the rudder, while I shoved out a set of oars and began to row, pulling the bow of the boat around and pointing toward the island. *Excalibur Pacific* had drifted past the southeastern corner of the island and was headed in a southwesterly direction, away from Efate. Curt joined in the rowing, and within a short time we were headed in the direction of Port Vila, the island's capital. I pulled in my oars after a while and went into the cabin to make a snack.

"Hey, do you realize how close we came to Efate? How close we came to crash-landing on a reef?" I called out to him as I cut up the Australian canned cheddar cheese. I handed out a couple of sand-wiches and poured two cups of hot coffee.

"Yeah, very lucky, the navigation was almost too accurate," he agreed. It was frightening to consider how we had very nearly carried out our post-Samoa fantasy to end the crossing

The row along the Efate coast was pleasant as we took turns rowing and reading. We were reading a book apiece and one Law-rence Sanders murder mystery together. I rowed while Curt read out loud about the vicious Sanders' murderer and her victims. Sometimes I would ask to have a passage repeated, and then he had to almost shout above the banging of the dagger boards as they knocked about. Once we heard an engine, and I looked over to see a large, ungainly motorboat coming our way. From the deck, a small group of Mela-nesian fishermen gestured with ropes in their hands, offering to tow us to shore. On the nearby reefs, locals waved a handkerchief, franti-cally cautioning us of the dangers. We refused the tow and headed away from the reef with a friendly wave and smile, though if I had rechecked the *Sailing Directions* and saw that the coast around Efate still contained pockets of mines from World War II, as I later did in port, we might not have been so blasé about our welfare.

"These people are very nice," I commented. "Come on, it's my turn to read."

Eventually, the range lights of Port Vila appeared, and we lined up *Excalibur Pacific* to row into port on the east side of Mele Bay without further trouble in the early evening light. Melanesia, in the western South Pacific, was different enough from Polynesia that we looked forward to a stay here. In port, we found international sailboats, including Greenpeace's anti-nuclear testing ship *Rainbow Warrior* that was later bombed and sunk in Auckland, New Zealand by the French government. On shore were the remnants of a joint British and French condominium, which was a curious mix of Anglo–Franco rule. The indigenous Vanuatuans spoke a pidgin English in addition to the many dialects of their own languages. The result was an extremely diverse independent nation of hundreds of islands.

Efate was rainy and windy the week we were in port. When news of high pressure and calm seas came from the weather bureau, Curt pushed to leave right away, though I wanted to spend more time in port. We bickered over the departure date, but with the boat restocked with fresh eggs, potatoes, and fruit, Curt reasoned it was important to leave on the same day we had begun the row from Callao the previous year. I didn't see the connection in the same way he did.

So it was on July 4, 1985, exactly one year after the voyage began at Callao, Peru, that we paddled the dinghy out to *Excalibur Pacific* after a farewell meal at the local restaurant. Though we were still at odds over the quick turnaround on Efate, Curt insisted we film ourselves getting ready to leave and waving goodbye. I hated when he pushed me around like that, but it was easier to put on a public show of collegiality than refuse to be filmed. I sat down to row, imagining Curt breathing a sigh of relief that he was not going out alone. He pulled up the anchor, and we began rowing with the last of the incoming tide, as the plan was to be partway out of Mele Bay by high tide, so that during the night the outgoing tide could carry us safely clear of Devil's Point, a low wooded promontory located on the west end of Mele Bay. A large French container ship, *Capitane Cooke*, was leaving Port Vila, and when it came abreast of us, there were three loud farewell blasts from the ship. At the same time, the French flag on her stern dipped three times in salute and the sailors lined the gunwales, waving.

Not since leaving Callao had I felt so apprehensive, though at the same time I was confident in my ability to complete the row. We said little to each other as we pulled at the oars, each of us already in another world. This was the last leg of the voyage and its crux: the Coral Sea, the Great Barrier Reef, and Cairns, Australia.

CHAPTER 36

Through the Coral Sea

July 1985

T HESE DAYS ON THE ROWBOAT, life was not easy. I was sure I was pregnant, though we didn't talk about it much because the possibility that I was not one hundred percent up to the job in this most dangerous part of the expedition was not acceptable. Still, I was in the best shape of my life, and morning sickness no longer bothered me. Unfortunately, I had to go out on deck to pee at all hours of the day and night, and sleeping with my leg pulled up against the cabin wall wasn't as comfortable as it once was. The days of sleeping on my right side while facing the cabin wall were gone. This meant Curt was also sleeping on just one side, because we were able to sleep in the cabin together only if we interlocked our limbs like parts of a complex puzzle.

Curt's log: July 9
The weather has been remarkably good up to now until the sky filled in today. Unfortunately, I've seen a sun dog or round halo around the sun, which means inclement weather within 24 hours. The wind has been northeast Force 2 or 3 for four days. There's also a bit more swell from the southeast. I tried to get the weather report from Honolulu but they were off schedule.

One morning, I left Curt to his navigation and went out to set up my oars in the stern rowing station. I noticed more pumice than usual in the foot well, though there had been a fair amount since leaving Samoa six weeks prior. Initially, they were a great novelty, but after a few weeks the little floating stones were no longer so interesting.

I pulled at the oars, stroke after stroke, my arm and back muscles straining with the weight of extra food and water stores bought in Efate. The wind was now more out of the northeast, but the ocean swell was coming out of the southeast. I looked up at the sky, and there it was, a rainbow sun dog encircling the sun that meant bad weather ahead. The week of sunny skies and low rolling seas was about to end.

As we came closer to the Coral Sea, any kind of bad weather made us more apprehensive than ever. Sailors and merchantmen on ships all across the South Pacific had warned us of the unpredictable nature of the weather in this subtropical sea. Violent gales that could pop up out of nowhere were not uncommon, nor were currents that split off and flowed in different directions. As we rowed toward Australia's east coast, we were in the lower reaches of the west-flowing South Equatorial Current, the current system we had crossed most of the South Pacific on. At approximately 15 degrees south, the South Equatorial Current would merge with the south-flowing East Australia Current. We were coming from Efate Island at latitude 17 degrees 40 minutes south and heading to Cairns, located at 16 degrees 55 minutes south, but the combining of the two major currents took place over a wide region. We were so vulnerable to adverse currents that could push us in the opposite direction or drastically cut down on our forward progress, such as we had encountered at times between the Galápagos and Marquesas, that we worried about the difficulty we would have reaching our destination once we made it into the Coral Sea. We could take comfort only in the fact that, after a year on the rowboat, we were well acquainted with bad weather.

After my rowing stint, I checked the deck hatches for water leakage because the port and starboard hatches of the boat now leaked on a daily basis. The rubber silicon gaskets under the plastic hatch covers that Curt had replaced in Samoa were not doing their job. Most of the canned goods purchased in Samoa were now rusty and slimy from the seawater. When I bent down to take the cans out of the hatches to dry, the stinky whiff of mildew that wafted upward made me feel seasick, something I could no longer control with pills. It wasn't morning seasickness but the familiar heavy feeling in my eyes, nausea, and the dull headache.

Curt's log: July 10, 1985
We're putting more time into the navigation these days. In American Samoa, a sailor who was crewing on a fancy yacht gave me a dog-eared extra copy of the tables for H.O. 211, a complicated navigation method once used by air pilots. I was able to figure it out and in fact it helps me to pass the long days at sea. H.O. 211 basically enables us to solve for stars near the horizon, beneath the cloudbanks, unlike the H.O 249 system that Kathleen, who's been navigating alongside me since Samoa, uses as a double check.

When it comes time for star sights, usually there are large billowing cumulus or more frightening stratus clouds in the sky. Both of us have to be quick about sighting a star and taking the altitude reading before it goes behind a cloud. Often we have to shoot first and then identify the star later. One of us flips through the star charts while the other checks out the tables to help make an educated guess about its identity. Hopefully when we work out the solutions, the stars can be plotted on the same LOP [line of position] as our course. Most times it does.

Curt and I sat on deck and talked over the impending transit of the sea directly north of the Recife de Cooke. The reef was the first major obstacle to be negotiated as we began to make our way towards the Coral Sea and the Great Barrier Reef, which was littered with a maze of hundreds of coral reefs. The Recife de Cooke is part of the archipelago of the New Caledonia islands and reefs. From his star sights and my sun shots, Curt figured we would pass the reef at a comfortable distance of fifteen miles.

After dinner, though the seas were increasingly choppy, we planned to finish the day with several star sights to confirm our distance from the Recife de Cooke.

"Mark! Just one more in the southern sky." I wrote the time down and grabbed the navigation tables to start working out the sights. We had developed a healthy competition between us to see who could figure out where we were first.

"Did you end up with the same position I have?" I asked, hoping I was wrong. Curt took the plotting sheet and laid down his fixes. He looked at me, and we both grimaced at the same time. Our navigation showed us to be only five miles from the Recife. Incredibly, there seemed to be a gravitational force in the form of strong south-flowing currents. It was dark outside, with no stars to be seen. The sky had filled in, and the night looked menacing. With memories of the Hormigas off the Peruvian coast still vivid in our minds, though it was a year later, we set up an all-night watch. As I sat on the deck, huddled in a light jacket because the night air was cool, I listened for sounds of surf, though the wind could have carried any noise away.

It was an uneasy night in the choppy waves that were undoubtedly rebounding off the reef. In the early hours of the following morning, the waves lengthened out, and we knew we were past the reef and into the Coral Sea. By noon, the sun sights confirmed that *Excalibur Pacific* had cleared the reef.

The weather deteriorated, and the wind swung from the northeast to the southeast. The wind strength increased, and Curt put out an extra-heavy sea anchor that I had sewn in Efate. The boat pulled hard on the sea anchor, only to be jerked back with each wave. The weather was so difficult to row in that we spent most of the next two days in the cabin, coming out only when its walls became too confining.

"How're you doing out there?" Curt shouted from the cabin as I was setting up the bench one morning.

"I'm watching the storm," I shouted back. Though the sun was shining, the wind was blowing a mean Force 6 and the seas were breaking fast and furious. After two days of sitting cramped together inside, I needed some space to myself. Besides, Curt was in a cooking mood despite the nasty weather, and he had to use my side of bow cabin floor as well as his for the stove, flour, yeast, and tomato sauce. We were only able to cook in crazy conditions like this because we'd been doing it for almost a year now. With legs crossed and the food mixed up before we'd even light the stove, our bodies would sway back and forth easily with the motion of the boat.

While Curt worked on the afternoon's delicacy, I watched the stormy seas. They were both frightening and intimidating as they formed, dissolved, and reformed their pyramidal shapes, and I was fascinated. At one point, so focused was I on the whitish green waves off the stern that I didn't see one wave that grew and grew in height beside the boat until it crashed down on my head. I screamed in shock as gallons of cold seawater poured over me and nearly filled the deck. Inside the bow cabin, Curt protested as I frantically rocked the boat back and forth to empty the deck of the excessive water.

The new, bigger sea anchor was working hard off the stern. After the rough crossing from the Galápagos, we had bought extra cone-shaped ones in Tahiti, and in Efate I had sewn a couple of heavy ones that were bucket-shaped. Thanks to the loan of an extra-heavy grommet riveting kit from a German sailboat in Port Vila, the bucket-shaped anchor was turning out to be very effective at controlling the boat's drift. But as I watched, the brass swivel Curt had tied between the anchor and retrieval line was not really functioning properly to pivot the anchor and avoid any unraveling on both lines. I was contemplating whether to do anything about it, when I heard a shout from the cabin.

"Hey, Kathleen, it's done." I made my way to the bow hatch, holding tightly to the safety lines on the gunwales. I looked inside and saw Curt holding up a mouth-watering tomato cheese pizza in the fry pan. "I hope you like it!" I couldn't think of anything else that looked so good; Curt's Coral Sea pizza was simply the most delicious food I could imagine.

The stormy weather continued for another day, and when the sea anchor was pulled in, the retrieval line had completely unraveled and twisted out of shape, and was no longer useful. The power of the sea to destroy a heavy-duty rope like that never failed to impress us.

On the evening of July 11, we heard on Radio Australia that a mine in Auckland harbor had sunk the Greenpeace ship *Rainbow*

Warrior, their Portuguese photographer had been killed. We remembered seeing its crew in Efate working on the ship, which was anchored not far from *Excalibur Pacific*. We both felt it must have been sabotage. Later, a scandalous plot by the French government was uncovered, revealing the extent to which France was willing to go to censor outside knowledge of what they were doing with their nuclear testing program in the South Pacific.

The nearer we came to northeastern Australia and the end of the voyage, the greater was the danger of crashing onto a reef. The chart showed most of the reefs, but a number of uncharted reefs still existed on the approach to the Coral Sea. As we rowed into yet another reef area one day, the skies, which had been sunny, began filling in with a mixture of clouds. It was at a point in the voyage when we most needed good weather conditions. There were many reefs we had to go south of, and there were others that we had to go north of, to thread our way into the reef corridor that would lead us through the Coral Sea and to the middle of the Great Barrier Reef.

Shortly before we reached the corridor, another low pressure system moved into our area. Gale force winds began blowing out of the south with increasing speed, producing mountainous seas that crashed on and around the boat. The bucket sea anchor went out again as we tried to control our drift in the storm.

Despite the horrible conditions, we still needed to know where we were either through sun or star sights. To grab the sun or a star in those conditions was extremely difficult, because the seas were so rough and breaks in the clouds so fleeting. Curt or I would stagger along the deck clipped to the safety line and make our way to the aft cabin to pull on our waterproof jackets before bracing ourselves against the cabin bulkhead to take a sight, while the other would watch anxiously out the Lexan bow hatch.

In recent weeks, as we had closed in on the Coral Sea, I made regular contact with a couple of ham radio operators in Australia who were now following reports to our yachting friends and maritime nets of the horrendous weather conditions. Because we might need to signal for help as the weather deteriorated, Curt left up the dipole radio antenna, but one night amid strong winds, breaking waves crashed over the bow cabin and tore the radio wires down. From this point on, we were out of touch until we reached land.

We had just come through the corridor of outlying reefs, with dangers on either side, when yet another storm with gale force winds arrived on the heels of the last one. The Great Barrier Reef was less than one hundred miles away now; the wind blew hard, and huge waves thundered toward the boat. Rowing was out of the question. We double-tied everything as the conditions worsened, and I pumped saltwater into all the empty water bottles. The first night of this latest storm, Curt put out a bucket sea anchor to better hold our position. By the second day, it was far too rough to stream the sea anchor, so Curt pulled it in, and we just let the boat go wherever the waves pushed her, hoping it wouldn't be onto a reef.

Sleeping was impossible in the stormy weather, with the boat in a state of violent motion all the time. In the middle of the night on July 23, we were wedged against the cabin walls and trying to rest when there was the freight train sound of a wave roaring like no other we had heard before. It came closer and closer until it hit *Excalibur Pacific* with such impact that the boat was thrown onto its side, and in the next second, the wave rolled the boat over. One second we were on the wall, the next we were on the ceiling of the cabin. *Excalibur Pacific* had capsized.

"Aagghh, get off my elbow!" I screamed. The boat continued to roll, and we were back on the cabin floor in a jumbled heap on each other. She had righted herself. Bravo, Ed Montesi, *Excalibur Pacific*'s designer! She didn't roll over again, but the sea continued to throw us around violently. In the cabin, everything was in a state of disarray, though very little water had come in through the air vents. We mopped it up with a towel and flopped down to sleep.

CHAPTER 37

Black Clouds in the Coral Sea

July 1985

Black-gray waves broke hard everywhere. With each hissing crash, white foam slammed broadside to the boat. Overhead, threatening masses of steel-gray nimbostratus clouds grew steadily in bulk and size. Everywhere I looked, from the water to the sky, a gray cotton cocoon was smothering us with no way out.

The day had begun quietly when Curt went out to row at dawn and I stayed in the cabin to sleep another hour. The boat rocked as he pulled the oars in and out of the water, his hands moving forward and then, with a quick flick of the wrists, dropping his oar blades into the water against the enormous opposing weight. Over and over he rowed the same stroke, the boat making headway, steady as a tortoise moving over bumpy terrain.

In the cabin, sounds from his rowing seat mingled with the popping of millions of tiny bubbles outside cabin walls beside my head. Whoosh, the bubbles rushed by and I could almost feel them, as I lay wedged between the floor and the two-inch hull of the boat. The wall of the cabin was pleasantly cool against my skin.

The sounds and sensations were comforting and flowed into my half-wakeful state. I was suspended between two worlds: one of the illusion that I was floating in air, and the other of reality, where my mind connected what I was hearing to what I really knew. For an all-too-brief moment, I didn't know where I was. I didn't feel the fear and anxiety of rowing through the Great Barrier Reef, though another part of me knew it was one of the most treacherous areas of coral reefs in the world. I felt no concern for our safety and no dread for what might come as we navigated through a body of water notorious for sudden gales and high seas. It was completely restful. I rocked back and forth as if in Curt's hammock during the quiet days after leaving Ua Pou.

And then, *bam*, a fast-moving wave slammed hard against the port gunwale, and I was jarred awake. On deck, Curt swore as the oar handles dug into his gut and the boat tipped over hard to the starboard gunwales, burying his starboard oar.

"Damn shit fuck," he screamed, his favorite trio of swear words.

By now, it was no use trying to sleep anymore, because I had come down hard to earth and to the reality of what was outside the cabin. I sat up, reaching for the handholds on the ceiling. Without those yellow woven straps placed directly above our heads to hold on to, many things we did on the rowboat would have been impossible. I stuffed the sleeping bag into the forepeak, under the radio shelf. The foam sleeping pads were crammed on top of the bag. I was ready to make breakfast and coffee on the Camping Gaz stove. My head was still woolly from my deep sleep, but I took the floor hatch cover up to pull the stove and food items out and started the relaxing ritual of making a meal.

Curt stopped rowing and went to the rudder in the stern. I heard the tiny squeal of the Autohelm as it pushed the tiller back and forth to keep us on course. I imagined our course so much more efficient and safer at this stage of our voyage than if we'd had to tie off the tiller and adjust it only a couple of times a day. Having the Autohelm was like having an automatic 24/7 helmsman on board. By now, we had become so attached to it that we both grew anxious when we couldn't hear its electric squeal from the bow cabin. It was company for us, part of our carefully constructed world of isolation and self-sufficiency.

The dagger boards banged their muffled, comforting, calm thudding sound back and forth as Curt and I sat eating breakfast on the bench straddling the mid deck. As with the Autohelm, we listened for their rhythm as they banged back and forth in their slots.

I was tired and not much interested in conversation. Getting up at all hours to go out on the deck for bathroom matters was exhausting. The weather in the Coral Sea had proven unlike anything we had seen so far in the South Pacific. The waves were irregular and the wind would pick up with frightening intensity out of nowhere. To help calm our fears of another rollover or a swamping, we had decided to keep adding more weight to the boat by filling empty fresh-water bottles with saltwater. Just the act of hand-pumping gallons of saltwater in the empty bottles made me feel as though I had some control over my environment. Curt was spending most of the day calculating distance and plotting and re-plotting the course to the Australian mainland, which was now only fifty miles away.

This morning we sat in silence as the sun shone brightly, while a brisk breeze ruffled the blue sea slightly. It was as though the demons of the Coral Sea came out only at night, in the darkness when we were left to imagine the chaos they were creating.

"I'm going to work on the morning sights and see where we are now," said Curt. I nodded and reached for his bowl to wash with mine. I planned to row for a few hours and then sit on deck to read or think.

Curt's log: July 25, 1985
It was during one of the brief periods of sleep last night that I had the same dream I'd had before on Aconcagua. I was walking up the meadow on the hillside. Trees were sparse as I gained altitude. This time I didn't wake up before I reached the top of the mountain. The summit was the most perfect, idyllic setting. The meadow was beautiful; the trees around the large clearing were perfectly formed. There was a wall around the grounds of what seemed to be a monastery. From the gate, a man dressed in white walked toward me and shook my hand and pointed the way to the pass.

Now it is clear, southeast wind Force 4 to 5. We are approaching the reef by Noggin Pass where we'll transit the Great Barrier Reef. We should be there by tomorrow.

After rowing, I sat on deck lost in daydreams. In my mind, I was not on the boat. The ocean surrounded me, but I was not here. In physical form, I was sitting on the boat bench, legs stretched out in front of me, ankles crossed. My back was propped against the sweep oars with a pillow to cushion the hardness of the carbon fiber oars. My baseball cap lessened the brightness of the Australian sun while a light wind blew gently over me.

First, I went into past memories and visualized them in my mind. I began to see what I was remembering and I was becoming different people so that those memories had a multitude of variations. In each one, I was someone different, even though the events were the same.

Hours passed in this game of mental charades. The environment no longer affected me because I was somewhere else now. I was in Ecuador, on the dockside, the day we were told it was a bad idea to row out of Guayaquil. I remembered my stomach tightening as the shipping agent told us that squads of speedboats tracked down people in small boats to kill and rob them throughout the Gulf of Guayaquil. All we needed to do was row out of this port in our big orange rowboat with all our gear on deck, and we were instant targets. These pirates knew we had money and valuable equipment on the boat.

I visualized again the drive into Guayaquil, sharing the back of the shipping agent's truck bed with young kids who had stowed away on *Santa Paula*, the freighter we had traveled on for the past three weeks. It was the second or third time for these Ecuadorans to flee their country for America. Presumably, they would survive in the shipping container for the month or so it would take to reach Philadelphia. I imagined myself as one of those stowaways and wondered how to stay alive in a twenty-foot metal box deep in the bowels of a freighter.

In my mind's eye, I saw again the shocking poverty along the road into Guayaquil, where people lived in cardboard huts with rusted sheet-metal roofs. The garbage scattered along the road and throughout the shantytowns boggled the mind. How could any government official drive by these slums and ignore their existence while living in fancy villas with maids and air conditioning? How could they hold their heads up?

My thoughts moved to what we were doing: rowing across an ocean. Doing something that was entirely hedonistic. Something that would not benefit anyone but ourselves. I stopped before my thoughts went too far in that direction, and I fast-forwarded to memories of *Strider Fearless*, the feeder ship that took us south to Callao, Peru, for a safer departure point. I focused in on the captain and first mate of the ship and my mood began to lift.

I saw myself walking about the ship in my little red shorts and red T-shirt. Everyone seemed to be crazy about me, and my mood lifted even more. "Kathy, Kathy!" the Philippine crew and British officers called when we walked down the gangplank after arriving in Callao.

"Good-bye, everyone!" I called back, waving my hand like a movie star. Intuitively then, I knew I had gathered enough fantasy memories to last me for months on the ocean crossing. I knew because I had been a great daydreamer for years, and all good daydreamers know they always need a cache of juicy memories to review and dissect at any moment. Especially at the moment when it's time to slip away from the "madding crowd."

Except this time there was no crowd to escape from. There was only one other person on this boat, and he was in the cabin at the moment. My daydreaming at sea may not have been the same as on land, but the intention was similar. I wanted to go somewhere else for a while in my mind.

Now I was in the captain's quarters with Curt, drinking shots of Johnny Walker Red and laughing hysterically with everyone at the sight of our newly purchased bottles of Johnny Walker Black sliding back and forth on the captain's desk with the ship's movement in the rolling seas. I turned to say something silly to the captain and saw a dark, almost black cloud in the porthole behind his head.

I blinked, and the *Strider* memory was gone. I looked hard at the real blackness spreading on the horizon in front of me. I was back on the rowboat in the Coral Sea, and the skies were no longer filled with pretty white clouds. A gray blanket covered the sky and was reflected in the waves, which had sharp, breaking peaks.

I sat up straighter and dropped my legs on either side of the bench. The wind had increased noticeably, and I resettled the baseball cap on my head. My stomach began to tighten, as it had for days since we left Efate.

The blackness was coming closer, and the waves were growing. I jumped up and grabbed the cabin hatch and yanked it open.

"Curt, you should see this weather coming at us. Close the ports on your side."

He looked up startled from his reading but reached, without a word, for the knobs on the ports to batten them down. I backed away from the hatch, but I had to hold tight to the safety lines that ran alongside the gunwales. The wind was now blowing a Force 6, near gale-force strength.

Curt came out and turned his head toward the nightmare that was coming our way. He headed directly for the stern cabin, clutching the safety lines hard.

"I'm going to put out the sea anchor!" he yelled in the rising wind. His words were torn from his mouth, but I saw what he was doing despite the diminishing light.

"Okay, I'm going to tie down the bench and stuff on deck," I yelled above the keen of the rising wind and tried to balance myself on the heaving deck. I looked over my shoulder and saw with horror that the blackness was almost upon us.

"Get in the cabin!" Curt yelled as he gave me a hand with the last knots. I reached for the hatch, and the wind practically tore it out of my hand. I dove headfirst into the cabin and did a quick turnabout so Curt wouldn't crash into me. We held on to the ceiling straps for another wild ride in the Coral Sea.

CHAPTER 38

The Great Barrier Reef
and Landfall

July 1985

I WAS SCANNING THE HORIZON FOR a sign of Hedley Reef when a mass of coral heads below the boat caught my gaze through the emerald-tinted waters. My eyes widened as fear struck. Had we rowed unknowingly onto Hedley Reef? The very idea of it only a few feet below the boat was enormously frightening.

Earlier in the day Curt had plotted a course to Hedley, which was at the entrance to Noggin Passage. Between the many reefs that make up the Great Barrier Reef are navigation channels of varying lengths that usually go in a north-to-south direction. As the wind and current generally flow north, we had chosen Noggin Passage because it went from a northeast-to-southwest direction, making it easier for us to row sideways to the wind instead of directly into it.

The plan was that if we reached Hedley Reef in daylight, we would enter Noggin Passage. But now, it seemed clear that *Excalibur Pacific* had floated onto an entirely different reef, because we had been rowing for only two hours and could not have reached Hedley so soon—unless Curt was off in his calculations.

Curt grabbed the chart and guessed that we were in an area of uncharted reefs that were approximately fifteen miles south of

Hedley Reef. I wondered out loud if we would reach it before dark.

He sat down in the bow seat and began rowing while I stood at the stern cabin, steering in and out of reefs as the water alternated between dark blue and emerald. The wind gusted occasionally, and ripples on the water's surface indicated a shallow area.

"What's that?" We listened and turned toward the sound off the port side. In the distance, breakers crashed down on a reef barely visible above the water.

The afternoon was drawing to a close, and we had been anxious to be away from the reefs by now. I set the course due east and sat down to row with Curt for another hour. Hedley Reef was still distant by four o'clock, so we decided to put out a sea anchor to slow the boat's drift in the night. Tired and uncertain about what was to come, I crawled into the cabin and fished out a package of Kraft processed cheese to have with crackers, while Curt cut up citrons to mix with sugar cane left over from Tahiti for a fruit drink we liked very much.

A light tinkling interrupted our thoughts. It was vaguely familiar, like tiny pieces of broken glass falling slowly to a hard surface. We both froze. The sound was notorious in our memories. It was the sound of the shoal wave in the Galápagos. We rushed out on deck and in the waning light of the moon, I saw that the reef was there under the boat. The incoming tide had pulled us onto yet another reef, but one that was shallower than the others.

"Should we drop the anchor and stop this drifting?"

We knew very well the risks of such an action. The chart was explicit:

"CAUTION: *Former mined areas exist in the Barrier Reef.* [The mines dated from World War Two] *Trinity Opening, Flora Pass, and Noggin Passage have been swept and opened to surface navigation only. They are not safe for anchoring, trawling or bottom travel by submarine owing to mines.*"

"It's a risk, don't you think?"

"Yeah, but I think it's a good idea. We might already be on Hedley Reef. Besides, we can't take a chance floating around here at night with the extreme tides."

Curt was convinced anchoring for the night was better than floating freely. Another factor was also at work, unfortunately, because the sun's and moon's declinations were unusually high and were creating extra-high spring and extra-low neap tides. An extreme tide could carry us anywhere throughout the Great Barrier Reef in the night.

With fingers crossed, Curt let go the anchor while paying out two hundred feet of line that was connected to a couple of feet of chain directly attached to the anchor. It held, and the movement of the boat stopped. In the pale moonlight, in the middle of the Coral Sea, I looked around at the strange beauty of the largest coral barrier in the world that was surrounding the boat as it tugged lightly at its anchor line. The water covering the reefs was calm, and the air was quiet, though it felt charged with energy, with the gentle sound of waves raking backward and forward over shallows. It was one of those moments, as I had encountered so many times on the South Pacific and the Atlantic Oceans, when I knew I was experiencing something about the planet that no one could ever teach me. Later, when I went back on deck to wash up that night, I surveyed the moonlit sea covering the Great Barrier Reef only a few feet below the boat and wondered what the next day would bring.

The sound of heavy surf and bright sunshine welcomed us in the morning of July 29. At first I didn't know where we were; my mind was disconnected from the boat as I lay there, wedged on my side of the cabin. The boat rocked lightly side to side, and with my eyelids shut, I didn't want to come to the surface of full consciousness. I didn't really want to open my eyes to face another day in the Coral Sea.

Curt looked out the hatch and saw that the heavy surf was breaking only two hundred feet off the stern while the boat floated in relatively calm water. From the gunwale, he saw the barrier reef glittering below the boat. The high tide had come in during the night with a rising wind, and now there was a line of white foaming breakers at the edge of Hedley Reef that surged with barely restrained violence toward the boat. Somewhere in the midst of all that mayhem was the anchor buried with the boat's chain and line.

I sat up reluctantly and turned over to look out of the cabin hatch. The waves were scary, but as long as the anchor was holding, we could eat breakfast and figure out what to do next. Curt wanted to spend some time videotaping the scene, though I thought we should get off the reef as soon as we finished breakfast. When he pointed out the fantastic opportunity to photograph the reef up close, I had to concede he was right. Afterward, I planned to take a few sun sights to confirm our proximity to Noggin Passage.

We suited up in heavy-weather jackets and clicked on the safety harnesses. I put my arms around Curt as he lowered the video gear into the water in a bulky fiberglass box that he had built in Vermont. When we looked at the video later, the sight was incredible: iridescent tropical fish swimming in and out of coral heads as sea anemones waved back and forth in the surging water. There was a fantastic world beneath our boat and no sign of the coral bleaching that was to come years later.

The anchor would not budge, but we needed it for the next few nights before and after reaching Australia, so I sat down to the oars. Curt pulled hard on the line leading to the short chain attached to the anchor as I backed the boat toward the breaking waves. But the line kept slipping through his hands and burned his skin. He grabbed again and pulled as hard as he could, but this time only thirty feet of line came up. I stopped backing the boat just before the white lines of breaking waves. We tried together, but the anchor must have been wrapped tightly around a coral head. It was obvious we would have to let it go unless we were willing to row into surf that would swamp the boat. We decided to abandon the anchor. Curt grabbed the machete a Marquesan had given us last March and hacked at the thick nylon line until *Excalibur Pacific* gave one last jerk and we were floating free.

A quarter mile to the west, we could see the part of Hedley Reef that was above the water with heavy breakers pounding its edges. The exposed reef confirmed what the sun sight had told us:

we needed to row for another two miles or so, and then make a turn to enter Noggin Passage and begin the twenty-mile-long southwest row to the Inner Run that would eventually lead us north to Cairns.

"Look, it's land! That's got to be Clump Mountain!" In the late afternoon, I spotted the purplish outlines of land on the southwest horizon and then checked the *Sailing Directions* to confirm that the sketched version matched the one I was looking at. It was the same and our first sight of Australia. We laughed that our first sighting of the Australian mainland was in the lumpy, rounded shape of a mountain called Clump.

Once we rowed into Noggin Passage, the deep blue waters with a southwest tidal flow indicated we were going in the right direction. At about four in the afternoon, Curt took another sun sight and calculated that we were two miles from the end of Noggin Passage and just about into the Inner Run, a shipping lane inside the majority of the reefs that make up the Great Barrier Reef. It varies in width from five to ten miles, depending on the pass a boat enters from. At that point, the Inner Run was only five miles or so from shore, but in a rowboat with strong diurnal tides to contend with, it was difficult maintaining our position.

As we rowed, the usual bad afternoon weather set in and the entire sky and horizon were blanketed with grayness and heavy rain showers. Strong, gusty winds blew out of the south, and it was difficult to hold the course with the wind and waves battering the downwind side of the boat. Finally, the squall passed overhead, and the sun slowly disappeared in the western sky behind Clump and the rest of the visible mountains of Queensland.

Curt's log: July 29, 1985
We weren't able to get to Cairns today. This means an all-night watch, taking lines of position from the visible lighthouse beacons. Just before dark, after calculating our LOP, I found that *Excalibur Pacific* is safely within the Inner Run, though it would be better to be in the middle of the Run when the tide returns so we won't be carried back out the passage we've worked so hard to transit.

The winds died down as we headed into the cabin for the night. I've set the Casio watch for 20-minute intervals when I plan to take bearings from the lighthouses north and south of our position. Throughout the night, I'll give the bearings to Kathleen so she can plot them on the chart. At around 3 a.m., I plan to put out the sea anchor so when the tide goes down, we won't lose ground.

July 30. By first light, I saw that we were very close to land, in fact closer than we imagined. The tide was in the process of coming in through the passes and we had drifted a ways inland from Cape Grafton, a large rocky promontory to the north that protrudes into the Inner Run. To get to Cairns, we would have to row around Cape Grafton. The weather has deteriorated again with the wind and waves coming out of the south with the usual rotten rain squalls and darkening skies. The wind is pushing us toward shore and it is going to be difficult to row around the Cape today. A wide sandy beach only a few miles off the port side of the boat beckons. We're going to row for it.

With mounting excitement, we rowed *Excalibur Pacific* steadily toward the beach. Curt stopped to tie the video camera on the roof of the aft cabin and turn it on to record our arrival. Within a short distance from the beach, with the bottom coming up fast, I put down my oars to pull up the dagger boards, and when the water grew even shallower, Curt pulled up the rudder. The boat suddenly skewed to the side and we had to pull harder on the port side to bring the boat around as the waves broke faster.

"Damn!" The port oar in Curt's hand snapped in half. I paused for a microsecond and then reached wide to grab more water with my port oar. Exhilarated by the danger and perhaps playing to the camera, Curt jumped up and began shouting to row harder on the starboard as the boat began to zigzag. Without missing a stroke, I yelled at him to sit down and keep rowing with his starboard oar so the boat wouldn't go broadside to the waves and flip over. He looked at me and then sat down, and together we pulled the boat straight for the beach, where *Excalibur Pacific* hit the sand with a thud. Curt grabbed the mess of mooring ropes and jumped out of the boat in the shallow water while I slumped over my oars, exhausted but deeply content.

When I turned around in my rowing seat to see where we had landed, I saw a broad sandy beach that stretched for miles to the north and south with no sign of development. No one was waiting for us under the eucalyptus trees that fringed the beach or "bringing us kangaroo steaks" as Curt later joked.

With the video camera still running and the tide steadily going out, Curt whooped it up waving around the Explorers Club and Australian flags, while I pulled in my oars quietly and stood up to survey our choice of landing spot. For the first time since pulling *Excalibur Pacific* out of the water at Ua Pou island months earlier, we were aground.

We had completed the rowing voyage of ten thousand miles across the South Pacific in 392 days, or 189 days of just rowing, by landing on a remote and uninhabited beach in northern Queensland. The "official" ending to the voyage would come, 12:20 p.m., the next day, July 31, after we had pushed off at high tide, 9:00 p.m., from what is now known as the Wooroonooran National Park and rowed through the night north around Cape Grafton and west to the port of Cairns.

When we rowed up to the dock at Cairns after calling on the VHF to the port officials, the Australians who stood fishing at the quay stared down at us in disbelief. The immigration officials, dressed nattily in their khaki bush shorts and neatly pressed shirts, politely took our passports and waited with us on our boat while their main office confirmed that we had indeed rowed from Port Vila on July 4 and had in fact, rowed in and out of a series of island ports across the South Pacific: Puerto Arroyo, Santa Cruz island, Ecuador; Hakahau, Ua Pou island, French Polynesia; Pago Pago, Tutuila island, American Samoa; and Port Vila, Efate island, Vanuatu, before arriving in their Queensland port of Cairns over a year later.

One Aussie looked at us doubtfully and shook his head, saying he figured because we were Americans completing a rowing voyage across the broadest ocean in the world that there would have been masses of publicity, swooping helicopters, and honking boat horns broadcasting our arrival. After all, Americans never did anything modestly, he reckoned. But we surprised them; we impressed one older man so much he pulled out a five-dollar Australian bill from his wallet for us to spend on our first (second, really) night in the Land Down Under.

Within a week, we had been invited to appear on television with a well-known Australian celebrity talk show host. What had ended so abruptly on the Atlantic row in Antigua when family and friends had greeted us in English Harbour was more under our control in Cairns and later Sydney. Friendly Queenslanders who had heard about our row from the newspapers and news programs invited us to stay in their homes as we worked out the details of transporting ourselves and boat back to the United States. Thanks to our appearance on the *Mike Wilersy Show* in Sydney and a flattering article that called us "the quiet Americans" as though we were a breed of Yank far from the usual, the ACTA/PACE shipping company offered to ship the boat home for free.

Amid the busy days that followed our arrival, we were able to find moments of privacy to appreciate what we had accomplished. In a pub one night, the friendly barmaid offered her family's empty home in Avalon to stay in for a few days until we worked out the details of shipping *Excalibur Pacific* from Cairns by roadway to the port of Sydney. In the quiet of Avalon, a Sydney suburb that rang with the occasional crazy song of the kookaburra, we talked between ourselves about the row and my pregnancy, which we decided to keep to ourselves while in Australia. By now, I was nearly five months pregnant but not showing at all. As nice as the Aussies had been to us, people always made cracks about the supposed difficulties of living with a spouse in such close living quarters. Before the Atlantic row and at boat shows afterward, more than one person said they couldn't imagine paddling across a river never mind an ocean with their spouse. If we shared the pregnancy news, I could just guess what sort of questions and jokes that would provoke.

By completing the South Pacific row, we had become the first couple to row across the South Pacific Ocean, and I became the first woman to row across two oceans. It wasn't until 1988 that the *Guinness Book of World Records* officially acknowledged our long distance rowing record in a print copy of their book and later listed me on their online site for my two ocean rows. The *GBWR* is a British publication, and we couldn't help but notice that they tended to post the long-distance rowing accomplishments of their fellow Brits first, before other nationalities.

Despite the new records we had achieved, more important to me was what I had learned over the past year, combined with the lessons of the Atlantic row. This was something of far greater profundity than the physical aspect or the setting of extreme adventure records. With each successful leg of each row, when I touched land again after what had felt like an extra-planetary experience, I affirmed that I was capable of doing more than I ever thought possible. In the exquisite moments of danger, wonder, and beauty in isolation, I understood it was all about making choices and taking responsibility for decisions. It wasn't just a matter of sticking it out with Curt on the boat the whole way, I had to acknowledge in being honest with myself. There was something in me that always wanted to see what was around the next corner. Now, having finished the South Pacific row and expecting a baby in four months' time, I was ready to continue exploring our Thoreauvian "private sea" and discover where we might go from here.

When I completed my second ocean row, I was only twenty-nine but I knew then that I would always be "on the road," not as a sort of female Jack Kerouac but in my own never-ending journey as outsider and explorer, as Other who would travel to foreign lands and cultures, in and out of familiar space and time, leaving only when I was ready to return.

CHAPTER 39

Sydney, Australia

August 1985

T HE AUSSIE TOOK A SIP of his white wine and said, "You don't look like . . . uh . . . someone who could row a boat across an ocean."

I studied the shipping executive, dapper in his single-breasted blue suit, an expression of perplexity on his smooth-shaven face, and then I smiled. It was two weeks after finishing the South Pacific row and Curt and I were in Sydney at a reception given for us by the board of directors of ACTA/PACE, an Australian shipping company with interests all over the world. The executive's board was considering shipping our rowboat back to America gratis after our successful row.

"Yeah," I answered. I could hear my American drawl as it clashed with his Aussie twang. "Well, I've been rowing for years, you know. I started in college and, uh, I've been rowing ever since." I smiled broadly, and he nodded to the waiter to bring another glass of wine.

I went on to entertain the executive and his colleagues with a story about rowing through their country's Great Barrier Reef to complete the voyage, only to find we had chosen to make landfall at a remote aboriginal reserve with not a single person in sight. They laughed heartily at the image I drew of myself nearly getting sucked into a quicksand pit as we scoured the area looking for people and roads. I still felt the horror of the moment, as the ground beneath my feet slowly sank and how in desperation I flailed around for a bush, something to grab, and pulled myself out.

Curt came over and joined in the storytelling, describing the fright of the thunderous breaking waves on the coral reefs surrounding our boat that we'd felt only two weeks earlier, when our lives were all about rowing a small boat across an ocean and not corporate schmoozing. From their body language, as they leaned in close to Curt, I could tell the middle-aged men were thinking, "Crikey, that guy's got balls! He's unbelievable!" They nodded their heads vigorously, their eyes wide as he talked of the fright of the boat rolling over in the Coral Sea and the thrill of fighting sharks along the South American coast and during the row from French Polynesia to Samoa.

I sipped at my tonic water and listened. I wanted them to fund the $5,000 shipping fee and be impressed with my own accomplishments too. As the reception wore on, though, I found myself standing back from the crowd surrounding Curt and downplaying my role in the expedition's success so that these men would not be uncomfortable with me, a woman who had not only rowed across the South Pacific Ocean but had rowed across another ocean four years earlier.

In the weeks since finishing the South Pacific row, we were still processing what it had been all about. We had lived together, loved together, and fought together in a space and situation that few people in the world could ever imagine. Our lives on the ocean rowboat had been the result of a choice, not of the chance outcome of some unanticipated circumstance, like a shipwreck, for example. Between us, though, there was a difference in how each related to what we'd gleaned within the privacy of our little world on board twenty-five-foot *Excalibur Pacific*. She had been the best of learning environments, as far as I was concerned, and I was not sure that I was ready to share what I had learned on her deck with the rest of the world so soon.

While I recognized that part of accepting sponsorship was about sharing exciting stories of how we survived the expedition's challenges, I found it difficult to reduce what I felt to be the profoundness of my experiences to sensational life-threatening anecdotes. It was hard to talk about how difficult it was to keep going, island stop after island stop, to remain motivated and finish the voyage, with people who didn't know what it was like to be alternately scared to death, physically weary and mentally worn out by the drudgery of toiling on the oars day after day, and spellbound by the utter and absolute uniqueness of living on the ocean's surface alone and for so long. We hadn't been rowing just for our immediate survival but for a future that we were constantly trying to guarantee for ourselves and, soon, for our child.

For Curt, who lived in the present, that future time was now, in that boardroom with the ACTA/PACE executives, for they wanted to be entertained for their money and he reveled in recreating the adventure in the light of their admiration. As armchair adventurers, they were vicariously buying an adventure through us.

Curt and I had been perfectly matched on our rows in this respect, because he was an explorer who loved to push the limits of what was possible and then celebrate the achievement in ways that bestowed public recognition, while I was the explorer who, though I loved to go to that same edge, would be the cautious one who always knew when to pull back.

After our meeting, ACTA/PACE did give us free shipping for *Excalibur Pacific* from Sydney to the port of Newark, New Jersey, while Curt and I flew Air Zealand back to the East Coast of America. From our bulkhead seats across the aisle from a woman with her newborn baby, we watched as she gently put the baby in the fold-down bassinet, fascinated and knowing that we too would be parents in late December or early January 1986.

PART IV

NEW IDENTITIES AND NEW LIVES

CHAPTER 40

The Boat Shows
and Life on Land

WE ARRIVED BACK IN THE United States in late summer 1985 and took the train into Manhattan to meet with people from the National Marine Manufacturers Association (NMMA), which had contacted us while we were in Australia to participate in boat shows. In 1981 and 1982, we had exhibited *Excalibur* at the Norwalk, Connecticut and Philadelphia boat shows with the NMMA. Now they wanted us for the prestigious New York, Philadelphia, and Miami boat shows, which were going to bring in a nice bit of change for us. To make the most of our profits, we negotiated for full fees for the three shows, saying we would find our own lodgings and be responsible for getting the boat to each venue.

In Manhattan, we met with Frank Scalpone, the managing director at NMMA, and his assistants to talk about the shows that would begin in January 1986. They wanted us in New York for the first show at the old New York Coliseum right after Christmas. This was going to be a challenge for me, because the baby was due about that time. We did not share the baby news with Scalpone, because we thought he would cancel us out of our three-show contract. All through our meeting I held a coat in front of my stomach because by then I was about six months pregnant and beginning to show. They didn't notice a thing.

Return to Vermont

With *Excalibur Pacific* in tow, we returned to Morgan, Vermont, to housesit a family friend's house as we had done the previous winters. I pulled out my old Smith-Corona typewriter and wrote letters to a number of private schools and clubs I had researched at the local library. The response was good, and we scheduled a series of lectures in the Northeast and Middle Atlantic states. We charged $350 for each lecture at the suggestion of Beth Ruze, whom we had met in Pago Pago, American Samoa, in April 1985. Beth had completed her contract with the Tutuila public school system and was back in the United States.

We spent the fall of 1985 driving to schools with our trays of color slides and giving joint presentations on the Pacific and Atlantic Oceans, Mississippi River, and Labrador coast expeditions. Initially, we had prepped by looking through all our Kodachrome and Ekta-chrome slides and putting together a narrative that we could share back and forth. We worked well as presentation partners, easily picking up the thread of narration from each other. Our lectures mirrored our partnership on the boat: I talked about radio communication and boat supplies, while Curt spoke about the navigation. We both shared what it had been like to build the boat and overcome the doubts of people who told us it was impossible to row an ocean.

Throughout the fall, we continued the lecture tour, staying closer to Morgan as I advanced in my pregnancy. On or about January 1, my doctor said the baby was nearly due and could be induced. This was good news, because the boat shows were drawing closer, and within a couple of weeks we would have to be in Manhattan for the opening of the New York Boat Show.

On January 3, I went into the hospital and began the induced labor. At about 8:30 p.m. on January 4, our beautiful baby boy, Christopher Morgan Saville, was born safe and sound.

Within the day, Curt had to leave alone for New York with *Excalibur Pacific* in tow. He drove south to New York City and delivered the boat to the loading docks of the Coliseum, where Frank Scalpone and the other NMMA people were finally apprised of my pregnancy. Frank was not pleased—in fact, he was furious I wasn't available for the pre-boat show publicity they had arranged. Curt knew Frank was going to be mad, so he came prepared with a box of cigars to celebrate the birth of Christopher.

The day before Christopher's birth, we had arrived at the hospital with no insurance or other means of paying for my stay. Fortunately, I was informed that the hospital would cover most of the cost through their private donors' fund. I was embarrassed to be given such charity, though we had no other way to pay the bill. After all the glory and accolades about our successful South Pacific row, the humiliating talk with the hospital billing office brought me down hard to earth.

Our good friends Ruby and Ken Jenness took me and the baby back to their home from the hospital. The next day Ken drove us to Massachusetts, where I was picked up by Explorers Club friend Bobbie Cochran from Westchester, New York. Within three days, I was gingerly making my way up the West End highway with Christopher in arms to the Coliseum. The stitches from giving birth were still sensitive, and I had to walk very carefully for the next week and a half while appearing at the boat show every day.

After the New York show ended, we headed to Philadelphia, where *Excalibur Pacific* was exhibited and we stayed with a friend from Curt's Peace Corps days. From Philly, we drove south to Miami, stopping to visit Curt's parents in Durham, North Carolina. When the Miami Boat Show opened in March, the baby was two months old and was a regular road warrior. When we weren't staying with family or friends, we camped in the boat, and the shelf that had once held the TR-7 transceiver radio on the South Pacific became the baby's bed, which he took to readily. It was as though he instinctively knew the boat had been his first home.

When the boat shows finally ended in March, we drove back north on I-95, towing *Excalibur Pacific* behind the new used Datsun 810 sedan that friends had helped us acquire to replace the once trusty Pinto wagon. Rust had so consumed the body and framework of the Pinto that when Curt drove it to a car dump outside of Philadelphia, his foot went through the floor when he pressed on the brakes. He and the Pinto barely made it to the dump in one piece.

In April 1986, with the proceeds of the boat shows, we bought twenty-four acres of open and wooded land in northern Vermont. We began building "Casa Grande," our tongue-in-cheek name for a tiny two-story house that was only twenty feet by twenty-two feet square. One warm late spring weekend, my family came up from Rhode Island and we poured a cement foundation for the house along the edges of the original 1880s cellar hole. While my brother and father mixed bags of cement and my mother, sister, and I tamped down endless wheelbarrows of freshly made cement mix, Curt acted as the general foreman, measuring and determining where the house frames would go once the cement dried. The baby spent his days in the canvas tent we set up by the house site or slept soundly in his stroller under the apple tree, fitted out with a white mosquito net to protect him from the newly hatched black flies.

By early June, with the help of friends, we had the house framed and plywood sheets tacked on the walls. There was no insulation yet, but it wasn't a problem with the warming summer weather. Since there was no electricity on our end of the town road, we took some of the solar panels off the ocean rowboat and electrified the house with solar panels and car batteries. Until a well was drilled on the property later in the fall, we regularly filled two- and five-gallon water bottles left over from the rowing expeditions from the nearby Morgan town spring.

Christopher and I spent our first summer in the house while Curt returned to the Arctic with friends from the Explorers Club. The upstairs of the front of the house did not have windows yet, so when it rained, I covered things with a plastic tarp. At night the baby and I sat by flickering candlelight, playing and listening to the cicadas and the occasional owl hooting in the woods below the house.

In the fall, Curt and I made plans to go to Moosehead Lake in northern Maine with *Excalibur Pacific* for ten-month-old Christopher's first boating expedition. Across northern Vermont and New Hampshire, the Datsun towed the boat until we reached Rockwood on the western shores of Moosehead Lake. The baby sat strapped in his car seat while we struggled for almost an hour to get the boat off the trailer and into the lake's cold waters, until one of us realized that the two four-foot dagger boards were in place, which was preventing the boat from sliding off the trailer. It seemed strange that both of us would have made such a stupid mistake. I worried that I was losing my ocean rower's savvy and becoming a domesticated landlubber.

Once I pulled up the dagger boards and set them on the deck, the boat slid off the trailer easily, and Curt went to park the car in a lot nearby. It was late in the day, and we were anxious to row to a spot on Moosehead where we could pull the boat up on shore for the night.

Dusk was falling quickly as we set our course across the lake's choppy waters. The baby, whom I had put in the bow cabin so we could both row, screamed and cried out his frustration at being put in the cabin alone. I felt terrible listening to his mournful cries while I pulled on the oars. It was the first time since finishing the Pacific row in July 1985 that I was rowing in *Excalibur Pacific*. My heart was divided. Who was I: Kathleen, the tough-ass ocean rower, or Kathleen, the full-time mother to baby Christopher? My identity at that moment was in conflict. This boat I had built alongside Curt in a Rhode Island barn because we fervently believed in our ability to row across the Atlantic Ocean, and later the South Pacific, was now a different place. It was a place we shared with an innocent child of our own creation.

That night, we pulled the boat ashore in a remote cove on the eastern side of the lake. We had made the bumpy crossing with the baby intact, but I wasn't the same. Though I knew and loved *Excalibur Pacific* better than any house or home in my childhood years of constant moving, she was not quite the boat I had known on the ocean. I was less certain of myself with the baby on board. The boat and our lives were changing.

Early Explorers Expedition and Turning Points

It was late January 1988, and we had just completed boat exhibition gigs in Kansas City and Minneapolis. We were now driving west to southern California for the start of the "Early Explorers Expedition," our proposed epic journey to circumnavigate the North American continent. The idea of the Early Explorers Expedition, hatched over the long winter in Vermont, was to follow the routes of old explorers along the west and east coasts of America and Central America, through the Gulf of Mexico, eventually ending in a transiting of the Northwest Passage and south to California.

I drew up a simple design for an expedition logo and had stationery printed so I could send out letters to former ocean-rowing sponsors. We envisioned the expedition as an educational product we could sell to schools for an ongoing lecture series that would be given between legs of the journey. This time, though, we were out of luck. No one was interested in sponsoring the formerly successful ocean-rowing couple who claimed they could not only row around the entire North American continent but do it with a two-year-old child who would grow up along the way.

When we arrived in San Pedro, California, at the home of a couple we had met on the freighter to South America at the start of the South Pacific row, we had only a vague idea of how we were going to get the expedition financed and on the water. The couple very kindly allowed us to stay in their spare bedroom for a few weeks while the ocean rowboat was parked in the small parking lot of their ocean-front mobile-home community. Within a week, we were introduced to local legend John Olguin, who was director emeritus of the Cabrillo Maritime Museum and founder of the Cabrillo Whalewatch program. John took us under his wing and helped us to find sponsorship for a trimmed-down version of our expedition. He understood, somehow, what we were going through as a once-celebrity couple with a small child at odds with our altered identities. With John's enthusiastic endorsement, his friends and acquaintances agreed to sponsor our rowing and sailing down the Baja Coast to Mexico and maybe the Panama Canal. We would still have the added excitement of a two-year-old aboard the rowboat. In fact, one article written about us at the time was entitled "Rowing Family Explores the World by Sea," with a photo of Christopher perched on the roof of the bow cabin of the rowboat while it sat parked on a trailer.

Our southern California sojourn became a major turning point in our lives. After the South Pacific row, I had never given up my dream to travel around the world in a sailboat. Over the year we spent rowing across the South Pacific, and even at the beginning of the Atlantic row, we had met and been helped by many sailors. Meeting Corrine and François in Hierro Island before we set out across the open Atlantic had first sparked a desire in me to travel as freely as they did in their sailboat, instead of in our ocean-rowing boat with its obvious limitations. Wouldn't it be great, I thought, to raise Christopher on such a boat and educate him about the world through a round-the-world sailing journey?

Back in Vermont, when we had first formulated the idea of the Early Explorers Expedition, the circumnavigation was to be done in a sailboat. I worked hard on Curt to get him to agree, though I knew he wasn't really a sailor. He knew how to navigate a sailboat, but he wasn't crazy about the amount of labor it took to run one. Besides, he liked to say, a sailboat was a black hole into which one just poured endless amounts of money for maintenance and upkeep. Nevertheless, I had managed to convince him we could find a cheap sailboat in San Pedro, California. I was excited, because I had finally gotten him to consider doing something I suggested for a change that wasn't quite his style. Don't worry, I told him, I'll pull the sails up and do maintenance on the boat. You just navigate and drop the anchor. It will be great for Christopher, I promised.

For a couple of weeks, we scoured the boatyards for the right deal and eventually found a twenty-six-foot fiberglass sloop. The price of $6500 was within our budget, and we made a deal to buy the boat. It wasn't the ideal sailboat, or one we could expect to sail across an ocean without extensive outfitting, but I thought it was an excellent start to a new chapter in our ocean-going lives.

The afternoon after making our offer, I was happy. It seemed we were about to return to the ocean and all those survival skills we had learned the hard way over the past few years would be put to use again on our new sailboat.

I should have known better, though perhaps I knew what was coming. The day we were to pay for the boat, Curt told me he didn't want to buy it because it was old and wouldn't work for what we needed to do. It would be a disaster to buy that boat, he said. I was very upset, but I couldn't do anything about it. If he didn't want to spend his portion of our boat show proceeds on a sailboat, it was out my reach. I couldn't afford the boat on my own. Nor could I sail it without him. He called the owner, reached his answering machine, and left a message saying we had changed our minds.

John Olguin watched what was going on with us and wisely said nothing. It was he who then suggested that we re-outfit *Excalibur Pacific* to row and sail down the Baja California coast and, if we felt like it, continue on to the Mexican mainland. The expedition became the Baja California expedition, where we would row and sail down the coast of southern California to the Baja California peninsula and on to Cabo San Lucas at its very tip. Since some who had been told of our latest boating adventures had offered to sponsor us with products, we agreed to the re-outfitting of *Excalibur Pacific*. She would have a real sailing mast that would be cut down to size to suit the length of the boat, along with a specially made sail. A spray dodger to provide shelter on the forward deck was made and attached to the bow cabin. The dagger boards we had used so effectively on the oceans were replaced with heavier ones that could better balance the weight of the sail and mast, which sat on the bow cabin. A set of comfortable boat cushions rounded out the retrofit.

The day in early April that we left San Pedro, Christopher, who had been spending a lot of time with John and Muriel Olguin and John's wonderful friend, Lois LaRue, did not want to get on the boat. The local newspapers and a television crew were there, courtesy of John's contacts. It was the moment of truth, and little Chris said publicly that he did not want to go with us on the boat. I couldn't blame him: his new friends lived a much more predictable lifestyle than his parents, who were still negotiating their post-rowing identities.

Baja with Baby on Board

"Papa, Mama, I need help!" We looked at each other and then back at the pod of blue whales swimming off the bow of the boat.

"I'll go see what he wants," Curt said, and went to the open cabin door.

"Christopher, what's the matter, little guy?" I half-listened to their conversation while I held the course. We were sailing *Excalibur Pacific* in a fifteen-knot wind toward the entrance of Magdalena Bay on the west coast of Baja California. With my right hand on the tiller and my left holding the rope to the sail, I was threading a tight course around a pod of hundred-foot behemoths that had appeared as we were changing course.

"Ah, Christopher, what's this?" I heard Curt saying. Today it wasn't the toothpaste two-year-old Christopher had gotten into; it was something more significant. He was trying to toilet train himself in the boat cabin while his parents were sailing through a pod of whales. Curt reached in and held him still on his potty while the boat bounced through the waves.

In a minute he was done and grinning as he stood in the doorway of the bow cabin with his safety harness attached to the gunwales. I was ready for them and steered over a wave that brought the boat neatly beside the pod.

"Look, Christopher," I said, pointing. "Look at the whales!" He squinted and squealed with delight as one of the whales lifted its tail out of the water and splashed the boat. Curt slipped a pair of child-sized sunglasses over Chris's eyes and tied his canvas hat over his blond hair, though he didn't even notice, he was so mesmerized by the whales.

I switched places and sat beside him as Curt made a ninety-degree course change across the waves, the wind kicking up a fine spray. Christopher, sitting on my lap on the high side of the deck where the wind and waves were hitting hardest, turned his face toward the waves, fascinated by the machinations it took to keep *Excalibur Pacific* pointed in the right direction.

As the sun sank below the stark, jagged mountains of Magdalena Bay, a red glow spread throughout the sky and over the water. We sailed along the shore until we reached an anchorage across from a village of tin-roofed cement block houses. Christopher helped his father drop the anchor by holding on to a piece of the two-inch rope, while I gave the oars a couple of hard strokes to set the anchor in the soft mud of the bay.

Excalibur Pacific floated quietly as the three of us stretched out on the soft boat cushions, enjoying the stillness of the anchorage after days of hard sailing and rowing from San Diego. With our warm Mexican *cervezas* in hand, Curt and I were relieved to be finally off the coastal waters of the Baja, while Christopher drank his apple juice, oblivious to the work it had taken to row and sail so far from San Pedro, California.

Impacted Wisdom Teeth and Engine

Halfway along the Baja coast, after a stop at Punta Eugenia, the pain Curt had been feeling in his back molar developed into a full-fledged impacted wisdom tooth that left him almost immobile from the agony. Since I had not relearned coastal navigation because I was focused on taking care of Christopher, I wasn't able to navigate the boat on my own. After a week of difficult travel along the Baja coast, where Curt tried unsuccessfully one day to flag down a ship for medication, we decided to head for the nearest port, which was Magdalena Bay.

The next day we went ashore to find medical help. Later, with the aid of some of the villagers, *Excalibur Pacific* was towed to a remote cove, where we would spend a week while Curt went to Ciudad Constitución to have his molar extracted. In the long week we waited for Curt to return, Christopher and I sat at anchor in the cove. Its extreme tides left the boat sitting on soft, stinky mud flats for hours at a time, while we were able to paddle to shore by the high tides and explore the flotsam-filled beaches. After a successful extraction, Curt took a local bus north to California, where he picked up the Datsun and boat trailer and drove south to La Paz, Baja, on the east coast. Our new plan was to row and sail around the tip of Baja California and end the expedition in La Paz.

The day Curt appeared on the edge of the mud flats of our little cove, Christopher and I were sitting on deck making camp bread. It had been a lonely and uncertain week at anchor, and we were happy to see him.

The day we left Magdalena Bay, our expedition changed its mode of travel entirely. Hanging off the starboard gunwale of our

ocean-rowing boat was a brand new four-horsepower Suzuki outboard engine that Curt had bought in California. On deck beside it
was a 2.5-gallon plastic container filled to its spout with gasoline. Sitting on the aft cabin in the arms of his father was Christopher, happily steering the boat toward the Pacific Ocean and Cabo San Lucas,
from where we would continue north to La Paz on the east coast.

The Baja trip had evolved into something completely different
from what had originally been planned. Though, on one level, sailing around the North American continent was an attempt to gain
back our prestige as fearless explorers, it had also been my way to
get us to change our mode of travel and go into the cruising life, a
sailing lifestyle I thought had limitless potential while still appeasing
Curt's desire to continue doing expeditions. The problem was that
we couldn't agree as a couple, with equal voice, on what to do next. I
was getting the feeling that my life's journey, which involved making
my own decisions, was stalling and fast becoming an unguided bush-
whack into the unknown. Unlike the bushwhacking hikes I loved
to take with my good friend Ruby, who knew the old abandoned
town roads of northern Vermont so well despite the complete lack of
road signs, Curt and I were headed into uncharted territory through
a series of post-ocean-rowing misadventures, in which neither of us
knew which path was the best and safest to take.

CHAPTER 41

Solar Boat Voyages on the Mississippi and Elsewhere

1989–1990

Nonetheless, the Baja California trip resulted in new ideas for future expeditions. We had always carried solar panels on *Excalibur* and *Excalibur Pacific* to recharge the batteries for the radio, the lights, and the autopilot self-steering device. Now we were thinking of new ways to expand our usage of solar energy on the boat. It seemed obvious, after the experience of motoring with the outboard gas engine down the Baja coast that a solar-powered electric engine would be much safer and equally reliable.

Curt jumped into the solar electric project enthusiastically, and eventually all our time and effort were dedicated to converting the ocean rowboat into a solar-powered electric boat. To test the electric engine, we carried out several long-distance coastal and river trips.

One summer, we drove to Cape Girardeau on the Mississippi River south of St. Louis to launch the *Excalibur Pacific* with her newly added *amas* (Polynesian-style outriggers) into the river's fast-moving current. Curt planned to motor down the length of the Mississippi to the Gulf of Mexico while I drove the car and boat trailer with four-year-old Christopher along the Great River Road south toward Louisiana.

For six weeks or so, we ran parallel expeditions. Occasionally we met up, and once Christopher had a chance to travel with his father on the electric rowboat for a few days. I had never towed a trailer before, so it was a good challenge to drive, park, and back up the fifteen-foot trailer as we passed through small southern towns and campgrounds along the way.

One day I pulled into a state campground south of Vicksburg, Mississippi, that overlooked the river from cliffs high above the river's edge. Carefully, I negotiated the hairpin turns with the old Datsun 810 and trailer, noting the steep drop-offs on either side of the road as we ascended to the entrance of the park. The atmosphere in the camping area was eerie, with the scent of ancient cedar trees draped with Spanish moss hanging over the roadway. There weren't any campers or rangers in sight. I drove the campsite loop again and stopped by the outhouses. As I was getting Christopher out of the car for a bathroom stop, a man with a bucket and broom emerged from the men's toilet. He was the only person I'd seen in the park so far, so I asked him about camping for the night.

"Well," he drawled, "you might wanna think about that." My eyes widened. "Just yesterday, a woman opened her trailer door and almost stepped on a rattler sunning itself right below her foot." He went on to describe other incidents of rattler sightings, but before he finished, I had made my mind up to leave. Within five minutes of saying goodbye, I was driving out the entrance of the park without a look backward.

A few days later, Christopher and I were camping on the banks of the Mississippi near Natchez. I sat at our picnic table, writing in my journal and keeping an eye on Christopher, who was investigating a series of armadillo holes by our tent. Earlier in the day, we had seen one pointy-nosed armadillo scurrying through the campground in the direction of the outhouses.

A pleasant river breeze wafted through the open campground, and an elderly couple pushed their equally elderly hairless poodle in a stroller around the camp road. I looked up smiling at the sight and over at Christopher, who was patting another dog that had come out of nowhere.

"Hey, how y'all doing?" An older couple appeared by the dog, smiling at us. We chatted about the river and our road trip. As the red sun began to slip behind the cypress trees on the west bank of the river, the lady invited us to spend the night at their house. We could take a shower and come to church with them the next morning, she told me. I thanked them for the offer and tried to decline, but the lady wouldn't hear of it; in fact, she insisted we come for the night. That night, Christopher and I slept in icy cold air-conditioned comfort, and the next day we fed our souls at the Natchez Baptist Church. Afterward, when we had been returned to our campsite, the two of us stood at the river's edge watching for Curt, who was scheduled to pass by the campground that day. In the last rays of the setting sun, Christopher spotted a rowboat cum solar electric boat motoring our way and started shouting, "Papa, Papa!" We waved our arms until he spotted us and pulled in to shore.

Within a month, the Mississippi River odyssey was over and we were back in Vermont. Curt was convinced he would be able to refine and extend the adaptation of *Excalibur Pacific* so that one day soon, he or we would be able to make a solar electric crossing of the Atlantic Ocean.

With an increasingly strong sense of detachment and trepidation, I watched the modifications take shape. The sinuous lines of *Excalibur Pacific's* hull that Ed Montesi had designed so beautifully in 1980 were being badly distorted by the added piping and batteries, and soon she looked like a dejected workhorse weighted down with an ugly metal harness. Now, instead of using a donated electric engine, Curt began to build his own solar motor.

One evening in the late fall of 1990, when Curt and I had been skirting for weeks around who was going on the Atlantic solar boat trip, Curt decided to push me to say whether I was going or not. He walked up to the U-shaped counter in the kitchen.

"What do you think? This solar trip needs two people to run the boat."

My stomach clenched, as it always did whenever this discussion began. He wanted me to go; in fact, he needed me with him. This I knew and feared.

"Do you think there's enough space for all of us? We've got more equipment on the boat this trip, Curt. And little Christopher."

Curt's eyes narrowed and he said, "You know how much there is on the boat. Chris will sleep between us. The boat will actually be more stable with the *amas*. You know that."

"I still think there's more stuff on *Excalibur Pacific* than before, and, really, it's going to be hard to get around the deck and in and out of the bow cabin with three of us." I looked up and waited for his reply. He was getting annoyed.

His soft voice notched up and hardened as he spoke slowly. "Are you coming or not? Are you going to let me go out there in a boat, fully laden with a hundred pounds of batteries, a full display of solar panels, and God knows what else, while you sit on shore and watch? Is that what you want?"

He was almost yelling now, and I was feeling threatened. I left the security of the U-shaped counter and stood in front of him. He leaned in close, and I took a step back. "Don't threaten me like that! I don't want to go on the boat with Christopher, and you know it!"

My courage failed me at this point, and I ran into the master bedroom and locked the door. Over on the other side of the living room, four-year-old Christopher stood in the doorway of his bedroom, watching in puzzlement.

With each new change to the boat, we drove to a body of water on the East Coast for trials. On a placid New Hampshire lake one evening after two hours of preparation and an equal amount of time driving from Vermont, we motored its quiet, calm waters for one mile to a campsite. With a bit of extra power, the bow of the boat was nudged onto a remote sandy beach. I jumped into the shallow waters to pull *Excalibur Pacific* up while Christopher ran off to explore the beach. I set up camp while Curt checked out the battery consumption for our thirty-minute trip. I couldn't help but think the boat was overkill for this kind of experience.

In May of 1990, Curt received a grant from the Charles A. and Anne Morrow Lindbergh Fund that would largely finance a solar crossing of the Atlantic Ocean. He had to go now.

CHAPTER 42

In Casablanca Again

1991

In late June 1991, Curt, Christopher, and I arrived in Casablanca on board *MV Jean Lykes*, whose parent company had sponsored our free Lykes Lines freighter trip with *Solar Eagle* as deck cargo. The plan was to set off from Casablanca as a family and solar-power our boat across the Atlantic Ocean. That was the official plan. It was the scenario Curt wanted, but I continued to vacillate over it every day. I knew *Excalibur Pacific*—formerly *Excalibur*, now *Solar Eagle*—very well, but the idea of the three of us living on her for an ocean crossing worried me enormously. Over the past year, Curt and I had continued to have huge fights about the expedition. He didn't want to go alone, while I didn't think it was prudent for three of us to go. It was one thing for us to take chances on the boat, but it was another to place the life of our child in such potential danger. The Baja California trip had made this clear to me.

Curt continued to push for the family plan. After he contacted National Geographic for support and they had agreed to supply cameras and film, I consented to rethink my position. After all, the people at National Geo had examined the boat in Annapolis and knew what we were proposing to do. Perhaps there was something I wasn't seeing.

Solar Eagle was lowered slowly over the side of *Jean Lykes* and placed into the oily waters of Casablanca harbor. Curt climbed down,

I climbed down, and when we both looked up at Christopher with our arms upraised, he continued to hold on to Sparky, the ship's radio officer, who had become five-year-old Chris's best friend. I can imagine what he thought when he looked down at the deck of *Solar Eagle*, cluttered with last-minute supplies and a huge battery box that took up a quarter of the nine-foot deck. When he finally climbed down the rope ladder like a true sailor, I put him into the front cabin, which he protested mightily.

At the invitation of a friend's friend, Curt and I rowed *Solar Eagle* to the Casablanca Yacht Club, the very same place we had left from in 1981 at the beginning of the Atlantic row. Instead of being feted with fine meals at the club and being given a safe and clean berth for the boat as in 1981, we were told to tie up to the outside of several decaying sailboats. It was only for a day or so, we were told, but it wasn't easy climbing over the sailboats to get to the boat club's facilities.

From the deck of our boat, we watched the harbor goings-on: fishermen arriving at 4 a.m. to go out to sea, their deep-rumbling diesel motors starting up in the silence of the early lavender dawn. The harbor would be quiet after they left until 8:30 a.m., when the rest of the little fishing fleet would get going, with many Moroccans leaving for a day's fishing trip. The boat repair yards were busy, with their work laid out in front of them: sailboats, large fishing boats, military gunboats, and even a motor yacht complete with a white-capped crew and an impressive array of canvas-covered bollards lined up on their deck like a set of pins at a bowling alley. All of these boats would arrive before the tide went out and wait for the rope from shore to pull them up the tracks to the boat cradles that the falling tide would reveal.

It became apparent after a few days that the harbor was not a safe place for a young child. Diapers and garbage floated around the boat for hours. The boat club dogs defecated on the docks. A derelict who liked to sniff gasoline fumes wandered back and forth all day and part of the night. Rats scurried up the pilings that were exposed twice a day when the tide went down. Each morning brought a false air of cleanliness as quaint little wooden fishing boats and big, gaily-painted fantailed fishing liners set off. Everything was sharp and in focus. And then by 8:00 a.m., a white haze of phosphate from the nearby loading facility settled over the harbor, and the illusion was gone.

By July 7, Curt was preparing, albeit unhappily, to depart Casablanca solo on July 9. It had become increasingly obvious to me that the boat was terribly overweight and couldn't safely carry the three of us. Chris and I would stay at a US consulate member's home in Casablanca and act as Curt's communication team; I'd been invited to house-sit while the family went on their summer holiday. When Curt's sponsors wanted news of the expedition, I'd pass along his location and whatever else he wished to share.

On July 9, when Curt left, his radio wasn't working, and until he found the time to repair it, he wouldn't be in touch with anyone. Several of us begged him to stay until it was fixed, but he refused. The 9th was the date he had set for leaving, and he wouldn't deviate from that. In retrospect, Curt's departure was a farce. July 9, 1991, the King's Day, was a national holiday; he had hoped there would be fireworks and other celebrations for King Hassan II at the harbor, but there were none. It was just another miserable day in the filthy port of Casablanca. Though the weather was the calmest and the water the flattest they had been in a while, I knew that would soon change, which it did in the form of a thunderstorm two days later. Prior to his departure, a low-pressure system had dominated the weather in Casablanca and was creating heavy seas and strong winds. It would have been better to postpone leaving until a week or a week and a half later.

As the days wore on and we didn't hear from Curt, Christopher and I alternated between fear, anger, and great sadness. My moods varied with the time of day. After breakfast, when the security of the night was over, I pondered where Chris and I should go from there and when. When should we leave the country, and with what? I thought, because I had less than a couple hundred dollars in cash and no credit card.

What a fool I would sound like if I voiced the truth: "Why yes, I'm waiting to hear from my husband, who is at sea—in the Atlantic during hurricane season—in a small, overloaded, solar-powered boat with a broken radio microphone. Yes, we heard news of him, last Friday in fact: a ham operator heard a call sign in Morse code that sounded like his. Nothing else is known."

That our lives had come to this point made me increasingly upset. I knew Curt lived to take chances, but why, I asked myself, did it have to be like this? Close to tears, I pushed back on the emotions and tried to achieve some degree of detachment. Now was really the same as living on *Excalibur Pacific* at sea, I told myself, where we simply couldn't afford to sustain a state of constant fear. I would have to remove myself from the immediacy of the situation by imposing a bit of reserve. Then things would be manageable.

One day, after Curt had been gone more than a week, five-year-old Christopher showed his creative side by making a paper collage of Curt's face so we could look at it and think of Papa. We talked about it over dinner when Chris stated there were three things he was: mad, sad, and glad.

Mad—about the garbage floating in the harbor waters.

Sad—because Papa was gone.

Glad—because he had Nate, his new friend, to play with and his pool to swim in.

I was pleased I had called Curt's bluff, but, because he was out there alone, dealing with all his inventions with no one to help and cajole him though the difficulties, I did feel guilty for letting him go by himself in such a specialized craft. Yet, while he was refitting it, each time he had added some new feature, I felt he was pushing me further and further away. When he first talked about a solar voyage across the Atlantic, I thought, "Okay, you've pushed me off the boat, whether you know it or not. You've taken over a boat that's mine, too, and committed it to a project I cannot support."

Curt certainly hadn't looked happy going out to sea by himself, but when I'd surveyed the impossibly crowded deck of *Solar Eagle* as it floated in the garbage of Casablanca harbor, I couldn't help but think, "This is insane. I made the correct decision for Christopher and me."

As the days passed and we still heard nothing from Curt, people began to tell me what they thought of the situation. In response to my question, "Any ideas of what to do?" Mohamed, a Moroccan acquaintance, said, "I think your husband should not have left you and your son without his radio working."

After my conversation with Mohamed, I realized how absurd my position as official spokesperson of the Solar Voyage was from the outset, when there could be no messages to report to anyone because Curt had left with the radio broken. Being on the other side of an expedition for the first time, I was hearing things that I might not have otherwise.

One night I had odd dreams. In one, Curt told me he had been blown south to Senegal. In another, Christopher told me his father had gone quite a ways south and had almost made it to the coast of Brazil before having trouble. Both these routes, Curt's and Christopher's, I could see clearly drawn out on the chart in my dreams. The next evening, I heard Curt's voice saying, "Kathleen." I felt so sad afterward. Was it a bad day for him too? Was he trying to reach me somehow?

On July 29, to our great happiness, Christopher and I heard that Curt had contacted the US consulate to say he planned to go to the Canaries and his ETA was July 31. Later the same day, a new position report placed him south of the Canaries. The message received from a ship was: "We have heard from Mr. Curtis Saville of *Solar Eagle*, the experimental American boat by VHF. He has damages to the boat and plans to go into Villa Cisneros."

I looked up Villa Cisneros and found it was no longer called that since the Green March in 1981, the year we began the Atlantic row from Casablanca, when Morocco had seized it from Spain and renamed it Al Dakhla. It appeared Curt had not, in fact, escaped Moroccan coastal waters in the three weeks he had been gone. At 5:30 p.m., I received a phone call from him.

"Things are bad with the boat," he told me. The hull was badly damaged and the batteries and other equipment were lost. He went on to tell me that in the beginning, the boat motored well, then a storm hit with the wind blowing very hard, and he had to jettison the one *ama* and batteries.

I asked if he was okay. He said he was, but his voice was shaky. I said, "You had a bad time," and he answered, "Yes, I had a bad time."

Fleeing Morocco, July 1991

The hot and airless plastic tunnel was crammed full of hundreds of North Africans and Europeans waiting to get the ferry to cross the Straits of Gibraltar to Algeciras, Spain. The two of us stood shoulder to shoulder with little Chris between us among the crowd. My old cloth backpack was stuffed with a few food items, clothes, journals, and a couple of Chris's stuffed animals that he had left to keep his father company and that Curt salvaged from the boat before he left it in Al Dakhla, Western Sahara. The salt-stained duffle bag in my hand had a few well-folded navigation charts and boat ropes. Another duffle hanging off of Curt's shoulder held the metal sextant from the Pacific row, log books, and a couple of water bottles. Even five-year-old Christopher carried a backpack. The rest of his stuffed animals—moosie, seal, and his hand puppet, "the wolf"—filled his pack, along with a change of clothing. The only things Curt recovered from the boat, after three eventful months in Morocco, were in those bags.

The mob moved again toward the gangplank going up to a boat deck. Since our tickets had been checked before the tunnel, all we had to do was get on the ferry and find a place to sit with all our gear for five hours.

Like every crowd scene in Morocco I had been through, it was push and shove. But after three months in Casablanca, I was not above shoving a couple of men aside so I could secure the only two remaining seats in the saloon. I didn't care anymore, because we were leaving a country that was filled with bad memories and experiences. Curt looked as surprised as the Moroccans at my behavior, but he didn't apologize to them, and he followed me with Christopher. We sat down and staked our claim by fanning our bags around us like an American-style stockade. At a nearby table was a European family with two small children whose mother looked shell-shocked as the kids wailed. All around us was the usual mayhem: children screaming, men and women shouting in rapid-fire Arabic as mountains of bags from their relatives who were still on deck filled the bar room. If anyone was here for a drink, they were going to have a hell of a time making their way to the bar.

Curt stared out the porthole, undoubtedly occupied with thoughts of his recently aborted solo boat voyage along the Moroccan coast. Was he as upset and disturbed as I was by his abandoning *Solar Eagle*, aka *Excalibur Pacific*, our ocean rowboat, the boat we had built by hand ten years earlier to row across the Atlantic Ocean? How did he feel about fleeing Morocco because it appeared the government would detain us indefinitely on trumped-up gun charges? Did he feel a rising emptiness that came with every step we took away from *Excalibur Pacific*? Was he thinking of how we were going to get back to the States when we had only five hundred dollars and a handful of useless Moroccan dirham between us?

I looked up and saw people moving around, fussing with their plastic bags and luggage. We must be arriving soon. My stomach tightened as we struggled toward the door.

Like a stream of unstoppable floodwaters, the mob surged down the gangplank and broke into a run toward immigration booths; Christopher's legs pumped madly to keep up with us. Across the wet docks we rushed and then, strangely, past the closed customs booths into the steamy night air of Algeciras. No one stamped our passports or even stopped us to ask where we were going, so like all the other ferry passengers, we disappeared into the city and the Algeciras night.

CHAPTER 43

New Beginnings

1991–1997

ABANDONING *EXCALIBUR PACIFIC* IN MOROCCO badly depressed me, though I didn't share all my feelings with Curt. Undoubtedly, he was upset about the failure of his solar expedition, an expedition that had been a couple of years in planning. But losing our ocean rowboat meant a final change of identity, to boatlessness. For ten years, friends had called us "the boat people." In my mind, *Excalibur Pacific* was my identity. I had built her from scratch and lived a lifetime on her deck and in her cabins with Curt. Our son had been conceived on her deck. Not only had she been rowed thousands of miles on oceans, rivers, lakes, and coastlines, she had been driven back and forth across the United States twice and through hundreds of miles in Canada and up and down the East Coast.

There would never again be anything like that boat and what she represented in my life. But it was time to get going with the rest of my life, I decided, and I was finally going to take control of it. I would wrest my life away from the uncertainty of the expeditions Curt was still committed to and go in a direction I felt was right for us.

For now, in 1991, the days of wondering how and where we would explore seemed frivolous, especially with the boat gone. I might never forgive Curt for losing *Excalibur*, but I could be grateful to him for unknowingly pushing me off my self-appointed throne of heroic adventure. I remembered reading a book years ago by Chay Blyth, who had rowed across the Atlantic Ocean with John Ridgeway from Cape Cod to Ireland in the mid-1960s. They received a lot of publicity for their row, and Ridgeway was eventually knighted. Though Blyth was not knighted, the accolades were profuse enough that he took them to heart. But this hadn't been a good thing, he later said, because he let all the praise of his great abilities go to his head. In his self-inflicted conceit, he spent too much time lapping up the praise before he was finally able to recognize how rich the quality of his inner life had become as the result of the Atlantic row. He had gone to the edge, as I had, looked over, and pulled back in time to value what the experience had taught him.

I was worried that if I didn't pull back from that edge now, I would never get to value what each experience had taught me.

No Longer Famous for Five Minutes

In early fall 1991 we had arrived back in the United States from the fiasco of losing *Excalibur Pacific*. We were in Durham, North Carolina, at Curt's mother's house. My head was still spinning from the series of events that had brought us back from Morocco without it, and I continued to feel as though I had lost a part of myself, as I'm sure that Curt did. It was as if a gaping hole had been torn out of my heart and my identity was no longer Kathleen Saville—Woman Rower of the Atlantic and the Pacific, Builder of an Ocean Rowboat. Everything that defined who I had become since 1981 was gone.

It was time to come up with Plan B. Curt was under the impression that National Geographic and ETAP boats, a Swedish sailboat manufacturer we had visited at a boat show in La Rochelle, France, on our way from Morocco to England before returning home, were still interested in sponsoring us for a solar crossing, but he was wrong about that. National Geographic was upset because we had said that all three of us were going on the solar crossing of the ocean and only Curt did. They had given the expedition cameras and film. While Curt had filmed the entire trip from Casablanca to the Spanish Sahara and brought back the tapes to show them, he hadn't succeeded in completing the crossing and had lost the cameras. We spent a couple of months making many phone calls to our contacts at National Geo, and though they watched the salvaged films and one of the editors told us how eloquent Curt had been in describing his fear of traveling the ocean alone, they finally dropped us entirely. It was a miserable and humiliating period.

ETAP was also not interested in our proposal that they provide us with a sailboat to cross the Atlantic Ocean while showcasing solar energy. Perhaps we hadn't written a convincing proposal, or our lack of ocean sailing experience concerned them despite our ocean rowing and navigational skills.

We spent another month in Durham before heading to our home in northern Vermont. When we arrived, we found that while we had been in North Carolina, the US State Department had left a message on the answering machine, requesting that we contact them about a boat we had left in Morocco. We talked it over and decided to do nothing. There was no money to fly back to Morocco, and there was no money to ship the boat home. Basically, we had shot our credibility by abandoning the boat.

On an earlier visit to Durham in late 1989, I was watching television at my mother-in-law's home when I saw a program about teaching English as a foreign language. I asked Curt if TEFL was what Beth Ruze, our friend from the South Pacific row, was still doing for a living. He said yes, and I began to think about it. We needed to make a living somehow, and I had always wanted to do graduate work. When we got back to Vermont, I enrolled in a graduate TEFL certificate program at St. Michael's College in Colchester which I completed in the summer of 1990 before we left for Curt's unsuccessful solar expedition. I loved going back to school and the feeling I was taking control of my life while providing us with the possibility of foreign travel again. When we returned from North Carolina this time, I applied to and was accepted into a master's program in TEFL at St. Michael's.

In late spring 1993, after I had completed my master's, I was waiting to hear about an English teaching fellowship to Pakistan from the United States Information Service (USIS). The job would pay a relatively measly amount for a family, but the benefits were great. USIS and the sponsoring Pakistani college would employ me as a US State Department English teaching fellow and Curt as an English teacher. We would be provided with a house and Christopher's schooling at Aitcheson College, the most prestigious boys' school in Pakistan, which educated old-money and nouveau-riche boys from ages four to eighteen. Round-trip airfare for all three of us and a small insurance policy were also provided.

When the call came, I was offered the job. It was one of the most satisfying moments of my life. I had won a competitive fellowship to teach and do teacher training at two colleges in Lahore, Pakistan.

I worked for two years in Pakistan. The first year was spent learning how to teach and teacher-train. When the English language officer asked me to travel for workshops in Islamabad, Peshawar, Karachi, and Multan, I said yes. I wanted to learn, but I also wanted to travel as much as possible. Curt did well in his job as an English teacher in the Upper School at Aitchison. The faculty and students respected his ability to express himself well, and the older Pakistani staff admired his abilities as a classically trained musician. The problem was with Christopher's schooling. Unbeknownst to us, Aitchison College, where we would live on campus and Chris would attend second grade, was in the second half of its academic year when we arrived. No one had thought to tell us that Chris had missed the entire first half of second grade. Even with the help of a sympathetic teacher, it became apparent that Aitcheson's competitive, memorize-or-be-shamed curriculum was not going to work for us. We took Chris out of school and home-schooled him for the rest of the 1993–1994 academic year.

In the second year, I was offered a renewal of my fellowship and was moved to Islamabad, where I worked as a materials writer and teacher trainer at Allama Iqbal Open University. The TEFL work I did was enjoyable, but my personal life was not. Curt and I had decided that Chris needed to be schooled in Vermont for the next year because the first year in Pakistan had been such a wash for him academically. For a brief time, we had considered sending him to the Lahore American School, but my fellowship salary and the small stipends we received from Aitcheson had not been enough to cover LAS's tuition.

Saying goodbye to Christopher when I left for Islamabad was horrible. He didn't cry and make me feel guilty, but he looked so sad that I felt like the worst mother in the world. I said goodbye to Curt, who was going to take care of Christopher in Vermont and probably practice the horn. I didn't know what he was going to do to make money on his end; this was something we never talked about. He had worked a year in Pakistan and that was it. My fellowship salary was paid partly in dollars, which I had deposited in our Vermont bank account, and the other part in Pakistani rupees, which I lived on in Islamabad.

During the second half of my year in Islamabad, I began looking around for another job overseas that would pay well and bring us together. Living and working in our small town in Vermont was not an option, since I had a master's in teaching English but not certification for public-school teaching. One day, while thumbing through a listing of TEFL jobs in the Middle East, I saw an ad for teaching at Kuwait University's business college. I applied and didn't think anything of it until I had been home in Vermont for a couple of months in 1995. The call came in late fall inviting me to join the faculty of Kuwait University beginning in January 1996. Would I be able to sponsor my family? I asked. Kuwait's education office at their embassy in Washington, DC, told me that I probably would after a couple of months. I took the job and once again felt terrible saying goodbye to Christopher as I left to fly to Kuwait City, the capital of a Gulf country where expatriates from all over the world came to make their tax-free salaries and live lives very separate from the host country nationals, the Kuwaitis. The expatriates' salaries at the university were less than half that of the Kuwaitis', though they taught an equal number of hours and students.

One night after work in early September of my second semester, I lay on the living room couch in my solitary, two-bedroom apartment reading the *Kuwait Times* with its graphic color photographs of the daily bombings in Tel Aviv, the television going in the background for noise. I was depressed at being away from my family and feeling restless and trapped. I had yet another four months in Kuwait before completing a contract I had no intention to renew. The entire time I was in Kuwait, I had tried to find a job for Curt, but it turned out that, unlike a man, a woman couldn't sponsor her spouse and son for a job or even visitors' visas. I missed my son with a fierceness that never went away. I sighed and continued reading the newspaper until the On-going Activities section caught my eye: "Meeting of the X Sailing Association. All sailors and beginners welcome. Monday at 7 p.m. in El Sabahiyah."

When Monday came along, after a day of teaching at the university, I called the local taxi service in nearby Shuwaikh. Within a half hour I was sitting in a meeting room filled with other expats listening to the club captain extol the virtues of sailing and racing. It seemed the real purpose of the meeting was to recruit members for the weekly competitive sailing races. An intense-looking man glanced over at me and said, "I've got you on my team." There was no request or introduction. I stared at him aghast. There was a bit too much testosterone in the room, and I got up to leave.

But in order to leave, I needed to call a taxi. That was when I met Joe and Emma. They were looking for people to join their weekly happy-hour sails from the yacht club on the Kuwait City waterfront. They were definitely not interested in racing.

All the way back to my apartment, in Joe's four-wheel-drive Pajero, we chatted about sailing and recipes for making twenty-gallon trash containers of the best red wine from Kuwait Dairy products' red grape juice. Joe promised to bring a couple of bottles of his wine, and I promised to bring cheese and crackers for the boat. Things were looking up for my time in Kuwait.

For the rest of the semester, every Thursday's sail became a life-line I grabbed hold of tightly, and I suspect my fellow sailors did as well. For those few short hours that we sailed on a straight line, away from the Kuwaiti coast toward the calm waters of the upper Persian Gulf, it was like being on a different planet. I could turn my head with the wind in my hair and watch with pleasure as the sun went down in a soft, luminous, reddish glow behind the mosques of

Kuwait City. At times like that, I appreciated the beauty of the call to prayer as each note floated in melodious harmony over the blue waters of the Gulf. The tensions of being a bad mother far away from family, and of being an expatriate in a strange culture, dissolved in the blaze of the setting sun and the gentle motion of the breaking waves.

The nine months I spent in Kuwait, with a paid summer ticket home in between, gave me the teaching experience I needed to apply for better jobs. When I got on the plane heading home in January 1997, having sent my last paycheck ahead to Curt via Kuwait's very efficient banking system, I was certain that I would never want return to any country in the Gulf.

CHAPTER 44

Egyptian Lives

In March 1997, I was in Orlando, Florida, for the national convention for teachers of ESL/EFL to interview for jobs in the Middle East, where I thought the highest salaries were being paid. After two years in Pakistan and one in Kuwait, my chances were excellent for scoring a well-paying job that would have family benefits as well.

As I thought, there was no problem getting interviews with Gulf universities, but the only ones in the wider Middle East and North Africa region that I would consider were Sultan Qaboos University in Oman and the American University in Cairo, Egypt. Both interviews went well, but the job application I was given after being interviewed by two young Omanis, in dark suits like myself, was decidedly odd. Halfway through the question list was an item inquiring about my job habits. The questionnaire had been building to this question, but when I came to it I was appalled nonetheless, and because of it I dismissed the thought of going to work in Oman. It asked: "How long is your period and has it ever prevented you from going to work?"

The job description for a USAID (United States Agency for International Development) education project hosted by the American University in Cairo was more positive. I liked the people I interviewed with and the benefits even better, because they included housing, airfare for all of us, health insurance, a savings plan, and most importantly, educational benefits for Christopher at an American international school. I hoped our family would be on our way to Cairo by the summer's end.

When the offer arrived in late May for the AUC job, there was no question whether I would take it. We didn't have jobs or any particular direction in our lives, though Curt had been making noises about returning to the Atlantic Ocean for another solar voyage attempt. I chose to ignore them because I had finally found a position that covered the whole family and was in an exotic location. I knew that living in Cairo, a city of sixteen million in 1997, would be a tremendous contrast with any place we had ever been, including Lahore, Pakistan. I also knew that Curt, who was always happiest living in nature, might feel stifled within the confines of a big, third-world metropolis, but he had gone to the Juilliard School in New York City and lived in Bolivia and El Salvador in the Peace Corps, so he had a feel for life in the big city and in the developing world.

After having worked jobs that paid decent salaries, I wasn't willing to continue living in the economically depressed Northeast Kingdom of Vermont with a small child and without steady work, while waiting for another expedition eureka-moment to strike. I didn't want to continue buying our food from the "dented can" stores, places that sold out-of-date canned goods and damaged cereal products that Curt enjoyed visiting because of their down-and-out ambiance. Our few dollars left over from building a barn with wood from our land, financed by my profitable Kuwait year, were going into maintaining another used car and buying huge piles of wood cores from the local plywood factory to heat our tiny, leaky Casa Grande. During the days, I substitute-taught in the local public schools while Chris, who was now eleven years old, attended the Holland Elementary School and Curt hung out at the family summer camp in Morgan. It had become obvious to me that our lifestyle was not about choice; we were buying dented cans for food and driving a perpetually broken-down car because we couldn't afford anything better. I was not willing to stay in the North Country living poor anymore, and I was not willing to go back overseas without Christopher.

In late August 1997, an eighteen-wheeler arrived at the end of our one-mile dirt road to take trunks full of our clothes, books, and Curt's darkroom supplies for shipment to Cairo.

Though we had worked together as a family to prepare for our new lives in Cairo, Curt and I hadn't really been communicating well for months. Curt knew that living overseas had always been a stimulating experience for me, but the circumstances of how I had happened to be in Pakistan, Kuwait, and now Egypt were my own doing. Yes, he had agreed to go to Cairo, but this new life, like the other foreign stays, had come about through my, and not our, instigation.

Living on my own in Islamabad had reawakened the excitement I'd felt at the end of the Atlantic and Pacific rows. It was as though my inner being knew I was once again on the path of personal discovery. Where did he fit in all of this? I am sure he wondered, as we prepared to leave for an indefinite period of time in Egypt, perhaps through all of Christopher's secondary-school years.

Egypt
"Let me live where I will, on this side is the city, on that the wilderness, and ever I am leaving the city more and more, and withdrawing into the wilderness. . . . Every sunset which I witness inspires me with the desire to go to a West as distant and as fair as that into which the sun goes down."—From *On Walking*, by Henry David Thoreau

It was February 9, 1998, and a strange blue-white light flickered unevenly from all the light bulbs in our Cairo apartment. A faint crackling sound accompanied each flicker. When I had made my emergency maintenance request to the university's housing department the morning after Curt's departure to Vermont for a few months, an electrician came armed with only a bag of new light bulbs to replace the ones that he figured had burnt out or were in the process of burning out. The housing office hadn't believed me when I said all the lights in the apartment had been flickering oddly like this for a couple of days.

But when the electrician came out of the kitchen after checking out the fuse box, he was very pale. He walked up to my desk and said, "Doctor, the fuse box needs replacing. Can I use your phone to call the *gama* [university]?"

I nodded. After his call, he showed me the large fuse box by the kitchen door that led to a landing in the middle of our multistoried building in Maadi, a southern suburb of Cairo. Shockingly, most of the wires were melted. Why? I asked. He explained there had been a surge in the electricity and because the box had not been properly wired, the wires melted when the power jumped from 220 to 280 volts. He and a colleague would have to rewire the box immediately, before a fire broke out. I looked at him, not sure of what I was hearing and understanding. Our fancy seventh-floor apartment on the Nile River Corniche was so badly wired that we could be victims of a fire any day if it wasn't repaired now? He nodded unhappily. I didn't know what to say in response.

The flickering and crackling of the lights in the living room gave Curt's departure a strange aura. He hated the city from the moment of our arrival, and within a short time had begun making plans for the next solar electric voyage across the Atlantic Ocean. He would be motoring his way across the Atlantic in spring 1999 if all went according to plan.

In the summer of 1998, when we flew home to Vermont, Curt shared his progress on his latest solar voyage with twelve-year-old Chris because I wouldn't discuss it with him. It was wrong, I thought, for him to be planning yet another trip that would put his life in danger. It wasn't fair of him to put us through it again, and I refused to be part of a journey that would undoubtedly be an emotional rollercoaster for all three of us. Nothing, however, could persuade him to do otherwise. Some might think it was admirable that he refused to give up, but surely there had to be other ways to approach a solar voyage that didn't involve motoring a twenty-three-foot, untested, homemade electric boat, solo, across the Atlantic Ocean. The one time I had agreed to get on it was when we trailered it out to Holland Pond for a so-called boat trial of a couple of miles. With Chris in the center cabin, his head poking out of the square hatch, I sat on the deck and worried the boat might tip over, it was so tender.

In June 1999, after a year of a dedicated effort building the new *Solar Eagle* in our yard in Vermont, Curt launched it with the assistance of old friend Peter Wilhelm from the docks of Chatham on Cape Cod.

Less than a week later, he had to be rescued by a US Coast Guard helicopter a couple of hundred miles east of Cape Cod. The narrow and tippy *Solar Eagle* had begun taking on water in a storm that had blown up quickly. To save his life before the boat sank under him, he had set off the EPRIB (Emergency Position Indicating Radio Beacon), hoping the Coast Guard would catch his signal in time. He was in luck because his position was at the outer limits of how far a Coast Guard helicopter could travel on a rescue mission.

When Curt sent me an email on the evening of his rescue, Chris and I were still in Cairo. I could tell he was still flying high with the adrenaline rush of his near encounter with death. The rescuer, he wrote, had been lowered to *Solar Eagle* to pluck him off the deck of his sinking solar electric boat. A couple of years of planning and limited sponsorship sank beneath them. As they were winched back up to the helicopter, the line rocked violently back and forth in the high winds and waves. Clutching the only two waterproof bags he'd been able to save as he held on to the rescuer, Curt involuntarily dropped the one with his passport, money, and logbooks, and they fell into the sea. He arrived at the Coast Guard station on Cape Cod and called Peter Wilhelm, who came and brought him back to Rhode Island; from there he made his way back to Vermont.

During the whole of his latest adventure, Christopher and I had only the slightest idea of what had been going on until we flew back to Vermont in the summer. We found out that he had set off from Chatham only when Peter Wilhelm notified us of his departure. I knew Peter had been working with Curt on the solar expedition. Curt had spent time with him and his mother, whom I had known since 1980 when Peter, Curt, and I had begun building our ocean-rowing boat in my parents' garage in Rhode Island. Though Mrs. Wilhelm didn't approve of Peter's involvement with our ocean rowing at the time, she came to like us, and we felt lucky to be befriended by such kind people when others we knew from the Narragansett Boat Club thought we were crazy to believe we could row a boat across the Atlantic.

When Curt eventually returned to Cairo, he saw that we had built a good life and had a reliable network of friends there. Despite what had happened to him, he had a place with us, and we lived together as a family for the next two years. He found a job teaching music history at a new private university, and, when semester ended, signed up to substitute teach at the Cairo American College where Chris went to school. When he wasn't working, Curt packed up his old Peace Corps backpack and went on overnight camping trips in Wadi Digla, a remote, dried riverbed that was close to Maadi, where we lived. After every hike or holiday trip we took together to places like Malta and the Greek islands, Curt would process the exposed rolls of black-and-white film himself in the makeshift darkroom he had created in the back bathroom of the apartment, while sending his exposed color film out for developing. Our lives were coming together slowly as a complete family.

As parents, our goal had always been to give Chris a more anchored life than he'd had before we came to Cairo. I wanted him to have the stability of long-term friendships and a small but international community to grow up in. Before he left the Modern English School in Heliopolis to attend the Cairo American College in Maadi, we sent him for a couple of years in a row on the yearly school trip to the White Desert of Egypt, and then later to Verbier, Switzerland, on a ski trip. Chris's schooling was turning out to be a highlight in our lives in Cairo.

CHAPTER 45

A Call from the Desert

April 2001

T HE METAL BLEACHERS WERE HOT in the Cairo mid-spring temperatures as I sat watching Christopher flying down the red asphalt running track, his arms pumping as he easily ran the 500-meter sprint. Where was Curt? I wondered, wiping a soggy tissue over my perspiring forehead. He should have been back from his hiking trip over a day ago. He had gone to the Galala Mountains of the Eastern Desert, at the edge of Egypt's Red Sea coast, but he had promised Christopher to be in Maadi on Wednesday or Thursday at the latest for the track meet. It was now Friday, April 25, and we hadn't heard from him in a week. I walked over to where the track runners milled around, joking and laughing with each other. I smiled at Chris when he came over to me, lanky and sweaty in nearly ninety-degree heat. He looked happy and carefree.

The day had been a good one despite Curt's absence. It seemed his hiking trip must have taken longer than expected. Maybe he couldn't find a minibus back to Cairo from Zafarana on the Red Sea, where he planned to go when he finished. Or maybe the hike from St. Anthony's Monastery to St. Paul's, a distance of approximately twenty rugged, mountainous miles, was a lot harder than he expected.

The Call

The phone rang, and I put down my glass of ice water to run down the hall. Maybe it was Curt and he was delayed in Zafarana.

"Hello, I am looking for Katzleen Sabille."

I frowned and answered, "Yes, this is Kathleen Saville. Who is this?"

"I have a message from your husband." I held my breath and waited. "He has a accident in Wadi ———. . . . . His leg is injured." I didn't catch the name of the dried riverbed. "He wants you to help. He says to send a helicopter."

"What? Excuse me? What did you say?" What he had just said was incredible. Curt had fallen down somewhere near the monastery and he needed a rescue? A helicopter? It was unbelievable.

"What? He needs me to get him a helicopter? Where is he? How serious are his injuries?"

"Your husband give me this message for you." He simply responded and repeated his original message. This man's English was limited. "I will call again. Thank you. Goodbye."

I sat very still on the edge of the bed in Chris's room, staring at the receiver in disbelief. Based on what this man had just told me, I imagined Curt lying in pain somewhere amid the rocks and sand of the desert floor, parched and unable to move in the 100-degree Fahrenheit temperatures. My notes of the conversation were a bizarre web of single words and question marks and exclamations.

The phone rang again a few minutes later. This time it was a Frenchman who was at St. Anthony's, where he had just encountered the Bedouin.

"Yes, yes. I met this Bedouin, his name is Gamel Mowad. He is right; your husband is in great danger. You must come down right away. We can hike into the mountains to find him."

"But where is he? How does this Gamel know Curt is injured?"

"The Bedouin says he saw him last Friday when your husband left the monastery. He says he saw him again on Wednesday on the plateau. He must have been lost. Then the Bedouin saw him today on the plateau and he came down here, to report a dying American on the plateau above the monastery."

I stared at the phone, anxiety building in my gut by the moment as I struggled to figure out what was going on with Curt.

"You have to come down here now," he repeated.

I thought about it for a second, but I realized it was impossible to drop everything as the Frenchman suggested and hire a driver to take me three hours south to the monastery. I needed to put my thoughts together and then plan for a rescue of Curt, who was apparently stuck on a plateau, dehydrated, injured, and unable to hike back to the monastery. Mowad said Curt wanted a helicopter. Where would I get a helicopter? I wondered.

I thought some more about it and wondered why Mowad went back to Curt a second and then a third time on the plateau. What was he doing there? It seemed obvious to me that Curt had gotten lost and had climbed to the plateau to look for the trail. Or maybe he had been trying to get away from something or someone. I got up to find my book of numbers at the university.

The door to the apartment banged shut. At the sound of his sneakers trudging down the hall to his room, I looked over to see Christopher, who was glaring at me for being in his room.

"It's Pop."

His face changed instantly to a look of uncertainty. I hated to burden him, but the words came tumbling out. "He seems to be lost somewhere between St. Anthony's and St. Paul's. He wants me to get a helicopter to rescue him."

His frown deepened, and he said in some alarm, "What? What's going on?" I told him about Gamel Mowad and the Frenchman and left the room with shaking hands to find my phone book.

Waiting and Hoping

It was nighttime, and Chris and I were in the darkened living room talking about Curt and the impending rescue I had arranged through my university's security office. We were both upset that Curt's expedition had gone wrong. Christopher sat at the small desk that was pushed up against the wall, writing the things we would say to Curt once we saw him again. I lay on the old couch, a product of the university's storeroom, and rested, though neither of us could really relax.

I looked over to Chris, who was intently writing his notes. He looked tired. I reminded him that it was time to go to bed because the last day of the track meet was an early one. He needed to be rested for his last two races. We both got up and went out to the balcony off the living room. In the distance across the Nile River, garish multicolored lights flickered over the pyramids of Chefren and Kufu from the Sound and Light show that ran every night of the year. We thought of Curt lying out there, in the cold empty desert.

Early the next morning, the Frenchman, his friends, and a couple of monks from St. Anthony's planned to hike to the plateau where Curt lay. The helicopter that I had arranged was going to the same spot. A doctor from my university's clinic was on standby.

The Frenchman had pushed hard for me to go down to the monastery right away and climb with them. I balked, because we didn't have cell phones and I needed to be able to call people for this rescue attempt. From what I perceived of the situation, hiking to where Curt was and rehydrating him was not going to be enough. What about a hospital and proper medical care for someone with severe dehydration? If rehydration was all Curt needed, why hadn't he come down to the monastery with Gamel Mowad in the first place?

And what about an ambulance and doctors? This was a developing country we lived in; nothing good happened without a lot of effort in planning. I had been on the telephone continuously since the previous afternoon trying to arrange the helicopter, an ambulance, a doctor, a hospital, and then the financing for everything because none of it would be done without guarantees. I called people at the university, the US embassy, my insurance company, and my father in the States, who helped me in reaching other representatives of my uninterested insurance company. I even talked to the monks who were planning to hike with the Frenchman. One of them, an older man, was a physician. The list went on. The nerves in my right elbow were completely numb from resting it on the table with the phone in one hand so I could write with the other. I barely had any feeling in the wrist and fingers of my writing hand as I talked to person after person.

It was more important to be with Christopher and support him in his competition. While I made the calls, my resentment toward Curt was building—for getting himself into another screwed-up situation and leaving his son so he could go off and live the hero's saga again. I was also afraid of losing Curt for myself.

The next morning, we were up early so Chris could be at school for his remaining races. The sun shone hotly once again in the deep sapphire of the Egyptian sky while the air pulsed in the humidity of ninety-degree-plus heat of the early dawn. I thought of Curt in this heat, and my whole body clenched in tension. Apart from the rescue plan I had put in place for today, there was nothing more I could do for the time being. My job now was to support Chris as he ran his races. He had already won a third-place medal in the 500-meter sprint.

I left him with his track team, huddled under the shade of the red flame tree, drinking water to keep hydrated before their races, an irony that I was sure was not lost on Christopher. I walked over to the PTA office and found the mother I had been in touch with about my promise of a cookie contribution. She nodded in understanding, her eyes widening as I explained our situation: we were waiting to hear about Chris's father's desert rescue. I would not be able to make cookies for the post-meet party.

Between something so banal as cookie making and the sickening reality of Curt's rescue in the desert, the contrast couldn't have been any starker. The coolness of the office, the air conditioning pumping away belied the fact that something was terribly amiss in our world. Everywhere I walked on the school campus, I felt as if I radiated fear, but no one looked at me differently. Cairo American College was an exclusive international school for grades kindergarten to twelve, set in a five-acre campus that was a green, flowering oasis in a suburban area south of Cairo in Maadi. Students, parents, and staff entered through an impressive security portal and walked into gardens of tropical foliage, filled with exotic flowers like birds of paradise and shaded by expansive palm trees. CAC's long white modern buildings framed a full-sized running track, and a cool, inviting swimming pool was located beside the arts building. In contrast, Egyptian public schools less than a mile away had broken glass windows and dirt schoolyards.

In the grassy center of the track with the other parents proudly waiting for our sons and daughters to be called up for their medals, I stood watching Chris get up on the winner's pedestal with the other students, hoping with all my heart that we would be sharing the results of the day's events with Curt.

The Waiting Game Continues

I turned the key in the door and walked into the cool, welcoming darkness of the apartment later that afternoon. As I was throwing down my baseball cap and heading for a chair by the air conditioner to cool off, the telephone rang.

It was the university security officer. He was calling to say that Curt had been picked up by the helicopter in the early morning and was now being taken to El Salaam Hospital in Hurghada, which was south of where he had been found. I was surprised to hear that he was being taken there, because the monks had told me he would go to their monastery for initial treatment. Maybe the hospital would be better. Whatever the reason, an enormous feeling of relief washed over me.

The phone rang again, and it was the police in Hurghada. They were upbeat when I asked for news about Curt's whereabouts and pooh-poohed my concerns. I had to fight down an impulse to scream, "Shut up! Stop laughing and just tell me how he is," but I didn't, because they held his passport, and I would need their help once I got down to Hurghada. I thanked them for the information and told them I would be flying down right away to bring Curt back to Cairo.

"Yes," the policeman said with a giggle. "You can come down and get him tomorrow." Maybe his condition wasn't that serious, I thought as I hung up the phone. I grabbed my new credit card, went downstairs and around the corner to the travel agency, and booked our flight for the next day because there was nothing available that evening from Cairo. Things were beginning to feel almost normal now. He would be back with us soon. Chris and I would fly to Hurghada and check Curt out of the hospital. I made sure to pack my international insurance card and went to the bank for cash. Egyptian hospitals charged much higher rates to foreigners than to locals and most wanted cash.

When I walked back into the apartment an hour later, the phone was ringing. It was the university doctor, who told me there was a problem. Though the El Salaam hospital in Hurghada claimed to handle renal disorders, they had refused to treat Curt. The doctor said we needed to know if Curt had already been moved, and if both of us called the numbers at the hospital, one of us would reach someone who could say what was happening. Would I pay for the ambulance to Cairo if he had to be moved? Yes, I practically shouted into the telephone. Curt's condition was far worse than those idiot policemen had told me. Clearly, they had known nothing except that there had been a sick American brought into their local hospital.

With shaking hands, I dialed the numbers the doctor had given me, and eventually an Egyptian doctor in the emergency room answered, in English. "He's gone in an ambulance to Cairo." The doctor sounded annoyed. I couldn't tell whether his annoyance was with me, because I'd pulled him out of the emergency room, or because he was disgusted at Curt's being brought to the wrong hospital in such a dangerously dehydrated state.

Later I learned that the elderly monk had flown with Curt in the helicopter to Hurghada, though the monk had requested they be put down at the monastery. The monks wanted to take care of him and then send him in an ambulance to Cairo. But the governor of the region had ordered by radio that Curt be taken to Hurghada for treatment, regardless of the inadequate facilities. The monk doctor said that when he left Curt in Hurghada, Curt was joking with them and looked as though he would recover. The monks speculated that the Egyptian government had wanted positive publicity from their "rescue of an American."

I put down the phone, my elbow tingling in its numbness, and searched the desk for my list of phone numbers. Where was Chris? I wondered as I sorted through the papers. All he knew was that Curt was going to be picked up by helicopter today and brought to a hospital. He had no idea of the severity of his father's condition.

I dialed the university doctor and told him what I had found out. But he already knew that Curt was in an ambulance coming to Cairo.

"It's important that he gets to Cairo within six hours. He needs to be treated as soon as possible." He then asked me for basic intake information on Curt because he was going to be his doctor at the kidney hospital on the Corniche in Cairo. The hospital, he told me, specialized in kidney disorders and would be able to help as long as Curt got to Cairo within six hours.

Christopher came in the door as I put down the phone and looked at me inquiringly. With some reluctance, I told him the latest news: we were waiting for his father to arrive in Cairo, in an ambulance from Hurghada, whose hospital had been unable to deal with Curt's dehydration.

When Chris came out from the shower a few minutes later, we sat in the living room again, discussing what this meant. We now realized with a painful certainty that Curt's medical condition was far more serious than we had initially grasped.

We went over the facts as we knew them. Curt had left Cairo last Friday and it was now Saturday, over a week later. The Bedouin, Gamel Mowad, had seen him that first Friday when he guided Curt to the beginning of the trail, and the following Wednesday when he found him lying on the plateau with little water, and then again on Friday with no water. There was an anomaly in the recurring appearance of Mowad, but we couldn't think of what it was at the time.

A month later, in Cairo, the monks from St. Anthony's came to visit us and speculated that Mowad had followed Curt the entire time because Curt must have seen some sort of drug trading or refugee trafficking.

CHAPTER 46

Desert Petroglyphs

April 2001

For a long time afterward, I tried to imagine what really happened with Curt in the desert above St. Anthony's Monastery in 2001.

In my mind's eye, I see him getting out of the university car, saying goodbye to the driver, and grabbing his old patched and faded Peace Corps pack, to begin the long walk down the dirt road that leads to the monastery of St. Anthony's. Before hiking into the wadi, a dry riverbed, he decides to top off his water bottles and talk with anyone who can tell him about the trail between St. Anthony's and St. Paul's. He's happy to be returning to the rough desert landscape of eastern Egypt, the only place where he has found the peace and quiet that he craves while living with us in overcrowded and polluted Cairo. His plan is to hike in the desert for approximately five days before heading to the Red Sea resort town of Zafarana, where he'll catch a minibus back to Cairo.

From what he's been able to find in our Egypt guidebooks—and there isn't much information—it will take about three to four days to do the whole distance through the mountains and wadis. Though it's not well marked, the trail can be worked out, he figures, by using his hand-held compass and Xeroxed maps he's tucked away in the upper flap of his backpack. With his climbing experience in South America and the Arctic, he figures it'll be like any other expedition he's been on in the past, including the ocean voyaging he did with me. He's confident about finding his way south to St. Paul's through the wadis and over the plateaus. He's decided to go ultra-light by packing only two liter-and-a-half bottles of spring water, five flat loaves of the local bread, and a package of French Laughing Cow cheese, along with a bivy sack tent, a sleeping pad and bed sheet, a camera, and a small telescope for taking photos of the night stars and planets.

When he leaves St. Anthony's later that afternoon, his mind is full of directions that were confusing at times. A Bedouin offers to lead him to the entrance of the wadi that formally begins behind the huge stone walls of the monastery and leaves him. Curt picks his way through the desert scree until he arrives at a campsite that is still within sight of the monastery. He's exhausted by the day's travels, so in the late afternoon shade of the desert wadi, he settles on the sleeping pad and drops off, deeply asleep for the night.

The morning air is quiet and pleasantly cool as the blue walls of the tent lighten in the following day's dawn. When he crawls out and stands for a moment, turning slowly around, he tries to pick out a trail in a landscape made up of wildly juxtaposing lines of craggy rock and scree walls with a vertical dried riverbed down the middle.

Was it here? I wonder if this is where his seeds of uncertainty were first sown.

He grabs the pad from the tent and finds a comfortable spot amid the rocks and sand to eat his bread and cheese for breakfast. He finds himself staying longer, perhaps longer than he should, given the heat and lack of any shade later on. In a small spiral-bound notebook with a yellow plastic cover, he makes notes about where he thinks he is and his plans for the day. He looks over the Xeroxed topo map for details that he might have missed earlier. With the thick reading glasses from his dad's collection in their Vermont summer house, he sees that the trail is straight ahead or due east from where he sits this morning, as the Bedouin said. He rechecks his bearings with the compass and rises stiffly from the rocks. As each item goes back into the pack, the silence is soft; the small stones crunch quietly under the leather soles of his boots as he picks up the pack and continues his hike under the rose-colored morning sky.

The walls of the wadi flare backward in steep lines, but the trail that the Bedouin so blithely gestured to isn't there. "*Heneck, heneck* [There, there]." The Bedouin waved his hand toward the far distance where the trail went up to the plateau between two large boulders. He pointed down at the dirt path where they had stood by St. Anthony's and up again in the direction of St. Paul's. It seemed obvious enough.

Curt becomes hot and increasingly thirsty during the day, though he tries not to think of how much water he left at the monastery because the extra weight could have slowed him down. Despite his creeping misgivings about the direction of the trail, he decides to stop for the night further up the wadi and make camp after the moon sets. When he looks up, the sky is filled with an infinitesimal number of visible stars and planets that he wants to photograph, so he pitches the tent and takes out his portable Meade telescope and Nikon SLR. In his stuff sack, he finds the index card with the stars and planets and their altitudes that he copied out of the almanac he left in Cairo. He's happy because this is the best time of the day.

Almost all his life, Curt has loved looking at the night sky and reading the constellations. When he and I rowed the Atlantic and Pacific, Curt reveled in the art of navigating by sextant, calling the altitude readings out to me as he shot navigation stars like Regulus and Eridani and the planets like Venus and Mars so I could record them in the navigation notebook. It was always satisfying to figure out those calculations and come up with a position that could be plotted with the dividers on the ocean charts. Each day, he'd put a little X after the previous day's position and show me our steady progress across the oceans.

This evening he photographs seven stars—two that he's looked for a long time—and scribbles their declinations into the yellow notebook. The silence of the desert is almost eerie in its heaviness.

When he crawls into the tent well after midnight, he contemplates what to do the next day. The wadi is coming to an end and its walls are coming closer together with no obvious path upward. Could he have missed the trail up and out of the wadi? The Bedouin said the trail went left and sharply upward shortly before coming to the end. He's seen nothing like this so far.

The air is hot and oppressive the next morning when he wakes. It's the day that he will, hopefully, leave this godforsaken wadi by climbing upward. At breakfast, he briefly considers retracing his route from the monastery and takes another nibble of stale bread and cheese with small mouthfuls of water. Can he find his tracks again, though? Can he find his way back in this 100-degree Fahrenheit heat? It's only late April, but every day is scorching hot. In the end, he decides that it's better to go up and figure out where he is than to wander on the wadi bed any longer.

After an hour, he sees a trail between two large boulders. He looks down and sees tracks made by a pair of sandals, though they don't only go in between those rocks; they are everywhere. It's only a vague suggestion of what he considers a trail, and it's not much to go on.

Before he left St. Anthony's Monastery, one of the English-speaking monks warned him to be very careful to stick to the trails. There are bad things out there, drug smuggling, he seemed to say in his imperfect English. But before he could process that information, the Bedouin stepped up and offered to be his guide to the beginning of the trail. He took only one of the extra water bottles that the monk held out, with a quick thank you; he followed the Bedouin toward the wadi. When he looked back, the monk was still staring after him.

He walks up to the two large boulders and pats both with outstretched hands. They are close enough to each other to form an entrance of sorts. He's sure that this is the start of the trail that will lead him out of the wadi and up to the plateau where he can figure out where the hell he is.

With one last glance backward at the two boulders, he starts up the trail with a feeling of trepidation and some foreboding, though he really doesn't have a choice but to go up. He can't go backward anymore and risk getting lost in the wadi.

Though his frame pack is relatively light, his fifty-five-year old body hurts with each step. He's definitely out of shape. A blast of heat strikes as he moves from the shade of the wadi into the full sun of the upper wall. His water bottle is light as he takes a short sip of warm water.

He pushes on through his increasing fears. He wants more water to quench what is becoming an all-encompassing thirst.

Suddenly, there is the faintest wisp of a breeze on his face. He's sure the end of the trail out of this hellhole is up there. He's near the top of the plateau. Thank God, he's there.

The night air of the plateau is surprisingly cold, and the thin bed sheet he uses in the bivy tent is barely keeping him warm. His body aches everywhere as he floats in the blank space of a restless sleep. The desert floor is cold and he's shivering, but, finally overcome by exhaustion, he falls into a heavy sleep.

I imagine that he has the same dream that he had on Aconcagua Mountain in the Andes in 1970 and on the rowboat in 1985 when we were anchored on the Great Barrier Reef. Curt told me several times, and I've read in his logbooks, that during times of great distress on expeditions, he would dream about a man in white, perhaps from a monastery. In the dream, he is walking through a meadow on a hillside. Trees are sparse as he gains altitude. He doesn't wake up before he reaches the top of the mountain. The summit is the most perfect and idyllic setting. The meadow is beautiful; the trees around the large clear area are perfectly formed. There is a wall around the grounds of what seems to be a monastery. From the gate, a man dressed in white walks toward him and shakes his hand and only looks at the trail.

The white light of an early dawn breaks below the rim of the plateau and slowly brings a glow to the eastern horizon. It's like the dawn at sea when he would look out the cabin door and see the deep yellow radiance.

Today is the third or fourth day since he left Cairo. Though the trail into the wadi wasn't easy to follow, he's now sure that he's on the right path. After breakfast, he plans to find the trail again and continue walking to St. Paul's. The only problem might be the heat and low food supplies. He decides to wait until noon, and then if he's not comfortable with the way things are going, he'll turn back and walk in the direction of St. Anthony's. He's sure that from the advantage point of the plateau, he'll be able to see the monastery below, and then be able to pick out a route back down.

An hour later, he is turning back toward St. Anthony's. It's crazy, this trail. It's not there and he doesn't know why, because he's been hiking all his life and he should know how to pick up a lost trail. It doesn't make sense.

The temperature is over 100 degrees Fahrenheit, and there's hardly any shade. His brain is frying, despite his sitting in the shade of this boulder for the past hour or so. His water supply doesn't look good, though he tries not to sip more than one mouthful an hour. He's incredibly desperate for water. He can't eat this *baladi* bread without some moisture; it's like eating pages of a book. It's stale, and he doesn't have enough saliva to chew it.

The sun is at its highest point in the sky. He's hot and thirsty, but still he sits here because there is nowhere to go in these temperatures. He tries to remember why he came here in the first place. Why was it so important to him to hike this trail between two monasteries? It doesn't make sense, but he thinks it had to do with challenging himself and getting out of Cairo. It's hard to focus on anything but this incessant craving for water. The need for moisture is worse than anything he's ever known on past expeditions.

This morning he had another strange dream as he lay on the ground. It was so hot and he was too tired to get up and go anywhere. All he could do was lie there, little pointed rocks poking him in the back, and the fear of dehydration consuming him. His mouth was completely dry.

A shadow crossed his face, and he opened his eyes. Instead of glaring sunlight, there was a face leaning over him and then speaking to him. The English was broken, but Curt struggled to beg him to help.

The man's face creased in a frown and Curt thought he looked familiar. Was it the Bedouin who showed him this trail at the monastery?

He reached up and tried to grab the Bedouin's sleeve, to get him to pay attention. "Help me," he managed to say. The Bedouin passed him a water bottle and Curt grabbed it fiercely. The precious liquid went down his throat in a second.

"Take a note to my wife in Cairo," Curt rasped, and scrambled with sunburnt hands for his notebook and pen. The Bedouin watched impassively as Curt wrote out the telephone number for our apartment, but he took it and promised to take it to the monastery.

Later Curt lay there wondering if the dream was real and, if it was, how did the Bedouin know where he was? If he was the one who told him where to go that first day, how did he know he was here on the plateau? It must have been because he had never left. The Bedouin shadowed Curt the first two nights and then guided him with his footprints to the plateau. When Curt couldn't go any further, the Bedouin got worried and came to see him. He was going to call me and tell me that Curt need to be rescued.

Curt's mind wanders freely as he thinks of the impending rescue from this plateau. He thinks of Christopher and me and the strange dream he had the other night. Why didn't the man in white from the monastery point out the trail to him? He had always done that in the past.

I imagine that, at this point, Curt fumbles for his notebook and pencil stub and begins to write the note to us that we later received, explaining what happened here. It seems important to let us know he loves us. But after two simple lines saying, "Something happened. I love you both very much," he drops the notebook and falls into a dreamlike state.

In his fantasy, he sees himself standing at the edge of the plateau looking down at the wadi floor, feeling overwhelmed by the sheer distance. Why am I up here? he wonders. He looks at the wall below him for the way through the maze of paths that blend together in shades of brown and ochre. He starts walking down from the plateau on a zigzagging path. Lower and lower he goes, the hot air of the wadi smelling faintly of dry acacia. He passes rocks and small caves that he had not noticed on his way up to the plateau.

He stops at the mouth of one cave to rest and marvels at his ability to keep going when he is so tired and thirsty. He was sure that it was over, but he's having no problem getting down now. He stops in front of a large rock that appears to have lines etched into it. He looks closer; it seems familiar. He's seen this sort of carving before. And then he remembers: French Polynesia and Tahiti Iti. These stone carvings were everywhere. Along trails that led from one village to another and in places that were out in the middle of nowhere. We had wondered about those, the ones that were barely accessible to anyone but the rock carver.

Once, in the winter of 1985, we hiked to the southern end of Tahiti Iti to find a petroglyph of a turtle on a boulder that faced the setting sun in the west. To get to it, we had to time our arrival to coincide with the low tide because at high tide, it was impossible to cross the reef to the small headland, where the turtle petroglyph resided at the water's edge.

Turtles in ancient Polynesian mythologies were sacred, we were told, and could transcend boundaries between the worlds of the living and the dead. Their images were often used in memorial ceremonies to assist a spirit in a successful passage to the afterworld.

He looks at this rock in the Egyptian desert and wonders about it as he runs the sandy, cracked palm of his hand over the surface, feeling the outline of the turtle incised so finely into rock. It is company for him while he waits.

There's a dot in the distance that turns into a figure. It's moving toward him. Without thinking, he begins to get up and step away but he stops. The figure looks familiar, and as it draws closer, he sees it is the man in white from the monastery. As he comes closer, Curt sees his outstretched hand is not pointing, but it is beckoning to him. He has come to meet him.

CHAPTER 47

Understanding Desert Islands:
An Eastern Desert Trek

November 2011

T EN YEARS AFTER CURT'S DEATH on April 28, 2001, I traveled on a Thanksgiving holiday weekend to Egypt's Red Sea coast with a group from my university in Cairo. Though everyone else on the trip planned to swim at the seaside resort and enjoy learning about the history of the mountain monasteries of St. Paul and St. Anthony, which we would also take in, my specific goal was to visit St. Anthony's, where Curt began his trek to St. Paul's Monastery on April 21, 2001. I had come to see the Red Sea partly on holiday break and partly to revisit the place where he had fatally lost his way ten years earlier.

The first day we would tour St. Paul's and on the following day, St. Anthony's. Though a hiking trail of twenty-some miles, best traveled with a Bedouin guide, connects the two in a north–south direction, the drive to reach each one is far from the Suez–Hurghada coastal road, circuitous and stretching for long, desolate miles through the rugged terrain of the Eastern Desert.

November 24, 2011: Eastern Desert, Egypt
The bus winds its way slowly along the narrow paved road to St. Paul the Anchorite's Monastery in the Eastern Desert. I look out my window and see a landscape of brown ochre rubble-strewn hills

and limestone cliffs that mark the western edge of the South Galala Mountains. Except for an occasional acacia or tamarisk tree, the land is starkly barren and devoid of greenery. As we drive closer to the foot of the South Galala Mountains where the buildings of the monastery nestle, the bus passes a couple of young Egyptian Copts walking along the road's edge, pulling their rolling suitcases. Someone says they have probably just spent a few days at St. Paul's in retreat. Now, they are walking the seven-and-a-half-mile road to the Suez-Hurghada highway, where they will catch a minibus back to Cairo.

I wonder what the Copts found in their days of spiritual contemplation. Did they renew their energies to go back into the hectic world of Cairo, currently at the center of Egypt's latest version of revolution? The Coptic Christians were finding Egypt an increasingly stressful place to live, as Islamist factions vied for political dominance. Perhaps the quiet and spiritual vitality of the area would reinvigorate them and give them hope for a peaceful resolution to the country's problems.

Once we pass through the steel gates that close off the compound to outsiders, the tour guide points out two recently built churches with barrel-shaped roofs. I glance over at the churches, but my real interest is in picking out the hiking trail that I know traverses the Galala Mountain range behind St. Paul's and goes north for twenty miles to St. Anthony's. The two are the oldest working monasteries in the world, linked by the trail that passes over precipitous rock cliffs and navigates huge open desert wadis.

In April 2001, Curt set off to hike this trail, leaving from St. Anthony's to go south to St. Paul's. His motives were not much different from those of the two young men I saw this day. By taking on the challenge of a desert hike on his own and perhaps confronting the devil, as the desert fathers originally intended when they first retreated here in AD 300, he probably hoped to chance upon the same sort of renewal as the Egyptian Copts, and that he and I had found on our rowing voyages in the 1980s.

Each time we had gone out on a rowing trip, either on the ocean, a river, lake, or coastline, we came back happier than when we left. It seemed that rowing *Excalibur, Guinevere,* or the sleek racing shells took us to new landscapes that continually forced us to look at our surroundings with new eyes. It was about focusing on one thing without the distraction of other people or excessive environmental interference. The process led us each to personal renewal, like a cleansing of the mind and spirit. Every time Curt stepped into a natural landscape, I'm sure the tensions in his body went away as he moved forward to find again that essence of who he really was.

After a tour of the Cave Church, where Paul may have lived as early as the fifth century AD, and having admired the recently restored fourteenth-century frescos, our university group sits in an outdoor picnic area to enjoy lunch overlooking the mountains. Others kick back and suntan in the lingering warmth of the late fall afternoon. I wander over to a black-robed monk sitting in a chair by the parking lot. I hope he can speak English, because my Arabic is limited. "Excuse me," I say. "Where is the hiking trail to Mari Antonios?"

"Antonios?" he counters, his gray hair poking out the edges of his embroidered cap.

"*Aiwa*," I nod and repeat, "yes, a trail"—I make a walking gesture with my fingers—"to Mari Antonios from Mari Bula."

He nods and stretches out his left arm toward where I had seen a white sandy path behind the buildings. Then he curves his arm back and up to show me that the trail goes behind and then sharply up to the plateau that spans the distance between the two monasteries. He points to a towering flat-topped rock mountain in the distance and repeats, "Antonios."

I smile and thank him in Arabic, "*Shokran*," and walk back to the bus. In my mind's eye, I imagine hiking the trail myself, like Curt, going off solo to find my way between the two monasteries.

The Red Sea

The setting sun casts shadows of soft gray over the garden filled with magenta bougainvillea and hibiscus bushes at the resort. I stare at the Red Sea, in the solitariness of my balcony, a glass of bad Egyptian red wine in hand, my open journal on the bamboo table. A strong, cool, northerly wind ripples through the palms and sends the sapphire-blue waves tumbling down the length of the Red Sea and onto the beach of the resort. The sound of the waves breaking one after another accompanied by wind gusts sets off a flood of memories and I'm back on the rowboat, huddling with Curt in the bow cabin, listening to the ocean waves breaking hard outside the thin walls of the boat's hull.

The next day we will continue the bus tour to St. Anthony's. Maybe there will be the chance to see the trail that Curt took on his hike, though time is limited because of the tour group. Over the past weeks before the trip, I fantasized about quietly detaching from the group, a simple rucksack on my back with plenty of water and bread, unlike Curt, and walking in his footsteps. In my fantasy, I go along the monastery walls until I encounter the trail that goes freely into the desert wadi, and eventually climbs to the plateau in the direction of St. Paul's. My fantasy, though, seems to always end at some point between the edge of the walls and the open desert. I always return to the group.

I close my journal with barely a sentence added to the morning's notes and take one last look at the Red Sea before going to bed. The next day I'll be visiting St. Anthony's.

November 25, 2011: St. Anthony's Monastery

It is with some trepidation that I climb onto the bus with my fellow passengers this morning for the forty-minute ride to the monastery. It's another brilliantly sunny but fiercely windy day on the Red Sea; huge whitecaps break with the regularity of a metronome, gathering themselves up to crash down a second later, pyramid-shaped wave after wave.

The bus travels south along the narrow coastal road, the arid South Galala Mountains rising sharply on one side and the blue sea on the other. Supertankers, vaguely outlined in a white veil of sea fog, motor south from the Suez Canal. Small green wooden fishing boats with masts fore and aft bob up and down in the protected waters of marinas, their bows and sterns secured with heavy lines to cement quay walls. Their captains wait for the sea to calm itself.

Around a sharp curve and ahead in the distance, I catch sight of an enormous plume of blue-gray smoke swelling ominously into the blue sky. We continue and by now everyone on the bus has seen the smoke. A feeling of excitement comes over me; I feel like an accidental voyeur. Maybe it's an ocean-going tanker on fire or a building on land, because the smoke plume is thick and heavy as it extends high over the leading edges of the mountains.

The next curve in the road brings us to the shocking sight of a fuel truck lying across the road engulfed in thick, black billowing smoke. There is a sudden burst of orange-red flames as fuel ignites. The entire roadway in front of our bus is burning furiously, fanned by the wind from the Red Sea. Our bus screeches to a halt as cars, one by one in front of us, jam on their brakes at the sight of the flames. The bus driver flings open the door and one of the faculty jumps off to see if people need help. The rest of us wait, peering through the front windows. He returns to say that there has been a collision of two fuel trucks and the drivers were pulled out in time, though that seems doubtful from the apparent violence of the crash. Both fuel tankers, blackened and lying on their sides, are entirely swallowed up in deep orange flames.

As the flames burn, I realize that we will not get to the monastery this day, because there is only one road to St. Anthony's from here and it is blocked. It will be hours until rescue trucks with the proper equipment arrive from Cairo, three hours away. We all climb out of the bus and gawk with occupants of other buses and cars until our driver honks his horn madly, realizing the traffic is steadily building up behind us and that, in a short time, we will be locked into a traffic grid for hours. The bus turns around and we head back to the resort for the rest of the weekend.

The sea air is chilly in the evening. I meander along the resort beach, my bare feet shuffling through the cool sand as I look for shells and think about the day. The sun has set, and a yellow-pink glow outlines the sharp, jagged ridges of the Galala Mountains. I wonder how many secrets they hold of the people who came to renew themselves, like the two Copts we saw leaving St. Paul's or the desert monks who never leave or the hikers like Curt who seek renewal in a trek and then plan to go back the way they came. Is there a way to enter the desert of the mind and a way to leave?

Desert Islands: Beginning Anew

In 2014, I returned to the Red Sea with my university on its yearly trip to the Red Sea monasteries. This time we were successful in reaching St. Anthony's, where I had the chance to walk briefly outside the walls of the monastery. The forty minutes I spent in quiet contemplation on a small rocky hill, building a cairn from the sandstone rocks and pebbles that were scattered about as the light desert wind blew, reminded me of the hours I'd spent on *Excalibur*'s deck watching the hypnotic action of the waves forming and reforming around our boat. Like those times knowing Curt was in the cabin nearby, on that day at St. Anthony's Monastery, I felt him nearby again.

I thought of my conviction at the end of the South Pacific row that I would always be driven to explore anywhere and everywhere in the world, as Thoreau put it, "the Atlantic and Pacific Ocean of being alone." Now, more than thirty years later, I had done a lot of traveling in my life through working and living overseas, and what had driven me in 1980 to propose rowing across the Atlantic Ocean and in 1984 to commit to another ocean row almost three times longer than the Atlantic was still inside of me. I wondered, is there ever an end to the desire to explore life on another island and experience the pleasure of rowing to its shore as the Other?

Is it like what Giles Deleuze says in *Desert Islands and Other Texts*, his philosophical treatise on desert islands: "Dreaming of islands— whether with joy or in fear, it doesn't matter—is it dreaming of pulling away, of being already separate, far from any continent, of being lost and alone—or is it dreaming of starting from scratch, recreating, beginning anew?"

I resolved as I got up and left the tiny rock cairn I had built for Curt on that sandy hill outside of St. Anthony's that I would never stop looking for the answer.

Epilogue

This is how I began the talk I gave at the Extreme Women Conference at American University in Cairo, Tahrir Square, on March 22, 2016. It seems a fitting conclusion to this book.

Today's my birthday, but I'm not telling you this so you can wish me a happy birthday. It's the way I've decided to begin my talk for this Extreme Women's event at AUC because it's the starting point for the story I'm going to tell you today.

It was thirty-five years ago, to the day, that I celebrated my twenty-fifth birthday on the ocean rowboat *Excalibur*. Five days earlier, my husband, Curt Saville, and I had rowed out of the port of Casablanca, Morocco in our red homemade ocean rowboat to row over 3,000 miles across the Atlantic Ocean. Within hours of rowing into the choppy waters of coastal Morocco, I was hanging over the side of the boat throwing up everything I had in my stomach and wishing like hell that I could get off this miserable boat.

For five long, frightening days, we attempted to row south toward the Canary Islands, where we planned to turn right and row due west for the Caribbean island of Antigua. This is a distance of 3,600 miles according to the present-day GPS route, but in 1981, with our navigation instruments, which included a sextant, a compass, and the latest air navigation tables, the distance was more like 3,800 miles. Our route was not in a straight line because we were vulnerable to the current, wind, and waves.

In those first five days on the Moroccan coast we encountered gale-like conditions, a steady stream of shipping traffic, and southwest winds that kept blowing us back over the ground we had rowed so hard to gain. It wasn't until March 22, five days after waving goodbye to our new friends at the Casablanca Yacht Club and rowing our boat fully stocked with a hundred gallons of fresh water and eighty days of food, that the weather finally improved and the wind blew from the northeast. Finally, we were heading south toward the Canary Islands.

And it was my twenty-fifth birthday. I cooked up a fine meal of macaroni and cheese, and for dessert, we shared a soggy and salty slice of birthday cake given to us days earlier by Clementine Polizzi, whose husband was our host at the Casablanca Yacht Club. After dinner, Curt and I sat on deck eating my birthday cake slice, enjoying the warm air while the boat drifted south.

That twenty-fifth birthday in 1981 was the beginning of a voyage that was to change my life forever. It was a voyage that opened my eyes to how I could live my life while exploring what Henry David Thoreau called "the Atlantic and Pacific of our being." It was this unique form of travel, by water via a rowing boat over long distances, that I would come to crave the years that followed. During those years after the Atlantic row, we continued rowing long distances in the sub-Canadian Arctic, down the entire Mississippi River, along the east and west coasts of the United States, and across the South Pacific Ocean.

I feel fortunate to have this opportunity to share with you the story of these rowing expeditions. I have to say that I gained the impetus to be the Other, the adventurer and seeker of other cultures, from those ocean-rowing days. I would have to acknowledge, though, that I believe my own families' origins, as immigrants from England and Ireland on my father's side and from the Portuguese Azores Islands on my mother's side, also contributed to my impulse to be a lifelong seeker of new opportunities and ways to interact with the world. After all, how can we learn about who we are and what we are capable of without taking a chance and going outside our zone of comfort?

It has been my personal philosophy, brought about by the ocean rowing, that we have to take a certain amount of risk in life to bring about change and that change can be something we really need, perhaps without even knowing. Today I'd like to tell you the story of my ocean-rowing voyages from the days when I started rowing in college to the day, six years later, in July 1985, when we landed on a remote beach on the northeast coast of Australia after rowing ten thousand miles across the South Pacific Ocean. It's a story of how I jump-started my life by doing something that most people thought was crazy and impossible, though they knew nothing about ocean rowing themselves.

But happily, I didn't listen to them.